By HARRIS FRANKLIN RALL

NEW TESTAMENT HISTORY
RELIGION AS SALVATION
THE TEACHINGS OF JESUS
THE LIFE OF JESUS
THE CHRISTIAN FAITH AND WAY
THE GOD OF OUR FAITH

New Testament History

A STUDY OF THE BEGINNINGS OF CHRISTIANITY

HARRIS FRANKLIN RALL

ABINGDON PRESS
NEW YORK • NASHVILLE

NEW TESTAMENT HISTORY

Copyright 1914 by Harris Franklin Rall

SET UP, PRINTED, AND BOUND BY THE
PARTHENON PRESS, AT NASHVILLE,
TENNESSEE. UNITED STATES OF AMERICA

To
R. S. J. R.

CONTENTS

CONTENTS

PART IV

PAUL AND THE CHURCH OF THE EMPIRE

PART V

THE LATER CHURCH

MAPS

INTRODUCTION

THIS history might be more strictly called a study of the beginnings of Christianity. While designed primarily for use as a college textbook, it should be of equal value to any reader who wishes to trace the story of Christianity in its first days.

This is first of all a historical study. The average man has been wont to regard Christianity as a fixed and finished something that has been dropped down from the skies. If you speak of the Christian religion he will think first of all of a collection of writings, or of a body of doctrine, or of the institution of the church. But these three, Bible and doctrine and church, are simply the products of a greater movement that lies back of them. To understand Christianity we must go back to this great current of life, which was at once the greatest revelation of the divine Spirit and the greatest movement of the human spirit that mankind has known. What was the world to which this new life came? What did its Founder teach and do? How did the world brotherhood come out of the little company of Jews that followed him?

This book is a study of religion. That is why this history is of such supreme interest to us. It brings to us the religion that dominates the faith and conscience of men to-day, and shows us this religion in the person of its great founders and in the transforming power of its first great enthusiasm. It is a misconception of what New Testament study should be, to burden it with the elaborate discussion of dates and customs and the like. The supreme interest of the New Testament writers is in religion. What they bring us is not so much a history of this religion or a statement of its doctrines. Their pages reflect, rather, the religion itself, the rich and varied life out of which all doctrine and insti-

9

tutions grew. The study of this life is the best possible introduction to the understanding of religion.

The final aim of this volume is to secure the study of the Bible itself. To this end directions for reading and study are placed at the end of each chapter. The Scripture passages here given should be read carefully in connection with the text, after which the other directions for study should be carried out. The instructor will naturally modify these directions to suit the needs of the individual class. The text aims to set the biblical materials in their historical relations and to interpret them as part of a great movement. The instructor, however, should not be content with question and answer based upon the text, but should aim to secure first of all an interested and intelligent reading of the Bible itself.

While written frankly from the modern historical point of view, this book does not concern itself primarily with critical processes. Using the assured results of sober study, it aims to set forth reverently and constructively the great facts of this early history. It is a pleasure to acknowledge the aid received, especially in the revision of the manuscript, from my colleague, Professor Lindsay B. Longacre.

A brief bibliography is appended. The body of the work contains no references to other authors. The Bible itself is the only book needed. The student should have a copy of the American Revised Version with marginal references

HARRIS FRANKLIN RALL.

PART I

THE WORLD OF THE EARLY CHURCH

CHAPTER I

THE ROMAN-GRECIAN WORLD

WE cannot understand even the beginnings of Christianity without knowing something of the world to which it came. Jesus' life seems quiet enough in its little corner of the world; but Roman soldiers are present when he dies, Greek and Latin and Hebrew stand over his cross, and the story of his life goes forth to the world not in Hebrew but in Greek. Paul's case is even more suggestive. He was a Hebrew of the Hebrews, and he bore the message of a Jewish Messiah; but he spoke in Greek, he himself was a Roman citizen, and his field was the Roman empire. The world of the early church

These three worlds must be studied separately: (1) the Roman world, political and social; (2) the Grecian world of language and culture and religion; (3) the Jewish world which we study for its religion alone.

When Jesus was born in the reign of Augustus, Rome had fully entered upon her great career as a world empire. The nations about the Mediterranean had been merged under her rule. Great roads stretched everywhere for the Roman soldier. The sea had been swept free of pirates. Everywhere was safety and quiet. As a result trade and travel of all kinds increased enormously. The Mediterranean was one great highway. Travel was almost as general in the empire as it is with us to-day. Paul, with his long and constant journeyings, was not an isolated instance. We can imagine some of those whom he must have met upon the road: the wealthy merchant with his shipload of corn bound from Alexandria to Rome; a company of recruits traveling to join the army; university students bound for Athens or Alexandria; travelers for pleasure, numerous then as now; wealthy Romans journeying in The Roman world: safety and travel

13

search of health to baths, or to cooler climes; some throng
bound for the Isthmian games, or a company of Jews of the
dispersion on the way to a feast at Jerusalem; everywhere
the representatives of Rome, officials of administration or
officers and soldiers; and finally the common folks, merchants like Aquila and Priscilla, or artisans seeking for
work.

The lot of the common people

But the peace and increase of wealth meant little to the
common people. Rome was never a democracy, nor had
Greece ever been such. There was no great middle class,
prosperous and intelligent, to form the strength of the nation,
as with England or America. Of the fifty millions or more
in the Roman world the wealth and power belonged to but
very few. Rome was a constant drain upon the provinces.
Augustus declares that he gave eight gladiatorial exhibits
in which ten thousand men fought, and twenty-six exhibits
of conflicts with wild beasts in which thirty-five hundred
African beasts were slain. At the same time he was making
his donations of food and money to scores of thousands of
Roman citizens at one time. All this had to come from the
toil of the poor. There was also the support of Roman
armies. The temple of Janus was closed three times in
Augustus's reign as a sign of universal peace, but the cost
of that peace was an armed host ready to be hurled east
or west or north at the first sign of uprising. In addition
to all this was the procession of governors and officers of
all kinds moving out to the provinces, amassing wealth in
their brief term of office, and then giving way to others.
No wonder the people compared themselves to the beggar,
who would not chase away the flies that fed at his sores
since to do so would only be to make room for others unfed
and more hungry.

Slavery

Slavery is another side of this picture. Roman wars
brought in captives by the scores of thousands. They were
not necessarily of inferior race, and yet the power of the
Roman master was absolute. He could feed a slave to the

fishes if he would. And the Roman law provided that in case any slave killed his master, the whole household of slaves, young and old, innocent and guilty, might be put to death.

These common folks and slaves composed the mass of the members of the early church. To them Christianity's message of deliverance was indeed gospel—"good news." It showed them that their souls might be free though their bodies were in bondage. It introduced them into a fellowship where all men were brothers. And it gave them the sustaining hope of the new kingdom that was coming, which their Master would speedily establish upon earth. *The gospel and the poor*

Despite all this, Roman rule wrought great results for the spread of Christianity. It broke down the old barriers that divided race from race. The oneness of the empire prepared the way for that great conception of one brotherhood and one Father that Paul proclaimed. Peace and unity of the empire made possible that active intercourse and travel which did so much for the spread of the new faith. It gave broad and safe highways on land and sea, little dreaming that they would be remembered longest not for the tread of proud armies, but for the journeys of a humble Jewish preacher whose message was to lay the foundations of a new and greater realm. *What Rome did for Christianity*

Equally extensive with the Roman rule was the world of thought and culture which we call Grecian. Greek was the language of the West; the Roman conquerors had gone to school to their captives and taken from them language and philosophy and art. Greek was the language of the East; Alexander's empire had not lasted long politically, but he had carried Grecian culture wherever he went and this had remained. The east coast of the Mediterranean was dotted with Hellenistic cities, and they were found in the interior as far as Persia and India. One language could thus be used throughout the length and breadth of the Roman world. Into that language the Old Testament had been translated, and this Greek Old Testament was the *The Grecian world: the language*

Bible of the Jews outside of Palestine. It was in Greek that Paul preached from Damascus and Antioch to Rome, and in the same language our New Testament was written. The language was thus like another Roman road, and even more important. Along this road of the mind ideals and influences of the greatest power could travel: the great conceptions of Greek philosophy, the great religious ideals of the Greek Old Testament, and finally the religious conceptions that came from the farther east. To the consideration of these we now turn.

Religion in the empire

Christianity did not come to a world without faith, or to a time of religious decadence. It was a period of the most active and eager religious thought and life. In the number of religions and religious societies the situation was not unlike that with us to-day, except that our societies are mostly Christian. These religions were not all darkness and error, while even their failures helped prepare the way for Christianity. They may be studied under three headings: 1. The old national faiths and their decay. 2. Grecian philosophy and its religious meaning. 3. The new religions.

National religions

1. The National Religions. In ancient times religion was the concern primarily of the tribe or the state, not of the individual. It included all the life of a people. The founding of a city, the making of war, the planting of grain and gathering of harvests, the feasts and the mournings were all accompanied and directed by religious rites; and the welfare of state and people was held to depend upon a proper regard for such observances.

Polytheism could not last

With Greece and Rome this religion was polytheistic. It was not a religion that could last. (1) It could not stand the test of reason. The mind always seeks to find one cause and one meaning back of all things. Men could not rest in the thought of many gods. (2) It could not stand the test of the growing moral sense. It was a Greek philosopher, Anaxagoras, who wrote long before Christianity: "Everything that men count as disgraceful and immoral—theft, adultery, and deceit—that Homer and Hesiod have ascribed to the gods." (3) It could not meet the needs of men, and that was the chief reason for its passing. It was more the religion of a race in its childhood. It concerned itself with the simpler needs of life: harvests, health, safety, success in war. But men were asking deeper questions, about deliverance from sorrow and sin and death, about the hope of a life to come. The time of individualism was coming; men wanted a life for themselves, and not simply as part of a city or nation. The old faiths had no answer for these questions.

2. Grecian Philosophy. The story of Grecian philosophy is a noble chapter in human history. It has its great characters like Socrates, the man of whom Xenophon could write, "He was so devout that he never did anything without the counsel of the gods, so just that he never injured anyone even in the least, so truly master of himself that he never chose the agreeable instead of the good." In a later development, which we call Stoicism, this philosophy could show such spirits as Seneca, Epictetus, and Marcus Aurelius. So closely do some of the thoughts of Seneca resemble those of Paul that some writers used to hold that the former had borrowed from the latter. The Greek philosophy in the main was deeply religious. It was monotheistic; though the gods are often spoken of, it is one Divine Being that is meant. It was ethical. Plato sets forth a noble ideal of righteousness, of the just man who shows good to foe as well as friend. The Stoic picture of the wise man is even nobler, the man who is strong, self-contained, unmoved by outward conditions of good or evil, showing the same spirit toward the evil and the good. *Grecian philosophy*

But Grecian philosophy too failed to meet the needs of the day. It had nothing for the common man. It was a religion for the strong and the wise. The common man needs more than a high ideal, he needs some power to help him reach it. *Where it failed*

There was no message here of any God who cared for men, or who could redeem them. The world was waiting for a religion of redemption, a religion of hope and help. The Stoic God was like the Stoic wise man, serene and calm and self-sufficient, but unmoved by the needs of men.

The mystery religions

3. The mystery religions professed to meet this very need. We may call them the new religions, for about this time they began to pour into the Roman world from the east. We do not know much about these religions, for the classical writers of Greece and Rome looked down upon these cults as beneath their notice. It was for the very same reason that these writers did not mention Christianity. Like Christianity, these were the religions of the "lower classes." But the real religious life of the empire was in these faiths. These, and not the old polytheism or the noble philosophies, became the real competitors of Christianity.

Their character

Of these mystery religions there were many kinds, and yet they had certain aspects in common. (1) They were usually founded upon some story, the mystery, the tale of some god and of his life and death and coming to life again. Such is the story of Osiris coming from Egypt, the story of Mithra brought from Persia, and that of Dionysius in Greece. (2) These religions are no longer national. They come to men individually and unite them in societies, just as the believers were joined together in the Christian churches. (3) These religions were marked by ceremonies and sacraments. The members were initiated into the myth, or secret story of the god. There were sacred meals and washings and other rites, sometimes bloody and barbarous, sometimes involving gross excesses. (4) The great thought was that of redemption. The great end was deliverance from evil, especially death, by means of union with the god.

Differ from Christianity

Looked at superficially, there is much here that suggests the new Christian religion, and men have not been wanting who held that Paul, for example, was deeply influenced in his thought by these faiths. Here are societies like the churches, with sacraments of supper and baptism and the story of a dying and risen god. And these religions, like Christianity, appeal as religions of redemption, offering to save men. A very little study shows how deep the differences are. It is enough to point out two. (1) The salvation which Christianity offered was ethical. While these religions relied upon rites and magic, Christianity put at the center a new spirit and a new life. It met the final problem: not how to save men from sorrow, or even from death, but how to save them from sin, to make character. (2) These religions built upon a myth, a tale; Christianity came with a great historic fact—Christ as the revelation of the will of God, as the bearer of the mercy and help of God.

CHAPTER II

THE JEWISH WORLD

Christianity and the Jewish faith

GREECE and Rome and the Orient all had their influence upon Christianity and its development, but it was the Jewish world from which the new faith directly sprang. Its founder was a Jew and spoke a Semitic tongue. His work was done within the narrow borders of the little Jewish province. The early leaders of the movement, Paul, Peter, and James, were all of the same race. Above all, it was the noble faith of Israel in which Christianity rooted.

The Semitic world

What was the place of the Jew in the Roman world? The Jew was, first of all, a part of a larger Semitic world. Rome's old enemies, the Carthaginians, belonged to this race, as did the Phœnicians along the east coast of the Mediterranean; and other Semitic peoples extended as far east as Babylonia. Most of these used a common tongue called Aramaic. The Jews at this time used a dialect of this tongue instead of the old Hebrew in which the Old Testament was written.

The land of the Jews

Palestine was the old home of the Jews. It is usually thought of as having been shut off from the rest of the world and from the great movements of history. As a matter of fact, it lay on the great highways that joined the nations of antiquity. It was a meeting place for three continents. Along these roads swept in turn the armies of the great conquering nations, Babylonia, Assyria, Egypt, Macedonia, Syria, Rome. Israel had felt the influence of all these and yet had preserved her individuality. At the time of Jesus' birth she was ruled by Herod the Great, a selfish and cruel but strong monarch. The land had been separated by Rome, however, into several divisions. The province of Judæa was the principal one. This included

20

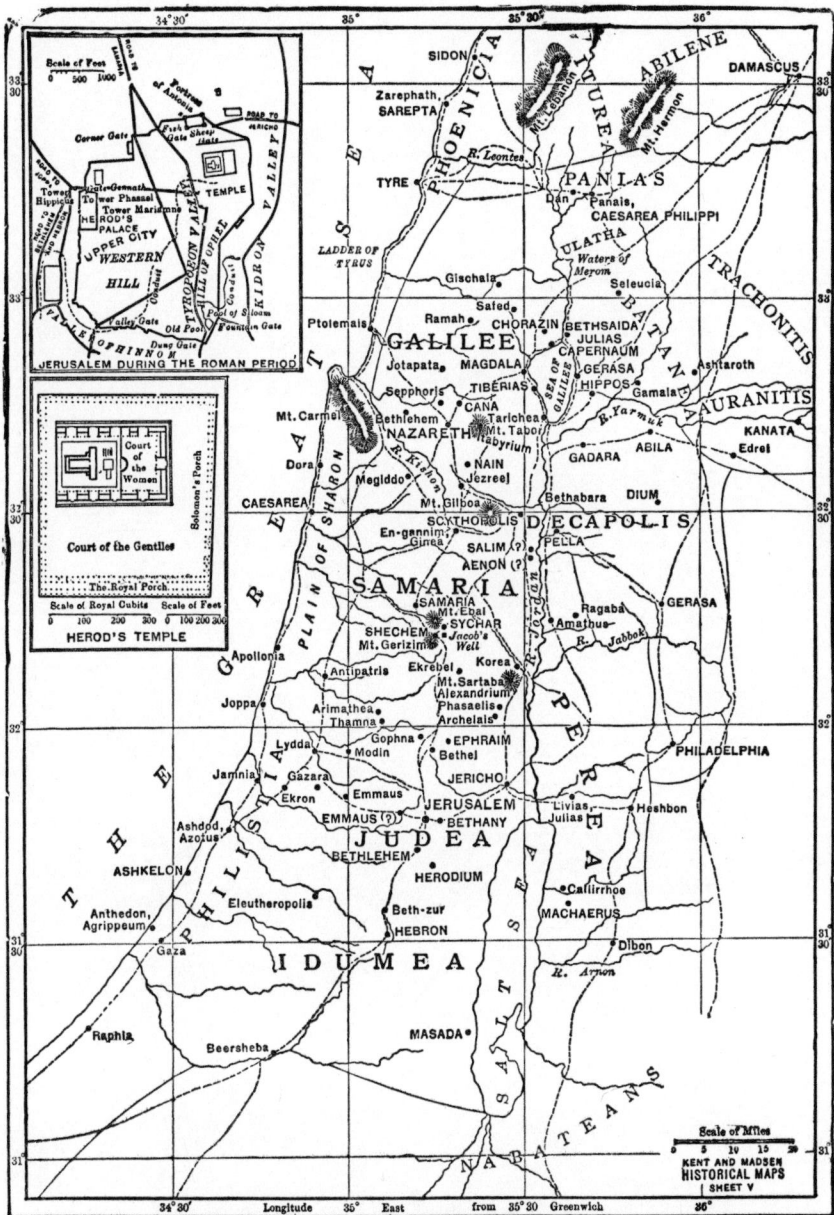

PALESTINE IN THE TIME OF JESUS. 4 B.C.—30 A.D.
(INCLUDING THE PERIOD OF HEROD 40-4 B.C.)

Scale of Feet
JERUSALEM DURING THE ROMAN PERIOD

Court of the Gentiles
The Royal Porch
Scale of Royal Cubits   Scale of Feet
HEROD'S TEMPLE

Scale of Miles
KENT AND MADSEN
HISTORICAL MAPS
SHEET V

Longitude   35°   East   from 35°30 Greenwich

Idumæa to the south, Judæa proper (corresponding to the old southern kingdom), and Samaria (corresponding to the old kingdom of Israel). The chief Jewish population lay in the two latter, which formed a territory but little larger than half of the State of Iowa or Illinois. North of Samaria lay Galilee, where Jesus' home was. It had not long been settled by the Jews and was still half Gentile. Across the Jordan lay Peræa, which was joined with Galilee to form a tetrarchy. After Herod the Great the kingdom was divided. At the time of Jesus' ministry the province of Judæa was under the direct control of the emperor. The governor appointed by him was called procurator, and at this time was Pontius Pilate. The tetrarchy of Galilee and Peræa at the time of the Gospels was under Herod Antipas, whom Jesus called the fox. The Jews had a very large measure of self-government in Judæa under their high priest and Sanhedrin, or Senate. For the most part their religious customs and scruples were respected. But the crushing burden of taxation was never intermitted. There were poverty and distress in abundance. The hated publican was always present as a sign of their bondage, and constantly smoldering underneath all was the religious-patriotic passion which flamed forth at last in the hopeless revolt against Rome that ended in the destruction of Jerusalem.

But the Jew was not limited to Palestine then any more *The Jew in* than he is now. In their earlier history the Jews had been *the empire* carried off by force into captivity, while in the later years vastly greater numbers had gone into other lands of their own free will. The scattered Jews were called the Diaspora, or Dispersion. The Jew had once been a nomad with herds and flocks, as his Arab cousin is to-day. When he settled in Canaan he became an agriculturist. But before the time of Christ he had begun the career of tradesman, in which we know him so well. Then, as now, he was scattered throughout the world. Over a century before

Christ the Grecian geographer Strabo wrote, "One cannot readily find any place in the world which has not received this tribe and been taken possession of by it." There were from four to four and a half million Jews in the empire, probably not far from a twelfth of the whole population. Then, as now, they were looked down upon and often persecuted. And yet they enjoyed special privileges. They usually formed in each city a special community with some measure of self-government. The synagogue was the center of the community, and over a hundred and fifty of these are known to have been scattered throughout the empire.

The dispersion a preparation for Christianity This dispersion of the Jews was of the greatest significance for Christianity. Rome built roads for the gospel, Greece gave it a language, but the Jews had prepared the approach to men's hearts and minds. Every Jewish synagogue was a center of religious influence. About it there was usually a fringe of converts, or proselytes, or at least a number of interested inquirers and attendants who were spoken of as "devout" or "God-fearing" (Acts 10. 22; 17. 4). Despite the prejudice against the Jews, the pure faith, the simple worship, and the high moral ideals must have proven attractive to many noble souls in the Roman world. Thus the leaven of the Old Testament moral and spiritual ideals was spread throughout the empire, and Paul's first and best converts were among these Gentiles that had already been touched by Judaism.

The religion of the prophets The religion of Judaism is of supreme interest to the Christian. Jesus did not profess to bring a new faith. He came to the Jews with the faith of their fathers; his God was Jehovah, "the God of Abraham and Isaac and Jacob." The highest expression of the Hebrew religion was in the prophets and the psalms. It was not merely the thought of one God, such as Grecian philosophy had reached; it was the character of that God as a God of righteousness and mercy. From this conception of God came the pure and noble idea of religion; for such a God asks of men not sacrifice and ritual, but "to do justly, and to love kindness, and to walk humbly with God" (Mic 6. 8). Upon this religion of the prophets Jesus built, and we cannot understand Christianity without it. Side by side with it in the Old Testament is a great system of ceremonial law, but with this priestly religion Jesus showed little sympathy.

There is a difference, however, between the Old Testament religion and the religion of Jesus' day, or Judaism. A living religion does not stand still. The last four centuries before Christ were of great importance for the Jewish religion, though we read little of this history in the Old Testament. The Jews had become a part of Alexander's empire. The Greeks, not contented with political rule, wished to change the eastern civilization and Hellenize it. At first they made some progress with the Jews. Grecian games and customs were introduced. There was a strong and growing liberal party. Then Antiochus, called Epiphanes, tried to force the process. He tried to compel the Jews to give up circumcision, the Sabbath, and the books of the law. As a result he merely strengthened the opposition and aroused the people. The party of the law triumphed. Everything that separated the Jews from the nations was emphasized. The passion of the Jews and the chief concern of religion became more and more the mere keeping of the many precepts of the law. All this bore its fruits in Jesus' day. Religion was not fellowship with God. God was far off. In his place were these laws which he had given. Religion was keeping these laws, and the endless traditions which had grown up about them. It was an almost impossible burden, and many made no attempt at all to carry it (Acts 15. 10).

Side by side with the law was the hope. We might describe the Jewish religion as an ellipse with the law and the hope as the two foci about which it moved. This hope we first meet in the Old Testament. It is the hope of the Messianic kingdom, that at some time Israel's enemies are to

[margin note: Judaism and the law]

[margin note: The hope]

be overthrown and she is to reign in triumph. Prophets like Isaiah give us a wonderful picture of the new earth that is to come, in which peace and righteousness shall prevail. Usually, though not always, the prophets spoke of a Messiah who was to bring in this new kingdom. Such a hope might be very broad and generous, as in Isa 19. 24, 25: "In that day shall Israel be the third with Egypt and with Assyria, a blessing in the midst of the earth; for that Jehovah of hosts hath blessed them, saying, Blessed be Egypt my people, and Assyria the work of my hands, and Israel mine inheritance." But it might be very narrow as it was in Jesus' day, when the Jews dreamed only of their own triumph and thought not so much of a reign of righteousness as of material blessings.

Influences from without The Jews had resisted every attempt to break down their peculiar faith and to engulf them in the mixture of religions and races which made the Hellenistic-Roman world. They did not, however, remain uninfluenced. This is especially seen in the changes that took place in the Messianic hope. We see this in Jewish writings of this period. We hear about angels and demons. The world is divided into two opposing forces of light and darkness, and these are to meet at last in a great conflict which is to bring in the new age. There are to be resurrection and judgment, heaven and hell. These ideas, which are lacking in the Old Testament, show the influence of the East, and especially of Persia.

Pharisees We have spoken so far as though there were no differences of religious thought among the Jews. The New Testament pages show us that there were different parties and classes. First among these are the Pharisees. They were the separatists, or Puritans, of their day. In the days of the struggle against Antiochus and the Greek customs they stood for the law and the separation of Israel from all the pagan life about them. They favored the strictest observance of the law and all the rules that had been built around it by tradition. There were not many of them—Josephus says six thousand—but their influence with the people was very great. With them are usually mentioned in the New Testament the scribes. They were the teachers of the law, the lawyers, and they usually belonged to the Pharisaic party. They studied not so much the law as the mass of teachings about the law which had been handed down from the older rabbis. Their teaching was simply a remembering and repeating of these traditions, a dreary and endless process that sank more and more to trifles and puerilities, while neglecting "the weightier matters of the law, justice, and mercy, and faith."

The Sadducees were the aristocrats, the party of the priestly nobility. They were conservatives in theology, disregarding the traditions of the scribes, holding only to the older written law, and refusing more modern doctrines like those of the resurrection and of spirits. In religion, however, they represented the more liberal and worldly wing. They were not so strict in observing the law and were quite ready to make alliance with the Romans if it would keep them in power. They had no influence with the people and their power depended upon their control of the temple. After the destruction of the temple and the city in the year 70 they disappear. *Sadducees*

With all their faults the Pharisees were the real representatives of the religious life of the people. But if they show the strength of Judaism, they show its weakness too. The religion of the law could not save men. With those who felt that they had kept the law, like the Pharisees, it gendered formalism and pride. With others it created either indifference or despair; the law was no help, but an impossible burden. Never did a people show more zeal for religion. "I bear them witness that they have a zeal for God," says Paul (Rom 10. 2). But it could not give men peace of heart or moral victory. Judaism trained the conscience which she could not still. She stood far above the other religions of the day. She saw that salvation must *The failure of a religion of law*

mean righteousness. Jeremiah had spoken of the law that
was to be written in men's hearts (31. 31-34). Ezekiel
had written of the new spirit that was to be given (36. 26,
27). The psalmist had uttered his great petition, "Create
in me a clean heart, O God; and renew a right spirit within
me" (51. 10). But the religion of law could not bring this
about. That remained for a new faith.

PART II
JESUS

PART II

ISSUES

CHAPTER III

JOHN THE BAPTIST

THERE is no more striking figure in the Bible than that John's impression upon his time of John the Baptist. Only a few words are given to him in the Gospels, and yet how clear the picture stands before us: the rude figure from the desert, the stern message of judgment, the thronging multitudes, the tragic end. For Christian thought he has been overshadowed by Jesus; on his own age he made a profound impression. He had no pleasant doctrine, and yet from Jerusalem and all Judæa there flocked to his preaching the people of every class—common folks and proud Pharisees, Sadducean aristocrats and plain soldiers. His name was upon every lip when Jesus was still unknown. Men asked one another whether he could be the Messiah. His stern words reached the palace and led at last to imprisonment and death. Yet even after his execution men could not think him dead, and the first reports of Jesus' work made them ask whether John was not risen from the dead (Mark 6. 14; 8. 28). Paul found disciples of his as remote as Ephesus, one of whom became a notable leader in the church (Acts 18. 25; 19. 1-7). The tragedy of the end helped to deepen the impression. Apparently at the height of his power, Herod laid hold upon him. The Gospels say it was because John had denounced Herod's sin. Josephus declares that Herod feared lest John, with his great influence over the people, might lead them to some rebellion. Perhaps both reasons entered in. In any case, the prison walls never opened for John again, and his murder must have followed soon.

We cannot class John with any circle or party of his The prophet day. He was, as Jesus said, a prophet. In him there came to life again that great line of men who were Israel's conscience and Israel's faith, and whose like no other nation of antiquity can show. Like them, he came with no pomp or heralding. His message constituted his credentials. He might have said with Amos, "The Lord Jehovah hath spoken; who can but prophesy?" John was a preacher, "the voice of one crying in the wilderness."

The message The message of John is essentially that of the great prophets. The great foundation for him, as for them, is the truth that religion means righteousness. But there is an urgency in John's message that comes from a special cause: the kingdom of God is at hand. To the Jews that was a welcome word. It meant that Jehovah was coming to judge the nations and deliver his people. The rule of the hated Romans was to be overthrown and Israel's glory established. Into this easy-going hope John cuts with the sharp sword of his word: "Repent ye. The judgment is coming, but it will not be upon the Gentiles. Rather it will be a sifting of Israel, and the test will be righteousness. The Jews will not be saved because they have kept the form of the law. The Messiah is at hand with his judgment. He will lay his ax at the root of every evil tree. He will winnow the wheat from the chaff with his fan. My baptism is with water. His will be with fire that shall burn up all the dross. The rule of God is at hand; repent and make ready."

The meaning of John's baptism It is in the light of this message that we are to understand the meaning of the baptism to which John invited the people. This was something different from the practice of the prophets. Was John, after preaching righteousness, falling back into the idea that a mere ceremony could have value in itself? There is no reason for thinking this. The form itself was familiar to the Jews as a symbol of cleansing in case of ceremonial defilement (Lev 15 and elsewhere). It was also used when a Gentile convert, or proselyte, was enrolled. Both these meanings appear with John, though not as mere ceremony. It was first a sign of cleansing, of

repentance and turning from evil; and second an enroll-
ment, a consecration to the new rule of God that was
at hand. It was the outward expression of the acceptance of his message: Repent, for the kingdom of God is
at hand.

The remarkable response of the people to John's message   The response
was due first to its declaration that the kingdom of God was   to the
at their doors. Chafing under the hated Roman rule, no   message
wonder that they flocked to him when the rumor of this
message spread. But the deeper and more lasting response
was awakened by his call to repentance. With all her
formalism Israel had a conscience, and a conscience like
that of no other nation of her day. True, her religion had
become largely legalism and her prophets had lost their
first place, but their work had not been in vain. She did
not want such preaching, any more than Florence wanted
Savonarola, but, like Florence, she answered to it, at least
for a time. John's message was fearless and searching.
He pointed out definite sins. And his appeal gained tremendous power because he pictured the Messiah and his
judgment at the door.

The limitations of John's work are closely joined to its   John's
strength. He represents the old at its highest. The moun-   limitations
tain peaks of the Old Testament are the prophets, and in
John we hear their message again. But John did not get
beyond the old. Men needed the message of sin and judgment; but they needed something more—a message of
deliverance. John had gotten no farther than Paul before
his conversion. Paul too knew of law and righteousness
and judgment. But if these were not enough for Paul,
the man of moral earnestness and mighty will, how could
they save the throngs of common folks who came to John's
preaching? That was what Jesus meant when he said that
they that were but little in the kingdom of God were greater
than John. They knew the God of mercy and had learned
to say, "Our Father."

John himself knew that his work was not final, but a mere preparation: "He that cometh after me is mightier than I." How much farther John went we cannot know surely. He did not cease his work after Jesus' appearance. He had disciples who continued faithful, and that, too, long after his death (Acts 19. 1-7). From his prison he sends a message to Jesus by his disciples asking whether he be the expected Messiah or no. Jesus' own estimate of John is significant (Luke 7. 24-28). He sees his courage, earnestness, and independence, and pays the remarkable tribute: "Among them that are born of women there is none greater than John." But the meaning of his work is preparation:

> "This is he of whom it is written,
> Behold I send my messenger before thy face,
> Who shall prepare thy way before thee."

John's greatest work was to make ready the way for Jesus and to call attention to him.

DIRECTIONS FOR READING AND STUDY

Birth: Luke 1. 5-25, 57-66, 80. Ministry: Luke 3. 1-20; Mark 1. 1-8; Matt 3. 1-12. Imprisonment: Mark 6. 14-29. Jesus and John: Luke 7. 18-25.

Read carefully the reports of John's preaching and make a list of the things he condemned and of the things he demanded.

Read Amos 3 and 4. What points of resemblance are there between John's preaching and that of Amos?

Write out a simple statement of the facts of John's life as learned from the Gospels.

CHAPTER IV

BIRTH AND CHILDHOOD

"JOHN STUART MILL, the great philosopher of positivism, Jesus as our central study once said, that humanity could not be too often reminded of the fact that there was once a man by the name of Socrates. He was right; but it is more important to remind humanity again and again that once there stood in her midst a man by the name of Jesus Christ." To understand the beginnings of the Christian religion one must first study Jesus. It is not necessary to construct a biography. The Gospels do not really afford the material for this. We may study his life in broad outline, but the great aim is to get a picture of Jesus himself, what he taught, what he wrought, and what his spirit and purpose in life were. This simple life, that came to so early a close, was the turning point of human history. What was this life to have produced this result?

The story of Jesus' birth is given by only two of the four Matthew's story of the birth Gospels, and these two give us quite distinct accounts. Matthew's story is as follows: Joseph is informed by an angel that Mary, to whom he is betrothed, shall bear a child. To the mother and child in Bethlehem (nothing is said of Nazareth) there come certain Magi with gifts, led there by a star. Warned by an angel, Joseph flees to Egypt, while Herod slays the little children of Bethlehem in the effort to kill the one that "was born King of the Jews." Joseph returns after Herod's death, but fears to go to Judæa on account of Archelaus and so settles at Nazareth in Galilee (Matt 1. 18 to 2. 23).

Luke's story is longer and introduces a larger circle. Luke's story Here it is Mary that is told of the wonderful child who is to be the deliverer of his people. From their village

33

in Nazareth, Joseph and Mary go to their ancestral home at Bethlehem near Jerusalem because of a census taken by the Romans. Here she brings forth her child, while simple shepherds, who have seen a light and heard a wonderful song, come to worship from the nearby fields. In Bethlehem they remain until they have fulfilled the requirements of the law, first circumcising the child, then after thirty-three days presenting the child in the temple and offering for the mother the simple sacrifice that was asked of the poor. This done, they return to Nazareth (Luke 2. 1-39).

The two stories compared

About these stories there has been a great deal of discussion, and principally for two reasons: first, because of the differences between them; second, because of the story of the virgin birth. As to the former, the differences include not only those in the two stories just told but in the genealogies which both give. It is plain that the writers had formed quite different pictures as to how the birth of Jesus occurred. How far they can be reconciled is not really an important matter. They agree as to the parents of the child, the place of the birth and later home, and the wonderful manner and meaning of that birth.

The meaning of the story

What is more important is to appreciate the beautiful simplicity of the story, especially as told by Luke. There is no stronger witness to its essential truth. It is not such a story as men would have invented for the coming of a king. The humble parents, the rude stable, the simple shepherds, the quiet return home again—nothing could be simpler, more human than this. The essential faith of the early church is set forth here in truest manner. For that church the life of Jesus was first of all a normal human life, just as is shown here. Secondly, it was a life from God, the life in which God came to men.

The virgin birth

As to the story of the virgin birth, it has been pointed out that the rest of the New Testament is silent upon this, and that in Luke there is but a single clause that refers to it. Two points should be made clear here. One is that the virgin birth was evidently not essential for the faith of the early church. Paul and John, who say nothing concerning it, are the two writers who give us the highest conception of the divinity of Jesus. The other is, that to the church it has always seemed the fitting conception of the mode of the coming of the Messiah. It is always to be remembered, however, that it is the character and life of Jesus which lead us to believe in the virgin birth, and not the virgin birth which leads us to believe in Jesus.

The exact date of Jesus' birth is not known, neither month nor day nor year. It was not till the sixth century that men began to date events from the birth of Christ. It was a Roman monk, Dionysius the Little, that proposed it. His reckoning was not accurate, and the date of the birth is probably about 5 B. C. So much is known, that the civilized world to-day, in every event that its histories record and every document of business or of news, pays tribute to that humble birth as the turning point of history. *The date of the birth*

Of the home life of Jesus there is little to be said. There is no reference to Joseph after Jesus' boyhood, and tradition says that he died early. That must have meant burdens of labor and responsibility for Jesus as the oldest son. There were at least seven children (Matt. 13. 55, 56), five of them sons. It must have been a very humble home, probably but a single room, and that used for the carpenter work as well. But it must have been a very rich home. When we think of the Jews of Jesus' day, we are apt to call up the New Testament pictures of the formal Pharisees or the worldly Sadducees. The first pages of Luke show us another circle. Here are Elisabeth and Zacharias, Simeon and Anna, Joseph and Mary. The songs of Mary and Zacharias and the words of Elisabeth and Simeon show us the atmosphere in which these people moved, the simple piety and the earnest expectation with which they looked for the day of deliverance of their nation. There must have been *The Nazareth home*

many such simple, quiet lives in which the noblest spirit of
the Old Testament psalms and prophetic writings lived on.
And such was Jesus' home. We are told that Joseph was a
just, or kind, man. A devout man he must have been. He
gave his sons the old patriarchal names: Jesus (or Joshua),
James (or Jacob), Joseph, Simon, and Judas. Jesus' own
words seem to give us suggestions of what that home life
was. When he prays in the garden he uses the simple
word that Mary taught him to call Joseph as a little child,
the Aramaic word for father, "Abba." He cannot think of
a father who would give his child a stone for bread. Many
of his illustrations must have been taken from the old
home: the dough swelling and bubbling with the leaven,
the housewife sweeping the dark room for the lost coin,
the hungry children crowding around for a bit of bread,
the father abed at night with his children about him in
the one room of the house and unwilling to get up for the
neighbor who comes to borrow a loaf.

We can form some picture also of the training which
Jesus received. No other nation had such a system of education as the Jews. It was for all children, not for the
few. The theme of instruction was the law. "Ask one of us
concerning the laws," says Josephus, the Jewish historian,
"and he can recite them all more readily than he could
repeat his own name." The mother began the work at
home, which was taken up by the father, and probably
carried on in the elementary village school connected with
the synagogue. The first words that Jesus thus learned at
home were probably the noble opening words from the
Shema, or confession of faith: "Hear, O Israel: Jehovah
our God is one Jehovah: and thou shalt love Jehovah thy
God with all thy heart, and with all thy soul, and with all
thy might" (Deut 6. 4). The various festivals of the
Jewish year, marking the great events in Jewish history,
were a part of this education, as were also the regular
gatherings at the synagogue. Luke tells how Jesus in his

early ministry "came to Nazareth, where he had been brought up: and he entered, as his custom was, into the synagogue on the Sabbath day."

At the same time it is important to realize that Jesus was brought up in Galilee, not in Jerusalem or Judæa. There was a wide gulf between the religion of the prophets and psalmists that filled his heart, and the deadly formalism, the slavery of the letter, the narrow bigotry and pride that opposed him when he came to work as a man. There is a humanness in his spirit, a breadth in his outlook, a simplicity and directness in his teaching, that we cannot associate with the streets of Jerusalem or the classrooms of the rabbis. The influence of Galilee

One incident from the boyhood days tells us how deeply the training took hold upon this youth. At the age of twelve or thirteen years the Jewish boy became a man in matters of religion and assumed the full duties of the faith. One of these was the journey thrice a year to the great feasts at Jerusalem. The story of Jesus' first visit is the only break in the silence that rests upon the years from infancy to the day when he began his ministry. Later legends tell of a precocious child confounding the learned doctors in the temple by superhuman knowledge. Luke's picture is very simple, though deeply suggestive. It is that of a boy already thoughtful about the deep things of life, and so stirred by the city and the temple and the solemn ceremonies of the passover feast that he forgets parents and all as he tarries in the temple. His one passion is already the business of his Father. But it is all normal and wholesome. He goes back as the dutiful son, and his life unfolds as a boy's life should, growing in mind and body, in the esteem of parents and friends, and in fellowship with God (Luke 2. 40-52). The first visit to Jerusalem

One other element in his training must be noted. As the boy grew older, he came to know a larger world than his home and village. We know how deeply the world of The training of the larger world nature impressed Jesus. Paul speaks of cities and soldiers and athletic contests; Jesus of birds and flowers, of fields and flocks, of storms and sunsets. The Galilee of his day was a beautiful and most fertile country. And then there was the larger world of men. It has been a common mistake to think of Nazareth as a quiet spot far from the life of the great world, where Jesus was nurtured in seclusion. That is far from the truth. The village itself was not large, perhaps of but a few thousand inhabitants, and it was hid away in a basin of the hills. But above it rose the crest of these hills some fifteen hundred feet higher than the sea level. How often Jesus must have looked out from those heights upon "the kingdoms of the world, and the glory of them." The smiling waters of Galilee lay scarce more than fifteen miles to the east. Only a few miles farther to the northwest was the Mediterranean. Near by ran north and south the great highway which for centuries joined the ancient kingdoms of Egypt and Babylonia, along which so many armies had marched to victory or defeat. Just below, to the south, was the great plain of Esdraelon, where so many of Israel's battles had been fought. All about was the teeming life of Galilee, with its numberless villages and cities. The Roman world had crowded in here. Jesus heard the Greek language spoken and the Scriptures read in the Greek translation, and must have known the language himself, though he probably preferred the Aramaic. From the hills above his home he must have seen at times the Roman legions on their march, and Roman rulers with their brilliant following. Something of what happened in the great Roman world he knew, for in one of his parables he uses the incident of the embassy that was sent after Archelaus, when this son of Herod went to Rome to get his kingdom.

DIRECTIONS FOR READING AND STUDY

Matt 1. 18 to 2. 23; Luke 1. 26 to 2. 52.
Write out the incidents of the annunciation and birth as given

respectively by Matthew and Luke. Note the apparent differences and points of agreement.

Read carefully the songs of Mary, Zacharias, and Simeon. What book of writings in the Old Testament do they resemble? What is their central thought or interest? What do they suggest as to the character of these persons? With the aid of a Bible that has marginal references, make a list of the Old Testament passages that are used or alluded to. Compare Mary's song with 1 Sam 2. 1-10.

CHAPTER V

THE CALL AND THE TEMPTATION

The years
of quiet

AMONG the hearers of John there had been many who came down from Galilee. Jesus had been among that number. It was John's word that called him forth at last from the quiet of Nazareth to begin his life task. He was about thirty when that work began. What had taken place in these years of boyhood and young manhood? Of all that time since he was twelve we have no record of a word. The life that we do know, however, seems to make some things clear about these earlier years.

The spirit of
the young
man

In the first place, Jesus' life shows no sign of any moral break in it. If we turn to great leaders like Paul and Augustine and Luther, we get a very different picture. Their Christian life stands forth from an earlier background of doubt and sin. They bear the marks of struggle and the scars of past defeat. That is true of all the great spiritual leaders—except Jesus. The spirit that is shown in the boy in the temple filled his young manhood: the sense of a close fellowship with his Father, and the passion to do God's will. With these two there was a third: the growing conviction as to the deliverance that Jehovah was to bring his people. He shared that hope with the rest of the nation, but with one great difference: with them it was the deliverance from the rule of Rome, while Jesus saw that it was the rule of evil in men's lives that was to be overthrown. How often at dusk or dawn had he looked out from the hill above Nazareth and asked what his part was to be in God's plan.

Jesus and
the preaching
of John

No wonder that the news of John's work found a response in him. "The kingdom is at hand." John was preaching not the overthrow of Rome but repentance for sin. And the people were answering to the call. This was God's doing. To Jesus it was a call to be about his Father's business. And so he joins John's hearers and offers himself for baptism. Many have wondered how Jesus could offer himself for a baptism of repentance. But we have seen that this was not the only or the final meaning of the rite. John was another Elijah, summoning the people to stand for this coming Jehovah or against him. Jesus was ready to stand with John and with them, only it did not mean for him repentance from an evil past as it did with them. He was but showing in public the pledge of allegiance which had ruled his whole life.

Mark's account of what happened at the baptism is the simplest as it is the oldest. "And straightway coming out of the water, he saw the heavens rent asunder, and the Spirit as a dove descending upon him: and a voice came out of the heavens, Thou art my beloved Son, in thee I am well pleased" (Mark 1. 10, 11). A young man's greatest question is that of his life calling. Not till he was thirty had the answer come to Jesus, for there is no sign that he knew before this time that he was to be the deliverer of the people. He had heard John's stirring words, had looked at the throngs that bent under them, and had realized that the day of deliverance was at hand. Now as he came out of the water he heard his call, "Thou art my beloved Son." These words are taken from the second psalm. It was a Messianic psalm for the Jews, and the Son meant the Messiah. It was the Father's call to him: "The kingdom is at hand, and thou art my Son; thou art to be the deliverer, the Messiah." *The baptism and the call*

Jesus had always lived in fellowship with God. Now there came a new sense of God's presence to his soul, stirred to its depths at the same time by the sense of what his life was to be. He must find solitude to meditate. Mark says that he was "driven" by the Spirit into the wilderness. It was the same need that drove him again and again in later *The forty days of prayer* days to places of quiet. When he chooses his disciples, in the hour before his arrest, and at other great turning points of his life, we find him on the mountainside or beneath the trees in prayer. So at this time he goes forth to gather strength and to meditate upon the work he is to do.

The temptation

Out of this last comes his temptation. We have it in strange picture form. The devil appears to him. He bids Jesus turn stones to bread, lest he perish from hunger. He carries him to a temple pinnacle and bids him cast himself down. He shows him from a mountain the kingdoms of the world and offers them to Jesus if he will worship him.

The story from Jesus

First of all we must remember that this story could come only from Jesus himself. It is not unlikely that he told it to his disciples in those last days when he had set his face to go to Jerusalem. They saw his danger from his foes. He was teaching them that death might come, that it was his duty simply to do God's will, and that it was such self-sacrifice that was to bring in the kingdom and not any outward triumph. At such a time he may have told them the story of his own first period of temptation. Studied thoughtfully, it is a story of supreme value for our understanding of Jesus' life and work. It is a bit of autobiography in which Jesus reveals his inmost self.

Jesus' use of picture language

We must remember, in the second place, that it is a picture form which Jesus uses. This picture language was Jesus' common method as a teacher, and he uses it not simply in the parables. He speaks of the devil here just as when he says to Peter, "Get thee behind me, Satan," and for the same reason, for he sees in Peter's suggestion the same evil that he discerned in the tempting thoughts that came to him in the wilderness. Thus, at another time, when he welcomed back the disciples who had been out preaching and healing, Jesus did not say, "This is the beginning of the overthrow of evil." He said, "I beheld Satan fallen as lightning from heaven." The significant fact is not that there was a literal bodily Satan whom Jesus allowed to carry him to temple and mountain, but that Jesus in the thoughts and conflicts of those days saw through many of the ideas which the people held as to the Messiah, and knew that they were evil.

What, then, was the conflict? The question which concerned Jesus in those days was this: What is the nature of the kingdom to be, and how shall the Messiah do his work? What the people expected we know. The enemies of Israel were to be cast down. Israel was to be delivered from want and oppression. She was to have her place of rule and glory, and the nations were to bow down before her. This was not the picture in the heart of Jesus. It was not this that attracted him to John. The kingdom of God, or the kingship of God, meant God's rule in the hearts of men, as well as the overthrow of all evil and suffering and wrong in the world. But in one point he agreed with them: God was to establish this kingdom and the Messiah was to proclaim it and bring it in. And so the personal question came at the end of his meditation: How was the Messiah to do his work and what was to become of him?

The conflict: how should he do his work?

The order of the temptations we do not know. Matthew and Luke differ. Both Matthew and Luke suggest that the temptation as to the bread came at the end of the forty days. We will put this last and follow Matthew in the other two. If such be the order, then the first question was this: How shall I announce myself to the people? If I am to preach to them and lead them, I must prove that I am the Messiah. Is it not written of the Messiah, that Jehovah's angels will keep him, lest he dash his foot against a stone? (Psa 91. 11, 12.) Why not cast myself down from a temple pinnacle before the multitudes? They will see that I am the Messiah and follow me. But Jesus' clear vision sees that such a plan is of the Evil One. That would be tempting God, not trusting him. It would be gaining

Jesus will not win the people by working miracles

an outward following, not a spiritual allegiance. Jesus refused to be a mere miracle-worker. He used his power to help men, not to dazzle them.

Jesus will not win by compromise

The next question also concerned the method of his work. How could God's kingdom be established in the world if all the power of the world were against it? Why not make some concessions at the beginning, perhaps make some sort of alliance with the regular leaders of the people? Or it might be possible to enlist the thousands who were ready to follow a leader if they saw it meant Israel's triumph. Once gained, it would be time enough to teach them the higher spiritual truth of the kingdom. Many leaders have yielded to this temptation of compromise. Not so Jesus. He saw that this was simply the prince of the world offering him its kingdoms if he would fall down and worship. "Thou shalt worship the Lord thy God," was his answer. His trust would be absolutely in God, and in God only.

Not self-saving, but trust and obedience

These temptations must not be conceived as coming at one time. They were at the heart of the whole matter which filled his mind in those forty days. The third temptation, we are told, came at the close of this period. He had forgotten about food. Now he was seized with sudden weakness and hunger. If he were the Messiah, why not turn these stones to bread? What would become of the kingdom if the deliverer should perish? Was it not his first duty to preserve himself? Here too he conquered. No, the first duty was not to preserve himself; it was to do the will of God. That in the end is what man must live by, not bread but the "word that proceedeth out of the mouth of God." It was the same answer as before, obedience and trust, and this too Jesus carried through his life. He knew his power and he used it, but always for others, never for himself. They taunted him when he was on the cross, "He saved others; himself he cannot save" (Matt 27. 42). But that was what he had been doing all his life—saving others, not himself.

Three things are made clear by this story. (1) The spir-itual insight of Jesus. How clearly he sees the principles at stake. What all other men are saying does not confuse him or lead him astray. (2) The moral victory of Jesus. Whatever powers may oppose him, whatever danger or apparent defeat may threaten, he trusts only in God and will obey him alone. (3) The human life of Jesus. He is victorious in temptation, but he is not untempted. There is real fighting here, and it comes not once but again and again.

DIRECTIONS FOR READING AND STUDY

Mark 1. 9-13; Matt 3. 13 to 4. 11; Luke 3. 21 to 4. 13.

Compare carefully the three accounts of the baptism and note the differences, observing that Mark is the oldest. Is the tendency to literalize figures of speech modern or ancient?

Are there any moral difficulties in the way of literalizing the story of the temptation? Would it have been a real temptation if a literal Satan had stood before him, or had carried him physically to a temple pinnacle?

Read the story of Gethsemane in Mark 14. 32-42. Note the nature of the temptation and the way Jesus met it. Is there any analogy in these two points between this and the wilderness temptation?

CHAPTER VI

THE BEGINNINGS

The Gospels not biographies

It is not easy to trace the outline of Jesus' life in the Gospels. The Gospels are not biographies, and do not claim to be. The fourth Gospel states what is the common purpose of all: "These are written, that ye may believe that Jesus is the Christ, the Son of God" (John 20. 31). The Gospels are sermons rather than biographies. In them the materials are collected which the early church used for its preaching. Their interest is to set forth Jesus, that men may believe, not to describe the development of his life or the progress of his work. The first chapters, it is true, give us the story of the beginnings, and at the close there is the story of his sufferings and death. But we cannot be sure of the order of what comes in between. It is not even known how long the period of Jesus' ministry was, and scholars have estimated it at from one to three years or more.

The stages of the life

But while we cannot trace out a biography, there are certain questions that must be raised. How did Jesus begin his work, and what was his aim? How did he win his disciples, and how did he make his enemies? And how, in the end, did his death come about? To these questions, the Gospel of Mark, the oldest of the four, gives some reply. If the suggestions of Mark be followed, five stages in the life and work of Jesus may be traced. (1) Jesus begins his ministry in Galilee, teaching and ministering to men, drawing great multitudes in apparent success, and gathering a few special followers about him. (2) As the meaning of his teaching becomes clear a change takes place. The people desert him because he does not fulfill their hopes of an earthly kingdom. The scribes and Pharisees grow bitterly hostile because he attacks their teaching and threat-

46

ens their leadership. The little group of his disciples, however, through Peter, confesses its faith in him as the Messiah. (3) More and more Jesus withdraws from the crowds and gives himself to the training of the inner circle of his disciples. (4) Finally he turns toward Jerusalem, realizing the danger, but convinced that by his death he is to save men, and that he will return again and set up the Kingdom. (5) His last appeal to the people fails after a brief outburst of enthusiasm, and his life closes with his trial and crucifixion. We shall study the work of Jesus according to this outline, taking up his teachings separately.

How did Jesus begin his work? According to the synoptic Gospels, Jesus began his work quietly and simply as a teacher. Why Jesus did this we can understand from the last chapter. The temptation story shows that he clearly recognized the gulf that lay between his idea of the kingdom and that of the people. With the latter, the kingdom meant an earthly realm. The Messiah was one that would come with splendor and deeds of power, overthrowing their foes and establishing this political realm. For Jesus the Kingdom was spiritual and ethical, a kingdom of righteousness and love. The great obstacle for them was their enemies. The great obstacle for Jesus was ignorance and sin. To have announced himself as Messiah would have defeated all his higher ends. There was only one thing to do. He had fought out the question in the wilderness. He must teach this people the true meaning of the Kingdom, and he must preach to this people and lead them to penitence and to a new life with God.

The fourth Gospel gives a most vivid and interesting narrative of the beginnings of Jesus' work in Judæa. We read here how he meets certain Galilæans among the followers of John the Baptist: Andrew and his brother Peter, Philip and probably John, with Nathanael. Such a meeting would explain how Jesus later called these men in Galilee and how they followed him. The later call was not

a chance meeting and was not at first sight; the men themselves were men whom he had thus had opportunity to meet
before.   There are other reasons for thinking that Jesus
began his work in Judæa. Mark suggests this when he
says that Jesus came into Galilee "after John was delivered
up" (Mark 1. 14). It seems implied in Jesus' words of
lament over Jerusalem, "How often would I have gathered
thy children together" (Luke 13. 34). If Jesus' ministry
lasted more than one year, it is probable that he would at
least have attended the yearly passover feasts at Jerusalem.

Jesus begins at Capernaum
It is to Galilee that we must turn, however, and to Mark's
Gospel, for the first clear and definite account of Jesus'
public work. Whatever he may have done in Judæa, it is
Galilee that he chooses for the real field of his labor. The
city where he begins is not Nazareth, but Capernaum. To
this he may well have been led because his friends Peter and
Andrew lived there. But there was a stronger reason. Capernaum was a populous city lying on the northwest shore
of Lake Galilee, being the chief port for the fishermen of
the lake. Round about it lay the most fruitful and populous
regions of the province. By it swept the great road that
led from Damascus to the Mediterranean. Jesus was here
in the midst of a busy pulsing life. Here he could bring
his message to the people and from this center he could go
through the villages of Galilee. It is Capernaum, with the
nearby cities of Chorazin and Bethsaida, that Jesus declared
had seen his mighty works (Matt 11. 20-24).

Jesus as prophet
We have seen why Jesus would begin his work by teaching and preaching, and this is the way in which the
Gospels represent it. "Jesus came into Galilee, preaching
the gospel of God" (Mark 1. 14). "He went round
about the villages teaching" (Mark 6. 6). "He was
preaching in the synagogues of Galilee" (Luke 4. 44).
The scribe, or teacher, was a familiar figure with the Jews.
Such a life on Jesus' part would excite no wonder. But
the people very soon saw with wonder the difference be-

tween Jesus and the scribes. The teaching of the scribes all looked to the past, to the law that God had once given and to the traditions that had been built up around it. Jesus spoke directly out of his own heart. "And they were astonished at his teaching; for he taught them as having authority" (Mark 1. 22). And so they called him a prophet, a John or an Elijah (Mark 6. 15; 8. 28). They rejoiced to think that God had thus come to them again (Luke 7. 16). Even after his death it was as "a prophet mighty in deed and word" that his disciples spoke of him (Luke 24. 19). His relation to the prophets was evident in his teaching. It was not the priestly and legal side of the Old Testament that appeared in him, but the prophetic. Their disregard of form and ritual, their appeal to conscience, their emphasis on righteousness, all reappear in his teaching.

And yet Jesus was not simply a prophet even in his teaching. The prophets had the special word which was given to them to speak. They came with a "Thus saith the Lord," and spoke only as commanded. Jesus' message is not simply a word given to him. It is a spirit and a life within him. Out of the fullness of that life he speaks. It is no formal message. It is the giving of a life. He gives it in the synagogue or by the wayside, to the thronging multitudes, to the little group of his friends, or to some single soul. He can speak with the passion and power of the prophet, but he can stop to comfort a poor woman or greet a child. And the difference is even more plain in his life. He is more than a messenger; he is a neighbor, a comrade, a friend. He is not the stern executor of fiery judgment that John saw. He can stop to caress the children in the marketplace. He has time for a wedding feast, or to meet Levi's friends at a dinner party, or to rest at the fireside of his intimates. He drew the line at no class. They criticized him because he accepted table hospitality even from "sinners." On the other hand, he was not afraid of the homes of the rich. But we must remember one other

Jesus more than a prophet

thing as we picture this ministry that was so different from that of rabbi or priest or even prophet: while Jesus lived this common life, he never suffered it to be commonplace. He touched all this life only to bless it, and his greatest blessing was to light it up everywhere with the divine life and meaning.

The call of the first disciples

Mark pictures to us with vivid detail the first days at Capernaum. We can understand this detailed knowledge when we remember the probability that it was from Peter himself that Mark obtained this story. Its first incident is the call of the two pairs of brothers, Simon Peter and Andrew, James and John, all of them fishermen. They had been among those that had answered to John's call, but they had seen in Jesus the One greater than John. Now that he was ready to take up his public work, they were ready to follow him.

Jesus and the synagogue

The Sabbath at Capernaum comes next. Luke tells us that Jesus was accustomed to go to the synagogue on the Sabbath (4. 16). The custom may not only have been for the sake of worship, but because the synagogue worship afforded him, as later on with Paul, an opportunity to give his message. No institution is connected more closely with the beginnings of Christianity than the synagogue. Its worship was simple and democratic. It laid stress upon teaching, as does the Protestant Church with its pulpit and with its Sunday school. It was no mere place of ritual, like the temple. At a stated place in the service there was opportunity for exhortation or for explanation of the Scriptures that had been read. Any one might be called upon here, but especially a visiting teacher or scribe. Here Jesus spoke and astounded them because he did not quote Rabbi This or Rabbi That, but "taught them as having authority."

In the synagogue at Nazareth

What Jesus' message was Mark does not record. Luke, however, reports a synagogue address which Jesus gave in his home town of Nazareth (Luke 4. 16-22). This must have occurred later in Jesus' ministry. We take it up here because it gives another synagogue scene and because in it Jesus speaks of the aims of his ministry. We can easily imagine the little village synagogue crowded with Jesus' neighbors and boy-time friends, eager to see and hear the young man whose teachings and doings had made such a stir. From the roll of the prophet Isaiah which is given to him Jesus chooses his lesson. The beautiful passage is the confession of his purpose, and descriptive of the work which filled his days at this time:

> The Spirit of the Lord is upon me,
> Because he anointed me to preach good tidings to the poor:
> He hath sent me to proclaim release to the captives,
> And recovering of sight to the blind,
> To set at liberty them that are bruised,
> To proclaim the acceptable year of the Lord.

Jesus' message begins like that of John. First comes the good news, the word which we translate "gospel": The longed-for kingdom is at the door, the acceptable year is at hand, the rule of God is about to be established. So near at hand did he feel it that he could say, a little later, "There are some here of them that stand by, who shall in no wise taste of death till they see the kingdom of God come with power" (Mark 9. 1). Men were to repent, as John declared, but they were to do much more; they were to live like children of their Father by being pure of heart and kindly and merciful in deed. This teaching we must study more fully later. The deeds of healing which Mark records in this story of that first Capernaum Sabbath will occupy the next chapter.

The good news

DIRECTIONS FOR READING AND STUDY

Mark 1. 14-28; Luke 4. 14-22; 5. 1-11; John 1. 35-51.
Locate upon the map Capernaum, Chorazin, and Bethsaida. Using the scale of miles, estimate their distance apart. Note the relative position of Nazareth to these three and its approximate distance.

Look carefully through the first five chapters of Mark and note (1) the number of passages which refer to Jesus as teaching, and (2) the number which refer to the crowds of people that came to him. Make a list of the passages in both cases.

Make a list of the different places and conditions in which Jesus taught as referred to in these five chapters.

Read carefully the accounts of the call of the first disciples as given by Mark, Luke, and John in the references above. Are they necessarily exclusive of each other?

CHAPTER VII

THE MINISTRY OF HEALING

WE have seen that, like John the Baptist, Jesus was a Jesus in contrast with John preacher, and he put his work of preaching and teaching first. But that was not all of Jesus' work, and a study of their lives shows the marked contrast between the two men. Jesus himself notes the difference in quoting the perverse criticism of their common enemies: "John is come neither eating nor drinking, and ye say, He hath a demon. The Son of man is come eating and drinking, and ye say, Behold, a gluttonous man and a winebibber, a friend of publicans and sinners!" Back of this caricature lay the truth. John was an ascetic and lived apart. He was "a voice crying in the wilderness." Jesus was a man among men. He had open eyes for the beauties of nature: he notes sunset and storm-clouds and lightning flash, the sprouting wheat and ripening grain, and all the life of out-of-doors. Above all, the world of human life appeals to him. He has his close friends. He craves companions. He accepts hospitality. He is found even at the table of the rich; indeed, to one rich man's home he invites himself (Luke 19. 5). He goes to the quiet places for prayer, but he comes back to the crowded ways to live. He chooses busy Capernaum, not little Nazareth, populous Decapolis and not the wilderness. We find him by the lakeside with the fishermen, at the customhouse, in the market place or the synagogue; and everywhere he is talking with men.

Two reasons lie back of this difference between Jesus The reasons for the difference and John. One lies in the spirit of Jesus, his broad humanity, his intense sympathy. The Gospels show this sympathy again and again: when the sick are brought to him, when he sees the people scattered as sheep without a shepherd, when he flames in anger against the Pharisees because these leaders are only leading folks astray, "blind leaders of the blind." He will not let the little children be pushed aside. He will not send the multitudes away hungry. He hears the cry of the blind man by the roadside despite the crowds. The second reason lay in Jesus' conception of his work. John was the herald. Jesus was the Messiah. The kingdom was already present in him, if only in its beginning. Men's sins were being forgiven and their sickness healed. That was what the rule of God meant, and that was what he was come for, "not to be ministered unto, but to minister." And that was why he pointed the disciples whom John sent to these works (Matt 11. 2-6). Thus both Jesus' spirit of sympathy and his idea of his work impelled him to a ministry far broader than that of John.

Demon possession

The ministry of service may be considered under two heads. There is, first, the ministry of healing, in which Jesus dealt with demon possession and other forms of sickness; and there is the ministry of forgiveness which shows Jesus in his relation to sinners.

The Old Testament has little to say about spirits, evil or good. The New Testament world seems to be filled with them. The belief in them came from without, from Persia, in the last couple of centuries before Christ. Men were thought to be in constant danger of having evil spirits enter them. Their presence was the explanation of special forms of disease such as seemed to demand some unusual cause. Among these were particularly mental and nervous disorders, like insanity and epilepsy, as well as diseases like paralysis and leprosy. There seem to have been cases also of moral degeneracy, where we read of unclean spirits.

Three healings

Mark's Gospel gives us three typical cases. The first occurs in the Capernaum synagogue on that first Sabbath. This may have been a man of evil life, whom Jesus aroused by the power of his appeal. The case served to stir the people and spread Jesus' fame at the very beginning. The second is the man in the Gerasene country across the lake from Capernaum, a case of violent insanity, the poor wretch living as an outcast among the tombs (Mark 5. 1-20). The third is a case of epilepsy, that of a boy whom the disciples had first tried in vain to heal.

Such cases of demoniac healing were an undoubted part of Jesus' work. We cannot, of course, be sure of all details. As to Jesus' own conception we cannot tell. So far as ordinary knowledge is concerned, we find him elsewhere sharing the opinions of his time. In any case his religious insight here is true. The evil spirits are here only to be overcome. There is no room for the superstition and fear which usually goes with the belief in demons, only the perfect confidence in the power and goodness of his Father. *For Jesus evil is here only to be overcome*

The same day at Capernaum brings to Jesus the second class of the needy to whom he ministered, the sick. Returning home after the synagogue service, he heals Peter's mother-in-law, whom he finds ill with a fever. This, joined to the case of the demoniac, rouses the city. No sooner is the sun set and the Sabbath over, according to Jewish reckoning, than they begin bringing the sick to the door of Peter's house for Jesus to heal. Mark does not say that he healed them all, but that "he healed many that were sick with divers diseases and cast out many demons." *Jesus and the sick*

It was enough to still further move the city. Jesus had no need to fear a lack of following. A great ministry seemed to be opening to him at Capernaum. But Jesus judged the situation differently. Here were the elements of danger that he had fought against in his temptation. It was not a spiritual following won by his message. It was a popular and outward success won by these signs of power. And Jesus puts it aside. He will not become a worker of signs. His great work is not here. It is to bring to men's minds a vision of God, to their hearts a new spirit in preparation for the coming Kingdom. The crowds that come early *Jesus will not become a mere healer*

in the morning do not find him. He has been meeting this
new crisis, as he met the first, in a desert place in prayer.
His decision is ready when the disciples find him: "Let us
go elsewhere into the next towns, that I may preach there
also; *for to this end came I forth*" (Mark 1. 38). He does
not cease his ministry of healing. He is moved with compassion when the leper comes. But he charges him sternly
to tell no man about it (Mark 1. 40-45).

The healings a fact

These stories of healing have been the cause of a great
deal of discussion. Scholars of all kinds to-day are generally inclined to admit them. They are so deeply embedded
in the gospel narratives that they could hardly be taken out
without giving up the entire gospel story. How they were
wrought it is neither necessary nor possible for us to
determine. It is important to notice that Jesus performed
these cures out of sympathy for men, and not to attract men
or win their faith. He did not want a following that was
due to signs and wonders. He wanted a moral and spiritual
faith and insight. Such a faith is still of most importance
with his followers.

DIRECTIONS FOR READING AND STUDY

Read and compare the three stories of the healings of demoniacs
found in Mark 1. 23-27; 5. 1-20; 9. 14-29.

Does Jesus' word of healing seem to have been conditioned by
what he found in others? Illustrate answer from following passages: Luke 7. 1-10; Mark 5. 21-43; 10. 46-52; Matt 15. 21-28.

Note Jesus' motive in this ministry as given Matt 9. 35-38.

Make a list of the passages in the first eight chapters of Mark
which refer to the crowds about Jesus, noting the indications as
to the reasons for his popularity.

What was Jesus' attitude as to the demand for miracles, and
his estimate of their value in his work? Read Matt 12. 38-42 and
note Mark 5. 43; 7. 36; 8. 26.

CHAPTER VIII

THE MINISTRY OF FORGIVENESS

THERE was another class of people with whom Jesus came Jesus and the sinners. in contact at the very beginning of the Capernaum ministry. They are referred to as the sinners. Nothing in Jesus' ministry caused more comment and more criticism than his relations with these people, and nothing is more characteristic of his spirit.

The word "sinners" in these references is not used in The Pharisaic idea of religion and of sin exactly our sense. We must not be misled by the fact that harlots and publicans are sometimes specially mentioned in this connection. By sinners are not always meant the morally reprobate. The idea of sin depends upon the idea of religion. With the Jewish leaders at this time, religion meant the keeping of a great sum of rules which touched every part of a Jew's life. These were supposed to be the laws of Moses, all taken from the Old Testament. As a matter of fact, they consisted for the most part of the "traditions of the elders," the endless rules on all subjects that had been deduced from these laws and built up around them. In large part they centered about the idea of ceremonial purity. Everything was divided into clean and unclean: food, vessels, people, acts, and objects. Minute rules governed all these points as well as the endless routine of sacrifices, gifts, washings, bathings, prayers, penances, and the like.

To live this life according to the highest standards of What religion required that time required knowledge and leisure and money. The scribes were the experts in this field, and so are sometimes called lawyers. It took leisure because it required time to fulfill such a round of duties. It took money because it interfered with ordinary business. That was especially true

57

in Galilee, where there were so many non-Jews, to mingle with whom meant impurity. The Pharisees were the strict keepers of the law. As such they were held in the highest esteem by the common people. This esteem they returned with contempt (John 7. 49). The poor Jew in our large cities to-day is handicapped in just the same way if he is strictly orthodox. Many of these work only five days in the week. They will not work on Saturday and cannot work on Sunday, and sometimes they are driven to the pedlar's pushcart because men will not hire them in other occupations for only five days.

Publicans

Of course the sinners included also the immoral. Among these the tax collectors especially stood forth. The tax-gatherer is not popular even to-day. He was doubly hateful to the Jews. In part the Roman system of farming out taxes was responsible. The contractor for a given province paid the government a fixed sum and squeezed this sum, and as much more as he could get, from the people. His officers, or agents, were the publicans whom we meet in the Gospels. Some occupied higher positions, like Zacchæus, and were correspondingly rich. Some were of the rank and file, as, apparently, Matthew. Aside from their exactions, the Jews hated these because they were renegades, men who took sides for hire with the hated Roman master.

Jesus' attitude

For all these people the heart of Jesus stirred with sympathy. They were as sheep not having a shepherd. He felt a special mission just to these classes, and he asserts it again and again. "I came not to call the righteous, but sinners." "The Son of man is come to seek and to save that which was lost." He felt himself sent to save "the lost sheep of the house of Israel," "to preach good tidings to the poor."

Jesus forgives the paralytic

Mark tells us in his second chapter of the beginning of this ministry. The crowds who followed Jesus because of the report of his healings had driven him out into the "desert places," that is, the untilled country. Now he comes back quietly to Peter's home in Capernaum, apparently for rest. But the people discover him and fill the house and the street. A poor paralytic, brought by his friends, can get to Jesus only by being let down through the roof. Jesus' first word to him, however, is not one of healing but of forgiveness. That seemed to Jesus the deeper need. The word stirred the ire of his enemies. What right had he to forgive sins?

A later event angered them still more. Situated on a great highway near the border of Herod's territory, Capernaum was an important place for the collection of customs, and contained a good many publicans. One of these, named Levi, had evidently heard Jesus' teaching and in turn had been noted by Jesus. Passing by the customhouse, Jesus calls him and invites him to follow, apparently to become one of the little circle of his regular companions. Not only did Levi, or Matthew, as he is also called, follow him at once, but he made a supper for Jesus, to which he invited his friends. All of them, of course, were "sinners," people who did not even make a pretense of keeping the ceremonial law; many of them were hated publicans like Matthew himself. The strict Jew would not have spoken to such men. To sit down at table with them was not only to scorn all the conventions of society, but to flout the laws which were the very essence of religion for these Pharisees. But Jesus saw in this his opportunity. *Jesus and the Capernaum publicans*

Luke records a similar incident, where Jesus sought out one of these men. It is the story of Zacchæus, a "chief publican" and a rich man. The time is the latter part of Jesus' ministry, the occasion is his passage through Jericho, and Jesus does not simply accept an invitation, but selects the house of this despised publican for his stay (Luke 19. 1-10). *A chief publican*

The Gospels show us that a large part of Jesus' ministry was connected with these people. Luke especially brings *The ministry to sinners*

out this side of Jesus' work. It was not simply that Jesus
saw their need and gave himself to them; these people in a
special manner turned to him. He found with them the
response which the scribes and Pharisees refused. John
had had the same experience (Luke 7. 29, 30). The religion
of formalism had left these people unmoved, or else they
were of the poor who could not keep these laws. They
had accepted the contempt of the Pharisees as a right ver-
dict, and there was no hope in their hearts. Jesus' message
of God and righteousness and repentance pricked their
conscience. At the same time he stirred them with hope.
They were to him not "people of the earth," but brothers.
He made them feel that God cared for each one of them.
He taught them to look up and say, "Father."

The response of the sinners
The response of these people to his ministry stirred the
heart of Jesus deeply. Luke brings this out in an incident
he relates (7. 36-50). Jesus had been invited to the home
of a Pharisee, when a woman of the city, evidently a
notorious character, came in and stood behind the couch
where he was reclining at table. She was one whom Jesus'
word of forgiveness had reached and to whom it had brought
a new life. Moved with gratitude, she had bought a flask
of ointment, and now, weeping and wiping his feet with her
hair, she poured the ointment upon them. His host, Simon
by name, paid no attention to this act of devotion which
supplied his own omission of courtesy, in that he had not
washed the feet of his guest. Simon saw only that this
was a sinner and that Jesus permitted her defiling touch.
He could not believe that Jesus knew what she was. Jesus'
answer was the story of the lender and the two debtors.
Like the debtor to whom the heavy debt had been remitted,
so these people showed a depth of gratitude which he had
not found with people of higher standing. He found even
more than this: a spirit of humility and openness and desire
which was so lacking with the Pharisees (Luke 18. 9-14).
He did not minimize their past disobedience, yet in the end

it was they who went into the kingdom of God and not the piously protesting Pharisees (Matt 21. 28-32). The parable of the king's wedding feast sets forth Jesus' own experience: the invitation is refused by the people of standing to whom it goes, and it is the poor and maimed and blind and lame that at last come in (Luke 14. 15-24; Matt 22. 1-10).

This entire ministry of Jesus, in its teaching and healing and forgiving, is the beginning and source of that marvelous development of education and philanthropy and missions which has marked the history of Christianity. The Jews laid great stress upon alms, but with them it was just one more precept to be kept. Their interest was in keeping the law; Jesus' center of interest was not in the law but in his brother. Nietzsche has criticized Christianity from this point of view, calling it the religion of the submerged, the morality of the weak. He felt that there was a certain superiority or contempt toward the weak in all this pity. That was a misconception. The ethics of Jesus was that of the strong, only not of the strong living for themselves but for others. In his service was no spirit of condescension or scorn. Like our modern social service, which he has inspired, it was democratic; back of it lay the reverence for men as his brothers, as sons of the Father.

Jesus as the ideal and inspiration of service

DIRECTIONS FOR READING AND STUDY

Mark 2. 1-17; Luke 18. 9-14; Matt 21. 28-32; Luke 14. 15-24; Matt 22. 1-10.

Read Luke 7. 36-50 and compare with the story told in Mark 14. 3-9 and Matt 26. 6-13. Give reasons for or against the opinion that these refer to the same event.

As against the identification, note the characteristic words of Jesus in both instances; state the difference in their point and meaning.

Carefully look through chapters 4 to 8 of Luke, making a list of the deeds of healing and forgiving. Do they warrant the assertion that the third Gospel shows a special interest in the poor and suffering and outcasts?

CHAPTER IX

THE MASTER TEACHER

The place
of teaching

It is as a teacher first of all that Jesus appears in his ministry. He began his work in this manner, and neither success nor defeat turned him aside from this course. When the crowds left him he devoted himself to his disciples, but his work was still that of teaching. It is as a teacher in the temple that he spends his last days at Jerusalem, making a final appeal to the people. His last night is given to his disciples in instruction.

The faith of
a teacher

The parable of the sower sets forth Jesus' faith as a teacher, which he passes on to the disciples for their encouragement (Mark 4. 1-9). He was like one with good seed, scattering it wherever he went. He saw the hard hearts upon which it fell in vain, and the shallow hearts of those who responded with quick enthusiasm only to turn as quickly away. None of these things moved him. He knew that there was life in the seed, in his message, and that it was his work to sow; and he saw the future harvest of thirty and sixty and a hundredfold. Jesus wrote no book. He established no church, and we have no record that he gave orders for its establishment. He was a sower. He scattered his living words constantly, prodigally. He gave them forth to all men, on all occasions, to eager throngs in Galilee, to hostile crowds at Jerusalem, to his little company of followers, to children in the market place, to folks met casually by the wayside. Only a few comparatively have come down to us, but they have justified his faith. These words, flung out upon the air like scattered seed, have lived on in the hearts of men and the lives of nations to comfort, to guide, to cast down, to lift up, to transform. And never

before have they been so closely studied, so widely spread,
or so mighty in their influence as to-day.

The first mark of Jesus' teaching is its freedom and
authority. It is truth welling up directly from life. That
is seen not merely in Jesus' attitude toward tradition, but
toward the Old Testament as well. These Scriptures were
indeed part of his inner life. In his moments of deepest need,
in the wilderness temptation and on the cross, their words
come to his lips. He quoted them too as authority against
his foes. And yet back of this we find an attitude of independence and sometimes of criticism. There are several
ways in which this attitude appears: (1) Jesus was not
simply dependent upon the Old Testament. He proclaimed
the God of Abraham and Isaac and Jacob; but this was a
living God, and Jesus saw him in the world and knew him
in his own life, and therefore was not limited to the record
of the past. (2) Jesus did not take from the Old Testament indifferently; he discriminated and chose. He preferred the prophetic writings, especially the second part
of Isaiah, Deuteronomy, and the Psalms. There were large
portions which he left wholly to one side. (3) He set
scripture against scripture. He went back of the Mosaic
law of divorce (Deut 24. 1) to assert a higher law that was
at the beginning (Mark 10. 2-12). (4) He definitely set
aside, upon his own authority, certain Old Testament precepts or laws. "Ye have heard that it was said, An eye for
an eye, and a tooth for a tooth; but I say unto you, Resist
not him that is evil" (Matt 5. 38, 39). In his own practice
he disregarded ceremonial laws, and not merely those of
the rabbis but of the Old Testament also. When called to
account he simply declared, that it was not what went into
a man's body but what came out of his heart that made him
unclean (Mark 7. 1-23). By this word he calmly set aside
entire sections of the law which the people regarded as
holy and unchangeable. And the evangelist points out this
conclusion (Mark 7. 19). (5) Finally, he recognized that

Authority and independence

a new day had come with him. He revered the old, but a better was now at hand; "one greater than the temple is here" (Matt 12. 6). The new wine had come; why should it be put in the old wine-skins that could no longer hold it? If the old forms interfere with the new spirit, let the old forms drop off (Mark 2. 18-22). That, indeed, was what Jesus did. He did not argue against the old. He simply let it slough off.

How Jesus fulfilled

One passage in Matthew seems to contradict this interpretation (5. 17-20). There Jesus seems to assert that every least letter of the law must stand forever. Against Jesus' clear and consistent teaching and conduct this cannot stand. Verses 18 and 19 may have been inserted, as some think. There is a more probable interpretation: that Jesus had been criticized as one who was destroying all law and overturning all authority, that he responded by saying: "You are the destroyers of the law, not I. I am fulfilling it by standing for its real spirit. There is not one truth that I am overturning. But unless your righteousness exceeds that of the letter, you shall never enter the Kingdom."

The teaching occasional and vital

Jesus' method of teaching was not systematic but occasional. He was not a college professor lecturing upon his subject, taking up one doctrine after another. He walked through the world of men and brought the truth to men as he saw their need. He saw men anxious and troubled, and showed them the birds and the flowers for which God was caring (Matt 6. 25-34), but he never sat down to give his disciples a lecture upon the divine immanence or providence. Two of his disciples came with their petty ambitions; he made it the occasion for his great lesson on the meaning of life as a chance to give, not to get (Matt 20. 20-28). Jesus' teaching was vital, practical. He was interested in life, not in ideas (Luke 13. 1-5).

Teaching by pictures

The materials for his teaching Jesus took from the life of the people to whom he spoke. He was popular in the best sense of the word. In pedagogical wisdom he was a teacher of the highest order. He spoke the language that people knew. He took their common world and made it teach his highest lessons. All the life of that day looks out upon us from his pages. We see the world of nature: the glowing sunset that promises fair weather, the red of the morning that suggests the storm, the lightning that flashes from end to end of heaven, the bright flowers and the quickly fading grass, the slow-growing grain, the field where wheat and tares are mixed together, the fig tree showing its first tender green, the vineyard ready for the gathering, and the bending heads of the rich harvest that promises its hundredfold. We see the living creatures: the birds that have their nests, the foxes with their holes, the carrion birds gathering where the carcass is, the hungry flock settling down on the new-sown field, the little dead sparrow whom God notices, though men do not. We see men busy at their daily tasks: the farmer, the merchant, the landowner, the judge. How many different characters he shows us!—the poor widow and the unjust judge, the faithful shepherd, the poor beggar, the successful farmer whom Jesus brands as fool. No pictures are more suggestive than those that show us the home and the children: the mother kneading her dough, the windowless house where you must search long for your lost coin, the closed house where the father and children are in bed, the picture of the children about the table with the dogs underneath, the evening hour with the lamp upon the stand giving light to all in the house. And the children! We see them busily playing their games of funeral or wedding as they might to-day, or coming hungry to their father, sure that they will get bread and not a stone, or placed once more by Jesus in the midst to preach the great lesson of th open, trustful heart. There are shadows too: the laborers that wait in the market place and have no one to hire them, that toil all day and then must serve their master at night before they can eat, or that feel the cruel scourge for some misdeed, the beggar lying at the gate while the feast goes on within, the debtor on his way to prison, the criminal bearing his own cross to the place of execution.

Effectiveness and art

Such teaching was of the highest effectiveness. It comes to us, indeed, from another world and a long-past age, yet so simple is its form and so human the relations it uses that every age since then has heard it as its own. There are vivid pictures, pregnant phrases, that have long since passed into common speech: salt of the earth, whited sepulchers, wolves in sheep's clothing, grapes from thorns, the house divided against itself. Jesus is an artist. There is a beauty in these words that neither the years of verbal tradition nor the loss through translation has destroyed. In beauty of phrase, in economy of line, in their picture language, and, above all, in the perfection of their thought, we have here poetry and painting at its highest. There is a finality of form which marks the highest art. And yet we hardly dare to use that word, which suggests effort and thought of effect, for everything here is free, natural, spontaneous.

The forms of the picture teaching

We have already seen how much of Jesus' teaching is figurative, and how he takes it from the life all about him. He took this common world which men knew and made them see the spiritual truths about which they were so blind. We may distinguish three forms in this picture teaching of Jesus: likenesses, examples, and parables.

Likenesses

First come the likenesses. Often the comparison is implied, not expressed. "Ye are the salt of the earth." "Ye are the light of the world." "A city set on a hill cannot be hid." "No man putteth new wine into old wine-skins." "Do men gather grapes of thorns?" Sometimes the comparison is stated, as in the picture of the perverse children. He found people like some children at play. Their comrades propose that they play wedding, and begin to pipe, but they do not want to play wedding and so will not dance to the music. And when their friends offer to play funeral and

start to wailing, instead of beating their breasts and playing
mourner they refuse this game also. John came as an
ascetic; they would not hear him but said, "He has a demon."
Jesus came and joined in all the life of men; him too they
would not hear, he was a glutton and winebibber (Matt
11. 16-19).

The examples form another class. These are usually **Examples**
classed with the parables. They are really impressive illustrations setting forth some Christian principle. There are
four of these: The good Samaritan (Luke 10. 29-37); the
Pharisee and the publican (Luke 18. 9-14); the rich fool
(Luke 12. 16-21); and Dives and Lazarus (Luke 16. 19-31).

The parables form the third class. The parable is an **Parables**
invented tale like a fable, except that the parable is something that might naturally happen. There are no talking
animals in a parable as in the fables of Æsop. The purpose
of the parable is to persuade or explain. It may be defined
as an argument or explanation from analogy, in which a
natural happening in a lower sphere is made to show the
truth in a higher sphere. The parable of the prodigal son
is such an argument. Jesus tells the story of a father who
forgives the returning son that has done wrong, instead of
casting him out. Men could understand and appreciate this
incident. Jesus transfers it to a higher realm and says:
That is the way with our Father in heaven.

Few parts of the teaching of Jesus have been more mis- **The mistake**
used than the parables. The common mistake has been to **of allegorizing**
treat them as if they were allegories. In Spenser's Faerie
Queene and Bunyan's Pilgrim's Progress we have good
examples of the allegory. An allegory is an extended simile.
Every figure or character in the allegory represents some
spiritual fact or truth. It is like two lines running parallel
with point corresponding to point. The parable is like two
curves which touch at only one point; it is an argument
usually meant to prove or illustrate just one thing. The
parable of the prodigal son proves one truth—God is

merciful as the best fathers of earth are. It is a mistake, then, to use it as is commonly done to prove a hundred other points, to find some hidden spiritual meaning in the swine and the husks and the strangers, the robe, the ring, the shoes, and all the rest.

The mistake of legalizing

The other mistake that has been made in interpreting the teaching of Jesus has been the attempt to make of it a set of rules or laws. Jesus had no thought of bringing laws to men. His whole teaching is a protest against a religion of laws. He was interested in the life of men, in leading men into the rich life with God which he himself possessed. To this end his teachings are designed to stir repentance, to quicken desire, to bring a higher vision, to lead men to decision for God and to trust in him. Like a good physician, he does not prescribe the same for every man. He calls Levi to follow him, but the Gadarene demoniac who wanted to follow him he sends to his home. Zacchæus and Lazarus may keep their home and their wealth; the rich young ruler he bids sell all and follow him.

DIRECTIONS FOR READING AND STUDY

Mark 2. 18-22; 4. 1-9; 7. 1-23; 10. 2-12; Matt 5. 17-48.

Using the marginal references of the Standard Revision, make a list of Old Testament quotations and allusions found in the account of the temptation and in the Sermon on the Mount.

In the first five instances of likenesses given in this chapter, write out the comparison in full.

What is the religious principle illustrated in the four examples given above.

Give the argument or analogy of the parables found in the following passages: Matt 7. 24-27; 13. 44; 25. 14-30.

CHAPTER X

THE KINGDOM OF GOD

"THE kingdom of God" is a phrase that meets us through- The interest in the Kingdom out the Gospels. As we have seen, John began with this message and Jesus made it his own. Both declared that the expected Kingdom was near at hand. The same thought was in the minds of all the people. They were ready to ask of John as of Jesus, "Is he the Messiah who will bring in the Kingdom?" Jesus' deeds of healing stirred their expectation: "Perhaps this is he." And when, at last, he entered Jerusalem the multitude was ready to shout, "Blessed is he that cometh in the name of the Lord: Blessed is the kingdom that cometh, the kingdom of our father David" (Mark 11. 9, 10). The people were especially interested at this time. Rome's rule was becoming intolerable. The deliverance must be near at hand.

The thought of the Kingdom was an essential part of Its place in Jewish faith Jewish belief. It sprang from their faith in God. It really meant the kingship of God, God's rule. The earth was the Lord's. If there was evil in it, if his people were oppressed, that could only be for a time. The day must come when he would overthrow every power and rule himself. "And in the days of those kings shall the God of heaven set up a kingdom which shall never be destroyed. And the kingdom . . . shall be given to the people of the saints of the Most High" (Dan 2. 44; 7. 27). Here was the heart of their hope—the rule of God meant for them the rule of Israel. God would overthrow her enemies and set Israel upon the throne.

Jesus too believed that the rule of God was coming in the Jesus' idea of the Kingdom and his idea of God earth, that there would be a new world without evil and oppression and wrong. He proclaimed the good news that this rule was near at hand. And yet the kingdom of God in

69

Jesus' teaching had a different meaning. Nothing is said about Rome, nothing of the overthrow of Israel's enemies and her triumphant rule. What he has to say does not concern men as Jews, but men as men. He even bids them render to Cæsar the things that are Cæsar's. He declares that many shall come from the east and the west and sit down in the Kingdom while Jews themselves are cast out. The real difference lay in the different thought of God. If the Kingdom means the rule of God, then it is the nature of God that decides what that rule shall be. For the Jews Jehovah was King of Israel and his kingship meant Israel's rule. For Jesus the King was Father, holy and loving, and Father of all men. The rule of such a God could not mean armies and thrones; it must mean the reign of righteousness and peace and good will which Jesus set forth as the heart of God.

The Kingdom as the highest good

For Jesus the kingdom of God was, first of all, a gift, the highest good that man could desire. It is like the treasure which the man found in the field, for whose sake he sold all that he had that he might buy the field. It is like the pearl to gain which the merchant parted with all that he possessed (Matt 13. 44-46). Having this, everything else would be added to a man (Matt 6. 33). At its highest this treasure means to see God (Matt 5. 8). For that reason the first gift of God's rule is forgiveness by which we are admitted to God's fellowship (Luke 1. 77; 24. 47). Elsewhere Jesus uses the word "life," or the term "eternal life," as meaning the same as the Kingdom, as will be seen by comparing Mark 10. 17, 30 with 10. 23 and Matt 7. 14 with 7. 21. For Jesus the rule of God was the great hope of men; it meant the overcoming of all evil, the coming of all good. For that reason the message is called gospel, "good news." Matt 11. 25-30, one of the most beautiful passages in the Gospels, breathes this spirit of joy, while at the same time its closing verses suggest some of the blessings of the Kingdom.

But the coming rule of God meant also a challenge and The Kingdom demands righteousness, repentance, watchfulness
a test. Who were the men who could meet such a God?
The test that Jesus puts is a very simple one. It is the test
of obedience springing from a true life within. The test of
the tree is the fruit. "Not everyone that saith unto me,
Lord, Lord, shall enter into the kingdom of heaven; but
he that doeth the will of my Father who is in heaven"
(Matt 7. 15-23). Only such a life would stand in that day
(Matt 7. 24-27). In another passage Jesus tells more particularly what this obedience means, that it is the service of
our fellow men in their need, no matter who they are
(Matt 25. 31-46). Such obedience is not simply a preparation for the Kingdom; it is of the essence of the Kingdom,
for the rule of God means the righteousness of man: "Seek
ye first the kingdom of God and his righteousness." Here
the sharp difference between Jesus and the people stands
out. The Jews were luxuriating in imagining all the joys
and delights of the future age of the Kingdom. Jesus was
summoning his disciples to earnestness and watchfulness.
This message of watchfulness is given us in two striking
parables, that of the ten virgins and that of the master and
the servants (Matt 25. 1-13; Luke 12. 35-46).

Is the kingdom of God in Jesus' teaching something The Kingdom as inner and spiritual
purely inner and spiritual, or is it something outer, a new
society? Undoubtedly it is the inner and spiritual upon
which Jesus lays stress. It means eternal life, as we have
seen. It works in hidden manner like the leaven, and grows
inconspicuously like the mustard seed (Matt 13. 31-33).
And what Jesus says about the people who enter the Kingdom or to whom it belongs, points the same way; it is the
inner spirit that is decisive. To enter the Kingdom one
must have the spirit of a child (Matt 18. 3). It is hard
for the rich to enter, for they are apt to be proud and
contented (Mark 10. 23). In beautiful yet searching manner
the Beatitudes set forth this inner spirit of the Kingdom,
whose blessings belong to the poor in spirit, the meek, the

pure in heart, and those that hunger for its righteousness (Matt 5. 3-12). When the Pharisees asked him when the Kingdom would come, he answered: "The kingdom of God cometh not with observation: neither shall they say, Lo, here! or, There! for lo, the kingdom of God is within you" (Luke 17. 20, 21). They were thinking of a political state; for Jesus the Kingdom was, first of all, the rule of God in men's hearts. It is true that the Jews spoke of repentance and obedience to the law as necessary before the Kingdom could come. When Jesus speaks of obedience and mercy, however, he is not speaking simply of the condition upon which men may obtain the Kingdom; these are for him the spirit and essence of the Kingdom itself.

The Kingdom as social   Yet while the Kingdom is, first of all, something inner and spiritual, it is social in its meaning and consequence. Jesus was neither political dreamer nor social reformer, but his teaching of the Kingdom has tremendous social meaning. Three points make this clear. (1) The Kingdom means God's rule in all the life of men. God is already in his world, but when the Kingdom comes, there will be no life not ruled by him. That means for us his rule in government and industry. That means no war, no oppression in state, no injustice in industry. The Kingdom begins in men's hearts, but it does not end until the spirit of God rules in every institution and relation of life. (2) The spirit of the Kingdom is essentially social. It must always be working out in the life of men. The love and service of others is the real test of God's kingship with men (Matt 25. 31-46). In his Kingdom the first is to be the last, the servant (Mark 9. 35). "Whosoever would become great among you, shall be your minister; and whosoever would be first among you, shall be servant of all" (Mark 10. 35-45). The fruit of this spirit has been the noble history of missions and philanthropies, the modern movements of reform and social service, and the modern passion for social justice. (3) The Kingdom involved a community, a brotherhood.

Jesus thought of the men of the Kingdom not as subjects but as sons, and sonship means brotherhood. The spirit of the Kingdom must bring the members of the Kingdom together. The first circle of Jesus' disciples was the promise of what was to come. The church as a fellowship was the inevitable expression of the Kingdom. The end could only be what Paul foresaw, the breaking down of the divisions and enmities that had separated men in classes and nations, and the final bringing together of all men into one brotherhood, the family of God.

Was the Kingdom in the future with Jesus, or was it already present? It seems certain that Jesus thought that the Kingdom was in the future, although very near. That is the meaning of the word, "The kingdom of God is at hand." It is at the door. "There are some here of them that stand by," he said, "who shall in no wise taste of death, till they see the kingdom of God come with power" (Mark 9. 1). On the other hand, it seems just as clear that Jesus thought that the beginnings of the Kingdom were already present. The rule of God meant the overthrow of evil in the world and the reign of God in men's lives. That he saw already taking place. He saw the sons of the Kingdom present (Matt 17. 26), the sons of the bridechamber (Mark 2. 19). He saw publicans and harlots going into the kingdom of God (Matt 21. 31). He pointed John's disciples to what was already taking place (Matt 11. 2-6). And he discerned it especially in his healings. He had entered the house of the strong man and had bound the powers of evil; he had seen Satan fallen as lightning from heaven (Luke 10. 18). It was God's rule even now displacing the rule of evil. "If I by the Spirit of God cast out demons, then is the kingdom of God come upon you" (Matt 12. 22-29). *The Kingdom as future and as present*

These were, indeed, only small beginnings. On every side the power of evil still lay, while the Kingdom itself was coming quietly and almost unnoticed. There are three *Parables of encouragement*

parables of the Kingdom that Jesus seems to have spoken
primarily to hearten his disciples who might be discouraged
by these facts. They are those of the wheat and tares, the
mustard seed, and the leaven (Matt 13. 24-33). The seed
which they were scattering was growing slowly and there
were tares, but it was growing surely, and grain and weed
would be made manifest some day. The Kingdom was only
a mustard seed now; it would be a tree by and by. Now
it was like hidden leaven, but it would permeate the whole
lump after a while. Above all, they were to remember
this, that it was theirs simply to scatter the seed; the fruitage
came from a power not their own. "The earth beareth fruit
of herself; first the blade, then the ear, then the full grain
in the ear" (Mark 4. 26-29).

The meaning
of the
Kingdom

These two convictions apparently lay side by side in the
mind of Jesus: first, that the Kingdom was already here
wherever God's will was being done and sinners were
turning to him and evil was being overthrown; second, that
in its fullness and power it should come some time in the
near future. The important element in Jesus' teaching is
not this thought of the exact time of the coming; he himself
said that no one knew the day or the hour except his Father
in heaven (Mark 13. 28-32). It lay, rather, in three great
truths: (1) there shall be a new earth in which the rule of
God shall prevail in all the world; (2) this rule, or kingdom,
will be ethical and spiritual, not an outer political reign, but
an inner spirit of righteousness and love; (3) this rule will
show itself in the way in which men live together, in all
the relations and institutions of life; and its final manifestation will be a family, or community, of brothers upon the
earth.

DIRECTIONS FOR READING AND STUDY

Parables of the Kingdom: Matt 13. 24-52; 25. 1-13; Luke 12. 35-
46; Mark 4. 26, 29. Other passages: Matt 11. 25-30; 7. 15-27;
5. 3-12; 11. 2-6; 12. 22-29; Mark 13. 28-32.

Read the following parables and state what thought concerning

the Kingdom each of these conveys: the hidden treasure and the
pearl (Matt 13. 44-46); the net and the fishes (Matt 13. 47-50);
the wheat and the tares (Matt 13. 24-30); the virgins (Matt 25.
1-13); the watchful servants (Luke 12. 35-46); the mustard seed
(Matt 13. 31, 32); the leaven (Matt 13. 33); the earth bearing
fruit (Mark 4. 26, 29).

CHAPTER XI

THE FATHER

Jesus' central thought

DESPITE the place which it occupied, it is not the idea of the Kingdom that determines the faith and the message of Jesus so much as the thought of God. It was this thought of God that filled his own life. His conception of the world and of men, of what man must do and what he may hope for, all depended upon God.

The God of the prophets

Jesus does not come proclaiming any new God. He brings to men Jehovah, the God of their fathers, "the God of Abraham, and the God of Isaac, and the God of Jacob" (Mark 12. 26). He speaks the simple ancient creed: "Hear, O Israel; the Lord our God, the Lord is one" (Mark 12. 29). We may note three elements in that lofty prophetic faith upon which Jesus built: (1) Jehovah was one God, God of all the earth; and not merely creator and ruler of nature (Gen 1), but ruling the nations and moving in their history (Isa 40 and 45). (2) He was the God of mercy, the covenant God who had chosen this nation and redeemed it (Deut 5. 6; Hos 11). (3) He was the holy God, and it was holiness that he asked from men. This holiness was not sacrifice and ritual, but justice and mercy to fellow men (Isa 1; Mic 6. 6-8; Amos 5. 21-24).

The God of Judaism

Israel had not kept this height. Her religion had become narrow, centered in her own welfare. She had lost the sense of Jehovah as the living God, present with her and speaking to her. A great system of laws and rules had taken God's place. God was a great bookkeeper, keeping record of men's obedience. Religion was to observe these laws. If she did this, Israel believed that at some future time God would again assert himself and rule in her midst. For the

76

present, since God was holy he must be separate from this
evil world.

Jesus goes back to the faith of the prophets; though not
dependent upon them. (1) For Jesus too there is but one
God, the God of all power, whom men are to reverence and
fear. He teaches his disciples to pray, "Our Father, who
art in heaven, Hallowed be thy name" (Matt 6. 9, 10). This
reverence is in his own soul; "I thank thee, O Father, Lord
of heaven and earth," he prays (Matt 11. 25). With this
God all things are possible (Mark 10. 27). Jesus chides the
questioning Sadducees with not knowing the power of God.
Their petty quibbling, with which they tried to make him
ridiculous, falls down before his great thought of God
(Mark 12. 18, 27). There is nothing here of the mere
sentimental good nature that some people have read into the
teaching of Jesus. He says plainly that men are to fear
God (Matt 10. 28). (2) God is the living God, present in
his world. As the parables show, this world was constantly
speaking to Jesus about God. The birds and the flowers
were witnesses of God's care (Matt 6. 26-30). He could
even say of the worthless sparrow dead by the roadside,
that it had not fallen without his Father's knowledge (Matt
10. 29). (3) That Jesus believed in the holiness of God
need not be pointed out. He did not often use the word.
because it had come to mean something ritualistic and external, but the Sermon on the Mount shows the prophetic
thought of a God whose supreme concern is the holy life,
and whose kingdom belongs to the pure and merciful and
those that hunger after righteousness.

The heart of Jesus' thought of God is the idea of Fatherhood. It is the mark of his influence over the faith of men
that it is this name by which men everywhere to-day call
upon God. The change is more apparent when we realize
that in the Psalms, Israel's book of worship, Jehovah is
never called upon as Father. The Old Testament shows us
God as the Father of his people, that is, of the nation, and

as Father of the king as representative of the nation; but
he is not referred to as the Father of individual men and
men do not pray to him as such (Hos 11. 1; Isa 1. 2; Deut
1. 31; Isa 63. 16). For Israel Jehovah was the King. The
King, like any ruler, would show fatherly kindness, but he
was first of all King, and religion was obedience to him.
For Jesus God is, first of all, Father. That is his nature,
his heart. And religion is being a son; it is fellowship with
the heavenly Father. There is no question that the source
for this idea of God and of religion was Jesus' own consciousness. It was out of this consciousness that Jesus said,
"All things have been delivered unto me of my Father:
and no one knoweth the Son, save the Father; neither doth
any know the Father, save the Son" (Matt 11. 27).

The law of Fatherhood   The law of Fatherhood Jesus shows to be forgiveness and
grace. The religion of Jesus' day was steeped in legalism.
It was a matter of earning and getting. It brought about,
on the one hand, a spirit of pride in those that were conscious of keeping the law, on the other hand a hard and even
contemptuous spirit toward others. "I thank thee, that I
am not as the rest of men, extortioners, unjust, adulterers,
or even as this publican. I fast twice in the week; I give
tithes of all that I get" (Luke 18. 11, 12). Men who could
pray in this fashion naturally criticized Jesus severely. For
Jesus, as we have seen, received men who were not keeping
the law, he sat at table with them, and even forgave their
sins. Jesus seemed to the Pharisees to be undermining the
very foundations of religion, which they saw in the ideas
of law and of merit and reward.

God values every single soul   Jesus answered them in a series of parables in which he
justified his own course by pointing out this nature of God
as Father. Three of these parables are found in Luke 15,
though probably not all spoken on the same occasion. The
first two have the same meaning. These sinners, he would
say, are the Father's children, his possession. Every one is
of value to him. The shepherd who has lost a sheep is not

satisfied, though he may have ninety-nine in the fold. He must find that lost sheep. Like the woman who has found her lost coin, he rejoices over his lost sheep that he has found. And so these sinners that are turning to the Kingdom are filling their Father's heart with joy (Luke 15. 1-10). The point of the parable is the value of the human soul. The same thought is in the story of Zacchæus. There too he was criticized because he had "gone in to lodge with a man that is a sinner"; and his answer was, "He also is a son of Abraham."

Luke's third parable is commonly known as that of the prodigal son. It might better be called the parable of the forgiving father. It is not meant as a picture of sin and its consequences. It is a picture of the forgiving heart of God. When the lost son comes back an earthly father does not weigh his desert. He rejoices that he has regained his son, and forgives. That is the way with God. All the rest of the parable, the boy's impertinent demand, his foolishness and wickedness, his degradation, his filth and rags—these are simply the strong colors that Jesus uses to bring out more clearly the wholly unmerited mercy of the father. But he makes us see that this is really the heart of God (Luke 15. 11-32). *The parable of the forgiving father*

The parable of the laborers is more drastic still in routing out the whole merit and reward idea of religion (Matt 20. 1-16). A steward, or overseer, is hiring men in the market place. Some he finds early in the morning and sets at work. He goes back in the forenoon, at noon, and in the afternoon, hiring others as he finds them. Late in the afternoon he finds still others, who work for him the brief remainder of the day. When night comes each man receives the regular day's wage, and the last named as much as the rest. At which the first complain, pointing to the greater work that they had done. The steward's answer was, "Is it not lawful for me to do what I will with mine own? or is thine eye evil, because I am good?" The old allegorical *The parable of the laborers* method, by which each point and person in the parable had a special meaning, would land us here in endless difficulties. If we are contented with the central point or argument, then the meaning is clear. God is giving the Kingdom to penitent sinners as the steward paid the late comers among the workmen; it is not what they have earned but what his goodness bestows. The complaining workmen are like the Pharisees, grudging this gift. But God is not the master, giving servants what they earn, he is the Father, giving and forgiving because that is his nature. Matt 5. 43-48 brings out the same truth.

God's King-
ship and
man's trust

The King is Father, therefore, not taskmaster. But that is not all, the Father is King. This gracious and merciful Father rules all the world and therefore men may trust in him and be unafraid. Very beautifully Jesus brings this out: "Behold the birds of the heaven, that they sow not, neither do they reap, nor gather into barns; and your heavenly Father feedeth them. Consider the lilies of the field, how they grow; they toil not, neither do they spin: yet I say unto you, that even Solomon in all his glory was not arrayed like one of these" (Matt 6. 26, 28, 29). Jesus saw love and power joined together. That was why men, when they feared God, could rejoice and fear nothing else. "Be not afraid of them that kill the body," he told his disciples, "but are not able to kill the soul; but rather fear him who is able to destroy both soul and body in hell. Are not two sparrows sold for a penny? and not one of them shall fall on the ground without your Father: but the very hairs of your head are all numbered. Fear not therefore: ye are of more value than many sparrows" (Matt 10. 28-31).

God gives
himself in
fellowship

But the greatest gift of this Fatherhood is not this care, nor even forgiveness, but fellowship. That is what the forgiveness of the Father means; it is the admission of the sons to the Father despite their sin and ill desert (Luke 15. 20-24). Such a fellowship meant peace of conscience and quiet of soul, and the strength that comes from trust when a man knows that all his life is under God's care. The deepest meaning of this fellowship, or sonship, Jesus showed in his own life. The disciples saw it in his praying, and asked him to teach his secret to them (Luke 11. 1). He himself was conscious that it was his great task to lead men into this life of sonship. That, indeed, was his double task: to show men the Father, to make men sons. That consciousness is expressed in a wonderful passage that rises to a lyric note: "I thank thee, O Father, Lord of heaven and earth, because thou hast hid these things from the wise and prudent, and hast revealed them unto babes. Even so, Father; for so it seemed good in thy sight. All things are delivered unto me of my Father: and no man knoweth the Son, but the Father; neither knoweth any man the Father, save the Son, and he to whomsoever the Son will reveal him. Come unto me, all ye that labor and are heavy laden, and I will give you rest. Take my yoke upon you, and learn of me; for I am meek and lowly in heart: and ye shall find rest unto your souls. For my yoke is easy, and my burden is light" (Matt 11. 25-30). It was this fellowship, with its love and gratitude and trust, that was for Jesus' followers the spirit and power of a new life.

DIRECTIONS FOR READING AND STUDY

Read Matt 6. 25-34; 10. 23-31; 11. 25-30.

Read the four parables in Luke 15 and Matt 20. 1-16. Tell the story and bring out the argument of each.

Read Matt 5. 43-48 and Luke 19. 1-10. Recall from previous study the instances of a Pharisee and of a publican from whom Jesus accepted hospitality.

CHAPTER XII

THE LIFE WITH GOD

Jesus' idea
of religion

JESUS' conception of religion may perhaps best be stated in the phrase, fellowship with God in the service of men; to live first as a son with the Father, second as a brother with men.

Jesus' idea of
righteous-
ness

The central idea of religion for the Jews of Jesus' day was righteousness. In the Sermon on the Mount Matthew has brought together the teachings of Jesus in which his idea of righteousness is set forth in contrast with that of the Pharisees, who were the acknowledged leaders of the people. The life with God that Jesus taught demanded righteousness also, but it is something far different from the keeping of rules which the Pharisees taught. (1) It was an inner righteousness; not many laws but one spirit. They had criticized him for his practice (Luke 15. 2); he declared that it was simply a higher righteousness for which he stood (Matt 5. 20). Outward deeds may do for a servant, but the son must have an inner spirit like his father. The angry spirit is a sin as truly as the deed of murder. The lustful glance is as truly wrong as adultery. It is not enough to avoid profanity; there must be a simple sincerity back of our speech. The mere rule of give as you get, both good and evil, will not suffice; there must be an inner spirit of good will such as our Father shows to all men (Matt 5. 21-48). Long before this, Jeremiah had spoken of the day when the law was to be no more an outward rule but an inner spirit (Jer 31. 31-34), and the psalmist had prayed for inner purity (Psa 51. 10). Such teaching Jesus was completing, or "fulfilling" (Matt 5. 17). (2) It was a social righteousness; men were to show it in serving their brethren. That was to be the test in the judgment

(Matt 25. 40). The way to show love to God was by showing it to men: "Whosoever shall receive one of such little children in my name, receiveth me: and whosoever receiveth me, receiveth not me, but him that sent me" (Mark 9. 37). To be reconciled to one's brother was more important than bringing a gift to the altar (Matt 5. 21-24). (3) It was an ethical righteousness. Mere religious rules and ceremonies did not count. Jesus protested against the Pharisees that they were defeating morality by their very rules (Matt 7. 1-13). It was the heart of a man that counted, not the ritual (Mark 7. 14-23). (4) This righteousness in one word meant sonship, "that ye may be sons of your Father who is in heaven" (Matt 5. 45). Higher than that it is not possible to go: "Ye therefore shall be perfect, as your heavenly Father is perfect" (Matt 5. 48). In a mere religion of law such a demand would be impossible. But Jesus' religion is one of grace, and not simply of demand. God does not ask men to become sons before he will receive them. Sonship is a gift, not simply a task. That is the meaning of forgiveness: God receives men as sons, though they are sinners, that by his help they may live as sons.

It is the term "sonship," not "righteousness," that gives us the best description of Jesus' idea of religion and the life with God. The first characteristic of this religion of sonship is the spirit of humility and desire. That follows from its very nature as God's gracious gift to us. God's first need is to find in us an openness and a longing for what he has to give. That is the meaning of his word about the child: "Whosoever shall not receive the kingdom of God as a little child, he shall in no wise enter therein" (Mark 10. 15). "Except ye turn, and become as little children, ye shall in no wise enter into the kingdom of heaven" (Matt 18. 3). It is the same spirit that he praises in the Beatitudes. The Kingdom is God's gift, but men must have the humble spirit and the earnest desire in order

The religion of sonship of humility and of desire

to receive it. And so his beatitude is for the poor in spirit, for those that mourn, for the meek, for those that hunger and thirst after righteousness (Matt 5. 3-9). It was this spirit that he found wanting in the Pharisees and in so many others. They were too well satisfied with themselves (Luke 18. 11); for Jesus there is a divinity in discontent. That is the meaning of the parable of the great supper. It was called forth by a pious ejaculation on the part of some man who was at the supper table with Jesus: "Blessed is he that shall eat bread in the kingdom of God." In reply, Jesus tells the story of those that refused the great invitation (Luke 14. 15-24). As a matter of fact, he says, when the great invitation comes men refuse it. That, as we have seen, was what stirred him with joy in his contact with so many sinners: these were humble and eager, were pressing into the kingdom of God, were even taking it in their eagerness by storm (Matt 21. 31; 11. 12).

The life of decision and surrender

This leads to the second quality that Jesus demands— a certain decision of character, a whole-hearted surrender of life. Religion was no incident with him; it meant a man's whole life. What God gives is everything; he demands everything in return. Jesus has a fine impatience with the superficial life: it is not saying, "Lord, Lord," that counts, but doing the will of his Father (Matt 7. 21). He has as little place for the divided life: "No man can serve two masters." Such a life means anxiety, and anxiety means wickedness (Matt 6. 24, 25). Jesus' own life was all of one piece. It had the strength that comes with a great and dominant purpose. The double life, he saw, meant not only weakness but darkness. Moral vision comes with singleness and sincerity of soul. "If therefore thine eye be single, thy whole body shall be full of light. But if thine eye be evil, thy whole body shall be full of darkness" (Matt 6. 22, 23). The stern demands that Jesus makes do not mean narrowness or asceticism, but simply spiritual vision and moral earnestness. "Narrow is the gate, and

straitened the way, that leadeth unto life" (Matt 7. 13, 14).
"He that doth not take his cross and follow after me, is not
worthy of me" (Matt 10. 34-39). The foundation of a strong
life is not a passing impulse but a clear decision that counts
the cost. The man who builds or the king who makes
war ought to look to the end and not simply the beginning.
A man must deliberately decide that if necessary he will
sacrifice the closest tie or give up life itself. That is what
Jesus means by the startling word, "If any man cometh
unto me, and hateth not his own father, and mother, and
wife, and children, and brethren, and sisters, yea, and his
own life also, he cannot be my disciple" (Luke 14. 25-33).
This is not asceticism. Asceticism is the denial of life.
Jesus' attitude toward life is everywhere affirmative. Cut
off thy right hand, he says, pluck out the right eye, but
make sure of life (Mark 9. 43-48).

These demands of Jesus raise the question as to his attitude toward the world in general and toward riches in
particular. As to the world of nature, Jesus' teaching as
we have noted it so far shows his simple pleasure in birds
and flowers and growing grain and all the life about him.
It was his Father's house, and it spoke to him of his
Father's wisdom and goodness. There is no dualism here.
But his clear vision showed him that all about him were
men who were losing their life because they saw and loved
only the world of things. No more searching words are
found in his teaching than those that warn of the peril of
riches. But it is not hatred of the world that sounds in
them, only the love of men. Three stories bring us this
lesson, each in some special aspect. The first shows us how
wealth blinds a man to the real meaning and the real riches
of life. It is the story of the rich farmer joining field to
field and adding barn to barn, as though that were the
end of life. Jesus writes his epitaph in two words: "thou
fool" (Luke 12. 13-21). The second shows how wealth
dulls a man's ears to any spiritual appeal and hardens his

*Jesus' atti-
tude toward
the world
and riches*

heart toward his fellows. Dives feasts and has no thought for Lazarus. Dives thinks that his brothers would repent if Lazarus were sent back to earth, but Abraham points out that his brothers have what he had on earth, Moses and the prophets (Luke 16. 19-31). Riches tend to make a man self-sufficient and proud. The rich man is used to having men defer to his judgment and bow to his will. He is usually far removed from that humility and sense of need which Jesus set forth. It is hard for such a man to enter into the kingdom of heaven. The third is the story of the rich young ruler. Here, at least, is a man of wealth and station who seems wholly in earnest: "What shall I do that I may inherit eternal life?" Mark says that he ran to meet Jesus and knelt before him. But he cannot meet the final test. Jesus finds his point of weakness. He would fain have eternal life, but there is one thing that he rates still higher. And so he turns away (Mark 10. 17-27). A man's wealth so easily becomes his master, and "No man can serve two masters. . . . Ye canot serve God and mammon."

The life of trust

The third principle of the life of sonship is trust. If the love of the world is wrong, as we have just seen, so also is the fear of the world. Jesus puts them side by side (Matt 6. 19-34). Both of them are paganism, putting something else up as a god, or as a power to stand beside God. For Jesus God stood not only first but alone. When a man really loved God everything else was given to him with that (Matt 6. 33). When a man really feared God, there was nothing else of which to be afraid. Anxiety, therefore, was a sin. In beautiful pictures Jesus shows us the God who cares for all the world, even the little worthless sparrow. His own life showed the strength and peace which came from such a trust, as he moved on sure of God and fearless of all else (Luke 13. 31, 32).

The place of prayer with Jesus

Prayer is the simplest and most natural expression of this life of trust. How important it was for Jesus himself we have already seen. The times of crisis in his life show Jesus at prayer. This is in connection with the days of meditation and temptation before he begins his ministry. It appears again at Capernaum. He spends the night in prayer before he chooses the twelve. It is the same at Cæsarea Philippi, the turning point in his work, and again at Gethsemane, when he faces the cross and death.

Jesus found men ignorant of the life of prayer and indifferent to it; God was master and religion was keeping laws and earning rewards. Jesus' doctrine of prayer followed inevitably from the teaching about the character of the Father and the nature of the life of his sons. If the fathers that we know give good gifts to their children, shall not the Father who is all goodness do this and much more? Therefore take courage; pray. If you ask, it shall be given you. If you seek, you shall find. If you knock, it shall be opened to you (Matt. 7. 7-11). This confident spirit, he said, is the greatest power in our lives. He puts this truth in his usual picture speech: "If ye had faith as a grain of mustard seed, ye would say unto this sycamine tree, Be thou rooted up, and be thou planted in the sea; and it would obey you" (Luke 17: 6). "All things are possible to him that believeth" (Mark 9. 23).

The encouragement to prayer

The same lesson of encouragement to prayer is brought by two parables that are often misunderstood. The first is the story of the unwilling friend, whose neighbor has had unexpected guests. These have come at night and there is no bread in the house. So he goes to his friend. The friend is in bed and does not want to be disturbed, but he gives in at last just because the neighbor keeps up his knocking (Luke 11. 5-13). The second is the story of the unjust judge. He has no interest in the poor widow, and no impulse of justice moves him to hear her case. But he yields at last just to get rid of her (Luke 18. 1-8). These parables do not teach importunity in prayer. It is the pagan heart that thinks it shall be heard for its

Two parables of encouragement

much speaking (Matt 6. 7). God is not an unwilling
friend or an unrighteous judge who will hear us at last
just to get rid of us. Jesus' argument is this: If such
men, evil or unwilling, will yet give in the end, how much
more will God hear us who is our gracious Father?

How to pray

Jesus not only encouraged men to pray, and showed
them the power of this attitude of faith, but he showed them
what prayer was and how to pray. He showed them by
his example, which moved the deeply impressed disciples
to ask him to teach them to pray (Luke 11. 1-4). He showed
them the difference between praying and making prayers.
They are not to say prayers, as the Pharisees do, who are
not averse to being caught upon the street corner when the
time for prayer comes, so that men may see how devout
they are. Prayer with him is fellowship, talking with God.
Let them go apart, therefore, and let their speech with God
be simple and sincere (Matt 6. 5-15). Then he gives what
we know as the Lord's Prayer. The spirit of Jesus' religion is nowhere more beautifully or truly expressed than
in the Beatitudes and in this prayer. Here is the utter
devotion to God, his name, his will, his kingdom. Here
is the quiet and strength that comes with perfect trust.
There is no clamorous petition here. The need of bread
and forgiveness and daily help is brought to God, but only
that it may be left with him.

Faith in God, not faith in prayers

Jesus' teaching as to prayer has often been misunderstood. The words that he used to encourage men to pray
(Mark 11. 22-24) have been taken as indicating a sort of
magical power in prayer, that prayers themselves must
bring certain results. And so men have talked about faith
in prayer. But this was just what Jesus protested against
in the Pharisees. With him it was not faith in prayers,
but faith in God. Petition has its place in prayer, but trust
and fellowship are the supreme words. This fellowship,
for example, demands that we shall have the forgiving spirit
when we pray to the forgiving God (Matt 6. 12-15). What

the trust means is shown us in the example of Jesus' own praying (Luke 22. 42). Jesus does not say, "Thy will be done," because he cannot get what he asks, but because God's will is his supreme desire. It follows from his trust in God that God's will is the highest good. It is the same spirit of devotion and trust that breathes in the quiet words of the Lord's Prayer.

DIRECTIONS FOR READING AND STUDY

Make a topical outline of the Sermon on the Mount (Matt 5 to 7).

Scholars agree that this is a collection of sayings made by Matthew, brought together here and arranged probably for purposes of use in instruction. Find the general subject, for example, of 5. 21-48 and 6. 1-18.

Using a synopsis or harmony, note that this material is wholly lacking in Mark, who deals more in incidents and less in teaching. Comparing Matthew and Luke, note several instances in which Luke seems to give the correct historical setting for some saying included by Matthew in his collection.

As to the spirit of humility and desire, read in addition Mark 9. 33-37; 10. 13-16; Matt 18. 1-6; Luke 14. 15-24.

As to the demand of decision and devotion, read Matt 10. 34-39; Luke 14. 25-33; Mark 9. 43-48.

Read the stories of the three rich men: Luke 12. 13-21; 16. 19-31; Mark 10. 17-27.

As to prayer, read Mark 11. 22-25; Luke 11. 5-13; 18. 1-8.

CHAPTER XIII

THE LIFE WITH MEN

ALL realize to-day that religion and morals must go together. It was not so in Jesus' time. In the Roman world religion was quite distinct from matters of conduct and character. The leaders of the Jewish faith laid the stress upon innumerable rites and rules which were to be observed for their own sake. With Jesus religion and ethics are one. He knows no such thing as a religion which does not issue in ethics, or a morality that does not spring from religion. The oneness is apparent from three considerations. (1) It is seen in the great commandment in which Jesus sums up all religion: "Thou shalt love the Lord thy God with all thy heart, and with all thy soul, and with all thy mind. Thou shalt love thy neighbor as thyself" (Matt 22. 34-40). Given in double form, the commandment really is one. The Pharisees summed up duty in six hundred and thirteen rules. Jesus has but one, and that is not a rule but an inner spirit. In that spirit faith and service are one; it is the same spirit whether turned toward God or man. (2) Jesus declares that our love of God must be shown in the service of his brethren, of God's children (Matt 25. 31-40). The mere forms of religion had no interest for Jesus. To be reconciled to one's brother comes before the gift at the altar. The Sabbath was not a form to be kept or a work to be done for God; it was a gift to man, and a good deed was the right way of keeping it. It was mercy, not sacrifice, that God wanted, as the prophet had taught long ago (Matt 12. 1-8; Mark 2. 23-28; 3. 1-5). (3) The heart of Jesus' ethics comes from his faith. To be a brother sums up the whole relation to men, but what that means we know only as we look to God. From his spirit as

Father we learn what we are to be as sons, merciful as he is merciful. And from his Fatherhood we learn that all men are our brothers, evil as well as good. Looking back to-day, we know that there never has been any real and full brotherhood except as there has been this faith in God as Father.

The first principle in the practice of brotherhood is that **The law of reverence** of reverence, the regard for humanity as sacred. Here, as at every point in the practice of brotherhood, the ideal is simply that men are to be "sons of the Father who is in heaven." God values men, as we have seen, and even welcomes back those that have been sinful (Luke 15). Human life is the one thing that is worth more than all the world (Mark 8. 36, 37). Not even the weakest and meanest of human lives may be injured with impunity; "Whosoever shall cause one of these little ones that believe on me to stumble, it were better for him if a great millstone were hanged about his neck, and he were cast into the sea" (Mark 9. 42). And even the spirit of contempt shown toward our fellow men brings down the judgment of God (Matt 5. 21, 22). Only gradually are we seeing the tremendous meaning for our social life of this teaching of Jesus, which has slowly been reversing the practice of the ages. The protection of property was the chief interest of law and government in his day. Gradually under this principle we are making human welfare our chief aim.

The second principle of brotherhood is the law of grace **The law of grace and good will** and good will. Here too it is the spirit of the Father that determines what the sons should be. We are to show the forgiving spirit to men as he shows it to us (Matt 6. 12-15). And it is not to be a grudging or limited forgiveness. As God forgives us freely and constantly, so we are to forgive, not seven times, but seventy times seven. Jesus enforces this by the parable of the wicked servant, who owed his king the enormous sum of ten millions of dollars. Such a sum he could not think of paying. According to the cruel law of the time, it meant not simply prison but slavery for himself and family. Instead his lord remits the whole. The servant, however, finds a man who owes him a few dollars, and throws his poor creditor into prison because he cannot pay this. We are to practice toward men the mercy that God shows to us (Matt 18. 21-35).

The strongest statement of this law of grace and good will is found in Matt 5. 38-48. Just as Jesus ruled out legalism between God and man, so here between man and his fellow men. He puts aside the old give-and-take, "an eye for an eye, and a tooth for a tooth." He stands for *justitia,* and not *jus,* for righteousness, and not rights. Against the assertion of rights and the use of force to obtain them Jesus sets up his new principle: unconquerable good will and trust in the power of love. It is easy to mistake these words by taking them literally, as Tolstoy did. By these figures of speech, by drastic statement, Jesus is trying to contrast a new principle with the old. As always, it is a spirit that he stands for, and not a set of rules that he is giving. The spirit of legalism says, "I will give what I get." God does not treat men that way. He shows men good, not to repay what they have earned, but because this spirit of mercy is his own nature and is right in itself. So we are to show to all men a good will which no evil on their part can overcome: not resistance, not force when kindness fails, but unfailing love all the time.

The law of service and sacrifice

The final law is that of service and sacrifice. The common rule with men is, Let us get what we can. Jesus' rule was, Let us give what we can. He illustrates it from the social life. To Jesus it seemed a sort of profanation of that hospitality which he himself was glad to receive to make it, as it commonly is, simply a give-and-take affair. "When thou makest a feast, bid the poor, the maimed, the lame, the blind: and thou shalt be blessed: because they have not wherewith to recompense thee" (Luke 14. 12-14). Such hospitality had in it the real joy of serving and giving. Such a spirit of unselfish service Jesus appreciated wherever he saw it. He rebuked the narrow spirit of the disciples who were suspicious of some man who was curing demoniacs, but not a member of their company. The man was serving men, that was the great matter. Even a cup of cold water counted if given in this spirit (Mark 9. 38-41).

This unselfish service was no mere duty for Jesus. It was a life, and the only way to achieve life. There are several instances where he set this forth. According to Mark, there were two occasions when the question of position came up among the disciples. Once the brothers, James and John, came to him asking that they might have chief places with him when he should come as King in triumph (Mark 10. 35-45). Another time the disciples quarreled among themselves (Mark 9. 33-41). For them the coming Kingdom still meant power and rule. "In my kingdom," says Jesus, "the way to reign is to serve. The chance to serve is the real throne of life. That man is first who serves best." *Service as the way of life*

The same principle Jesus set forth in even more searching manner on another occasion. At the turning point in his career Jesus began telling his disciples that instead of his winning an earthly triumph, his enemies were to gain their ends, and he must suffer at their hands and die. In answer to their protest he gave them this searching lesson. To try to save your life when duty brings danger or death is simply to lose it; and to give up your life in daily service or in some supreme devotion is to find it. Against the real life thus found the whole world cannot be weighed in value (Mark 8. 31-37). Keeping is losing, spending is gaining: that was Jesus' law of life. *Losing and finding*

Most important of all is the fact that this is the animating principle of Jesus' own life. On the one hand is the spirit of service. That was life's meaning for him, the opportunity of spending it for others. He was a servant (Mark 10. 45). On the other hand was his confidence in *Service and love in Jesus' life* the power of love as against all use of force. He had fought that out in the wilderness; he would not use the kingdoms of this world. To that principle he remained true. When they laid hands of force on him at last, he bowed to it; he knew that it was coming. He himself met alike the love of his friends and the deed of his enemies with love alone in return. The years since then have shown which was stronger, his weapon or that of his foes.

DIRECTIONS FOR READING AND STUDY

The relation of religion and ethics: Matt 22. 34-40; 12. 1-8; Mark 2. 23-28; 3. 1-5.

The law of reverence: Mark 8. 36, 37; 9. 42; Matt 5. 21, 22.

As to the law of grace and good will, read Matt 6. 12-15; 18. 21-35; 5. 38-48.

As to the law of service and sacrifice, read Luke 14. 12-14; Mark 9. 33-41; 10. 35-45; 8. 31-37.

What indications do you find in history and in modern social and legislative reforms of the reverence for human life which Jesus represents? Is this growing?

From concrete incidents in Jesus' own life, show that his actual method was the use of love and good will rather than force? How was that foreshadowed in the temptation experience?

CHAPTER XIV

FOES AND CONFLICTS

ONE of the paradoxes in Jesus' life is seen in the fact Conflicts that, despite his spirit of love, and his message of good will, his own life was one of conflict, a conflict that deepened and grew more bitter till it brought about the end. This conflict appears in different forms and degrees: there is the misunderstanding of his family and friends; there is the attitude of the Galilæan populace, changing from early enthusiasm to later disappointment and indifference; and there is the early and growing enmity of the scribes and Pharisees. These conflicts bring the element of change and movement into Jesus' life, and at last hurry him on to his death.

The first opposition that appeared was that of the Phari- The Pharisees and conflict about the law saic party. Mark shows this at the very beginning, when Jesus healed a man upon the Sabbath. The conflict about the Sabbath was the most frequent cause of their attack. Usually it was because Jesus followed the higher law of mercy and healed upon the Sabbath (Mark 2. 23-28; 3. 1-6; Luke 14. 1-6; 13. 10-17). They criticized him equally, however, for failing to keep other laws. He and his disciples kept none of the regular fasts, nor did they follow the innumerable rules about ceremonial washings (Mark 2. 18-22; 7. 1-5).

The study of Jesus' teaching and practice shows the real A different conception of religion ground for these differences. It was not simply personal hostility. It was a wholly different conception of religion and righteousness. For Jesus' opponents religion was a sum of laws that God had given, and of rules or traditions handed down by the fathers, which made clear the application of the laws, and which were almost more sacred than the laws themselves. A religion of life and the spirit faced here a religion of law and tradition. The great teachings of the prophets about love and mercy and justice had not been forgotten by the Jews; but the formal and ceremonial stood side by side with the ethical and spiritual, and in actual practice the latter were lost in the routine performance of the former.

The new religion

Jesus did not begin an attack upon legalism and formalism, but he left them at one side. He did not fast or observe the rules of washing, nor do we hear that he ever offered sacrifice. He paid no regard to ceremonial purity. He sat at table with sinners and publicans (Mark 2. 15); he touched the leper (Mark 1. 41); he did not mind that the woman with the issue of blood touched him (Mark 5. 27, 34). His principles were clear. Religion for him was (1) not outward forms but an inner spirit; (2) not rules performed for God but service wrought for men; and (3) the oneness with the Father of his children, who show to God reverence and trust and to men his own spirit of mercy and good will. Such fundamental difference had to bring conflict. With it went another fact: Jesus was conscious of bringing in a new age. He came with a message of joy, a ministry of deliverance and gracious service (Luke 4. 18-21). The bridegroom was here; why should the sons of the bridechamber fast? The new life was here; why try to press it into the old forms (Mark 2. 18-22)? To the Pharisees he was the revolutionist, overturning the old that was sacred. In his own heart he knew himself as the bringer of a new life and a new day.

The spirit of Pharisaism

Besides all this was the difference between his own spirit and that of the Jews. He calls the latter the leaven of the Pharisees (Luke 12. 1). In the terrible indictment of Matt 23 he charges the Pharisees with being hypocrites, religious actors. Religion meant to him humble reverence for God and loving good will to men. He found in them the opposite. They were selfish at heart, desiring applause and preference. They did not care for men. They bound excessive burdens upon them. They put their formal rules before plain human obligations, and the very multitude of their rules, which made them so strict and pious, was actually a means to defeat the real spirit of the law (Mark 7. 8-23). Finally he charged them with willful spiritual blindness (Matt 12. 22-37). He had been casting out demons. They declared that he was in league with Satan, and that was the reason Satan's angels obeyed him. He saw in the charge simply their willful refusal to see the truth. He charged them with the sin of sins, the sin against the Holy Spirit. It was not their rejection of him. It was the fact that they saw the light and called it darkness. They were sinning against the Spirit of God who was speaking to them. The man who thus willfully perverts his conscience shuts the only door by which God gets in. That was what he meant when he spoke of the evil eye and the darkened life (Matt 6. 22, 23).

In the same chapter follows another charge which Jesus sets forth in the striking parable of the empty room (Matt 12. 38-45). They had been asking for signs. He refused them. It was not light that they needed, but obedience. They were like the man who had been set free from an unclean spirit, who tried to keep his soul clean and fair and well ordered, but who would let nothing in. The last state of that man was a life of evil far worse than the first. These men were not guilty of the common vices. They prided themselves upon the order of their life; but their souls were empty, and when he came with the truth of God and the call to devote their lives, they shut the door. The fair outside did not deceive him. They were like the fresh whitewashed graves, seeming without, full of corruption within.

The sin of the empty room

These were not the only conflicts in Jesus' life. He had to face as well the misunderstanding and opposition of his friends and neighbors, and even his own family. At one

The conflict with friends and family

time his friends tried to carry him off, declaring that he was beside himself (Mark 3. 20, 21). He had not begun his ministry at Nazareth, and when he went back at length the fame of his preaching and healing had preceded him. His fellow villagers listened to him with wonder, but he read their unexpressed thought: Show us some of these wonders that we have heard of from Capernaum. Their proverb, "Physician, heal thyself," he answered with another, "No prophet is acceptable in his own country." "And they rose up and cast him forth out of the city" (Luke 4. 16-30). Still harder was the break with his own family, which may have occurred before the Nazareth incident. It was reported to him while he was preaching that his mother and brothers were without the house and had sent for him. But there was a tie even deeper than that which bound him to mother and brothers. It was the tie of loyalty to the work for his brother men in the kingdom of God. In answer he looked around at the gathered company in the house and said, "Behold, my mother and my brethren! For whosoever shall do the will of God, the same is my brother, and sister, and mother" (Mark 3. 31-35).

Jesus demands supreme allegiance

These experiences evidently lie back of the words of Jesus reported by Matthew as given in connection with the sending out of the twelve disciples on an independent missionary tour of their own (Matt 10). Matthew has probably brought together here, after his custom, sayings spoken on various occasions, but bearing upon one theme—the work of the Christian apostle. Such words may well have been used by the church in later years as an address of ordination or commission, when apostles or missionaries were sent forth, and they have probably undergone some changes in this usage. But the message itself seems to come from Jesus' own experience. His call was to a supreme allegiance: "He that doth not take his cross and follow after me is not worthy of me." Such loyalty might mean the breaking of all other ties. That had been his own lot: "I came not to send peace, but a sword." "I came to set a man at variance with his father, and the daughter against her mother, and the daughter-in-law against her mother-in-law." They must not hesitate to share what he had borne: "A disciple is not above his teacher, nor a servant above his lord." But they were to share his faith and courage also: "Fear them not therefore. Be not afraid of them that kill the body, but are not able to kill the soul. The very hairs of your head are numbered." This chapter may be joined with the story of the temptation as a bit of the autobiography of Jesus: the wandering life, here received, there rejected, with no sure place for shelter; the bitter experience of malice and hatred from men and misunderstanding even from nearest kindred; the courage to speak every hidden word, and the assurance that his life was in his Father's hand who marked his every step.

DIRECTIONS FOR READING AND STUDY

As to the attack upon Jesus, read Mark 2. 23-28; 3. 1-6; Luke 14. 1-6; 13. 10-17. State the charges against Jesus as you think the Pharisees might have framed them from their standpoint.

As to Jesus' criticism of the Pharisees, Mark 7. 8-23; Matt. 12. 22-45.

Read Mark 3. 20, 21, 31-35; Luke 4. 16-30; Matt 10.

CHAPTER XV

JESUS AND HIS FRIENDS

The inner
circle of
friends

ONE of the outstanding features in Jesus' life is the group of his friends and disciples. At the very beginning of his ministry we find these figures. According to the first chapter of John, Jesus meets his first disciples in the following of the Baptist. It is to the home of one of these, Simon, that he goes when he returns to Galilee to begin his ministry, and here he invites Simon and his brother Andrew, together with the other two brothers, James and John, to join his circle (Mark 1. 16-20). A little later a publican, Levi, is added to the number, who is probably the Matthew of Matt 9. 9 and 10. 3. From this time on we find Jesus always with a circle of followers. They are with him when the crowds follow him in Galilee. They accompany him on his journeys outside the province. They are the companions in the quiet days, and, though they protest against his going, they follow him to Jerusalem.

Jesus'
desire for
fellowship

What was the meaning of this special circle? It marked, for one thing, the friendly, deeply human nature of Jesus. There was in him not only a general love for humankind and a compassion for the needy, but this special capacity for friendship and the desire for it. "Ye are they that have continued with me in my temptations," he says (Luke 22. 28). At the Last Supper together he says, "With desire I have desired to eat this passover with you before I suffer" (Luke 22. 15). At special moments in his life he takes with him the three who stood nearer to him apparently than the others—Peter and James and John (Mark 5. 37; 9. 2; 14. 33); and in the garden of Gethsemane he misses the watchful sympathy which he craved in that hour of need (Mark 14. 37).

Deeper than this personal question was the purpose concerned with his work. Mark puts very simply this double purpose: "He appointed twelve, that they might be with him, and that he might send them forth to preach" (Mark 3. 14). The stress of Jesus' work was upon his teaching. He must teach men the nature of the Kingdom, and what the life of the Kingdom was, and how to make ready for its coming. The changing throngs could not give him the best opportunity for such work. He must have men who could stay with him, whom he could lead by constant patient tuition not only into an understanding of his message but into a sharing of his spirit, into the life that he himself lived with God. They were to take his yoke upon them and learn of him (Matt 11. 29). That is the reason for their name, disciples or learners. *The purpose of personal training*

The second purpose was to train these men for work— "that he might send them forth to preach." There was at least one occasion upon which Jesus thus sent them forth. Matthew and Luke report this with extended statements of the instructions that Jesus gave (Matt 10. 1-42; Luke 10. 1-20). As the statements agree in other respects, it may very well be that they refer to the same occasion, though Matthew speaks of twelve and Luke of seventy. How far beyond Jesus looked in this purpose we do not know. So much is clear, that in the early church this inner circle was regarded first of all as preachers, as those sent forth to proclaim the message. *The training of preachers*

It is this double purpose of Jesus that explains the demand that he made upon these disciples. It is not always clear in any given passage whether Jesus is speaking of what is required of all who would enter the Kingdom, or simply of what he asks of those who were to go with him. When he asks the rich young ruler to sell all his possessions and give them to the poor, it is because he wanted him to become one of his companions (Mark 10. 21). Upon the men of this inner circle he made a special demand. They *The demand*

must leave their homes and their business and follow him
(Mark 1. 17. 18; 10. 28-30). They must be men of single
and unswerving devotion (Luke 9. 57-62). They are to go
forth teaching and healing, like their Master, taking no
provision and trusting to hospitality where they go. They
must be pure men and fearless, ready to suffer, and yet
with faith that they are in their heavenly Father's care.
And they must stand ready to sever any tie or face any
foe as this loyalty may demand.

How the
inner circle
was formed

The inner circle was not composed simply of those who
came of their own accord. They were chosen by Jesus.
In some cases men asked to be enrolled, like the scribe
(Matt 8. 19), and the Gadarene demoniac whom Jesus
healed (Mark 5. 18, 19). Not all were accepted, for Jesus
sent the latter home. They were probably all Galilæans except Judas. We know, however, little of the circumstances
of any of them except the first five named above. The
limited group of the twelve was probably not fixed at the
very first. But even after the selection of the twelve there
was both a smaller and a larger group. The smaller group
that was especially dear to Jesus was composed of Peter,
James, and John. In the larger group there were men besides the twelve. Aside from the reference in Luke 10. 1,
we read in Acts 1. 21 of others that were in the company
of Jesus. There were certain women also who were members of the company for at least a part of the time—Mary
Magdalene, Joanna the wife of Chuzas, Susanna, and others,
who assisted also in meeting the expenses of the traveling
group (Luke 8. 1-3). Some of the women followed him
later to Jerusalem and we find them present at his death
(Mark 15. 40, 41).

The training
and its fruit

The Galilæan ministry showed less and less promise of
permanent fruit, and Jesus turned more and more to the
training of the inner circle. The final issue justified his
plan. It was not an easy task. He had to lament their
hardness of heart, their slowness to see the real spirit of

his work, his real aim. But in the end he won. Only one of the number failed him. Even the shock of his death could not overthrow their conviction. After the first few days we find them rallying the other disciples and standing forth before the people who had put Jesus to death as a malefactor, declaring their faith in him as the promised Messiah. We try in vain to imagine what those weeks and months meant during which Jesus gave himself to this little group. There were long days when they traveled together or remained in quiet retirement, when he poured forth for their ears alone the wealth of his teaching. More important still must have been the deepening impress of his personality, his tenderness and sympathy, his courage in face of every danger and disappointment, his simple steady faith in God, his deep sense of the Father's presence and his fellowship with the Father. There is one fact that shows as no other what the power of his person must have been: These men who walked and talked and ate and slept with him in that simple human fellowship were the ones who declared when he was gone that he was Master and Lord and King.

DIRECTIONS FOR READING AND STUDY

Read Matt 10. 1-42 and Luke 10. 1-20. On this basis state (1) what the work of the disciples was to be as they went out; (2) what qualities of character he demanded of them.

Make a list of the friends of Jesus outside of these immediate disciples, and mention any homes where he was wont to be entertained.

CHAPTER XVI

TURNING POINTS

WE can now see the rough outline of the course of events in Jesus' ministry. The period of popularity came first, the time when the crowds thronged about him wherever he went, following him out even to desert places. The quickly spreading reports brought the people not only from thickly settled Galilee, but from Judæa to the south and beyond Jordan to the east and the districts about Tyre and Sidon to the north (Mark 3. 7, 8). There were various reasons for this. John the Baptist had already stirred the people and they were ready to listen. Many were moved without doubt by Jesus' message. But there were less creditable reasons too. They hailed him as a healer and worker of signs.

Side by side with this popularity there were from the beginning misunderstanding and criticism and opposition. The opposition came from the Pharisaic party, headed by their professional teachers, the scribes. On the part of the latter there was jealousy, on the part of both the opposition to a religion that was directly opposed to the authority of law and tradition for which they stood. Meanwhile Jesus realized how little real understanding the people showed. Even his family and friends looked upon him as one beside himself. He confounded the Pharisees at first, but they persisted in the attack. They charged him with being in league with the devil. Leaders from Jerusalem came down to watch him, perhaps sent by the Sanhedrin (Mark 7. 1). These accused him of violating the rules of their religion and so sought to stir up the people against him. And finally opposition came from another quarter. The Jewish leaders got in touch with adherents of Herod (Mark 3. 6).

Herod had put John to death, why should he not lay hold
of this new disturber? He himself had begun to ask about
Jesus, and to wonder superstitiously whether this were not
John come to life again.

Meanwhile the tide was turning with the people. The
opposition of the leaders was taking effect. Jesus had refused to listen to their clamor for signs or let himself become
a mere healer. Some perception of his real message must
have come to them; it was not what they wanted to hear.
The fourth Gospel preserves a tradition of how the crisis
came. Together with the first three Gospels, it tells the
story of how Jesus fed the multitude, moved by pity for
the crowds that had gathered, hungry and far from home.
Such a deed stirred them with enthusiasm and they wanted
to make him king (John 6. 15). It showed how little his
teaching had accomplished, how hopeless the task was of
doing anything with the populace. What John states the
other Gospels imply. Matthew and Luke give his lament
over Capernaum, Bethsaida, and Chorazin. These had been
the center of his work. Here he had done his preaching
and healing. But the repentance that he had looked for
had not come. "Woe unto thee, Chorazin! woe unto thee,
Bethsaida! for if the mighty works had been done in
Tyre and Sidon which were done in you, they would have
repented long ago in sackcloth and ashes" (Matt 11. 20-24;
compare Luke 10. 13-15).

Desertion by the people

And so there came the first turning point in Jesus' plan
of work. He decided to leave Galilee. On the one hand
was the failure of his appeal to the people. On the other,
the danger that threatened from Herod. The leaders of
church and state were both lying in wait for him. How he
regarded the latter is shown by a passage which Luke has
preserved, though he assigns it to a later time (Luke 13.
31-33). Some Pharisees had told him of the danger from
Herod. His answer was: "Go and say to that fox, Behold
I cast out demons and perform cures to-day and to-mor-

Decision to leave Galilee

row, and the third day I am perfected. Nevertheless I must go on my way to-day and to-morrow and the day following." It was not a counsel of fear that moved him to leave Galilee. His life was in God's care who had planned its "to-day and to-morrow and the day following." But neither would he be reckless of danger and tempt God (Matt 4. 5-7).

The faithful circle

But while he had not moved the people to repentance or won them to his message, his ministry had not been a failure. Side by side with his denunciation of the cities there is his thanksgiving for those who had seen and believed: "I thank thee, O Father, Lord of heaven and earth, that thou didst hide these things from the wise and understanding, and didst reveal them unto babes" (Matt 11. 25). During these days Jesus had gathered around him the circle of disciples, and these now went with him on his journey. Here was his work for the next weeks, to use the quiet of the days thus spent together for the instruction and training of these men upon whom so much was to depend.

Did Jesus turn to the Gentiles?

The course of their wandering, according to Mark, was northward from Galilee through the regions about Tyre and Sidon, then southward again to the Sea of Galilee and down to Decapolis, probably passing on the east side of the lake. This journey into Gentile lands raises the question of Jesus' relations to those outside of Israel. Was this another turning point from Israel to the Gentiles? The one incident that we have from Jesus' stay in the region of Tyre and Sidon points the other way (Mark 7. 24-30; Matt 15. 21-28). Jesus had entered a house and did not wish his presence known. His fame had reached these parts, however, as appears from the statement that among the crowds in Galilee there had been visitors from these districts of Tyre and Sidon. And so a woman, a Gentile, who heard of his presence, searched him out and implored his help for her daughter. According to Matthew's report, Jesus at first was silent, and then in answer to her persistence said:

"I was not sent but unto the lost sheep of the house of Israel. But she came and worshiped him, saying, Lord, help me. And he answered and said, It is not meet to take the children's bread and cast it to the dogs. But she said, Yes, Lord: for even the dogs eat of the crumbs which fall from their master's table." The harshness of Jesus' answer is more apparent than real. The term he used for the Gentiles was not the opprobrious epithet, "dogs," but the diminutive, "little dogs"—a rather playful term. But though he yielded to the woman and praised her faith, yet there remains his first unwillingness, so unlike his usual attitude, and his statement that he was sent only to the Israelites.

How did Jesus conceive his relation to those outside of Israel? Did he proclaim a kingdom that was only for Israel? We must discriminate in our answer. Jesus felt that his own mission was to Israel, and when he sent the twelve out upon their special mission he limited them in the same way: "Go not into any way of the Gentiles, and enter not into any city of the Samaritans" (Matt 10. 5, 6). Just what Jesus' reason for this was we cannot say with certainty. It may have been a limitation of territory, that he did not wish to work outside of the bounds he had set. He did not refuse to help Gentiles as such, for he had already healed the centurion's servant (Matt 8. 5-13), and the Samaritan leper was cleansed as freely as the others (Luke 17. 11-19). There may have been the conviction that Israel, the people of the law and of special privilege, must first be called to repentance. How could he expect a response from the Gentiles, when Israel did not answer to his message?

Jesus' work was with Israel

One thing is clear—there was no national limitation in Jesus' thought of the Kingdom. John had declared that membership in Israel was not enough (Matt 3. 8, 9). Jesus approved and went farther. He promises deliverance not from the empire of Rome but from the kingdom of evil. And the Kingdom is to belong not to Jews or to Greeks,

His Kingdom universal

but to the poor in spirit, the meek, the merciful, the pure
in heart (Matt 5. 3-9). Moreover, it is the idea of God
that rules Jesus' thinking and not that of the Kingdom. And
God is not the Lord of Israel, but the Father of all men.
Neither in the nature of God nor in Jesus' conception of
religion is there anything national or limited. His religion
is universal.

Whatever the reason for limiting his work to Israel,
Jesus' own attitude was not limited in its sympathies.
He rejoiced over the faith of the pagan centurion and
the Syrophœnician woman, and over the Samaritan leper
that came back to speak his gratitude (Luke 7. 1-10; 17.
11-19). His own experience showed him Israel's refusal
and the open hearts outside his people. He condemned
the Jews with examples taken from the Gentiles, Nineveh
and the Queen of Sheba, Naaman and the widow of
Sarepta, and the Samaritan who proved the neighbor to
the man that fell among thieves (Matt 12. 41, 42; Luke 4.
25-27; Luke 10. 30-35). For the most part the examples
come in the latter part of his ministry, when his heart was
moved alike by the response that he found among individual
Gentiles and Samaritans whom he touched, and by the un-
responsiveness of Israel. It is in the last Jerusalem days
that he speaks of the temple as "a house of prayer for all
the nations," and declares in the parable of the vineyard,
"The kingdom of God shall be taken away from you, and
shall be given to a nation bringing forth the fruits thereof"
(Mark 11. 17; Matt 21. 43). Even before this he had
said, when praising the centurion's faith, "Many shall come
from the east and the west, and shall sit down with Abraham, and Isaac, and Jacob, in the kingdom of heaven; but
the sons of the kingdom shall be cast forth into the outer
darkness" (Matt 8. 11, 12). The great commission, therefore, which Matthew reports as being given by the risen
Christ, is in harmony with Jesus' principles: "Go ye therefore, and make disciples of all the nations" (Matt 28. 19).

The second turning point in Jesus' work that fell within these days came at Cæsarea Philippi (Mark 8. 27-38). It marked, not a change in his plans, but a stage in their progress. It probably fell within the later days of this period of wandering. Jesus had turned back again after having come south to Decapolis, and had led his company far to the north, where lay the city of Cæsarea Philippi among the headwaters of the Jordan. Here came perhaps the greatest hour in Jesus' ministry. The cities of Galilee had not turned at his preaching. The established forces of his native land were against him, Pharisees on the one hand, Herodians on the other. His life was in danger. He must have been considering before this the road to Jerusalem and what it would mean for him. He had turned from other work to give himself to these men. He had asserted no claims. He had lived with them and taught them and loved them. Did they understand him? What did they think of him? Would they be true to him? It was one thing to call him Master at the height of his popularity. What would they say about the fugitive and wanderer?

Here at last he puts them to the test. "Who do men say that I am? And they told him, saying, John the Baptist; and others, Elijah; but others, One of the prophets. And he asked them, But who say ye that I am? Peter answereth and saith unto him, Thou art the Christ." It was no allegiance of lips that Jesus wanted. It was no personal honor that he craved. Christ means Messiah, Anointed One, but it was not this title that he wished. He had brought them to see that the hope of Israel lay in him, in what he was and what he stood for. They had much yet to learn, but he had bound them to himself; and they had made the confession not in some hour of triumph when the multitudes wondered at his healings, but here in his hour of loneliness and reversal. It was the moral and spiritual power of his own person which had wrought this.

The crisis at Cæsarea Philippi

The confessio

The meaning of the confession

It is not easy to overestimate the importance of this scene which Mark has given us so simply. It has been called the hour of Christianity's birth. The Christian religion has always been more than a sum of teachings coming from its founder, or an ideal of life set forth by him. He himself has been the center, as one in whom men put their trust, upon whom they built their hopes. It was the first Christian confession. It was, indeed, the beginning of the Christian Church.

The first proclamation

The story of Cæsarea Philippi makes certain one other fact—that Jesus had not previously proclaimed himself as Messiah or allowed himself thus to be proclaimed. Our Gospels here state explicitly: "Then charged he the disciples that they should tell no man that he was the Christ" (Matt 16. 20). Later he publicly proclaimed himself as Messiah by the mode of his entrance into Jerusalem; but that was at the close. It is true that there are earlier references to the Messiahship on the lips of Jesus or accepted by him from others; but it must be remembered that the Gospels were written not to give the record of Jesus' life in chronological order, but to set him forth as Messiah and Saviour, that men might believe on him. It was natural, therefore, that the writers should use these terms in the earlier as well as latter part of his ministry, just as we find them indifferent to the order of time in arranging their materials, whether of works or teaching.

DIRECTIONS FOR READING AND STUDY

Read John 6. Note the difference in the style of Jesus' speech as reported here, and the difference in circumstances and form of Peter's confession. Note, however, the similar outline of events, giving in order Jesus' popularity, his withdrawal for a time, the falling away, and the confession of Peter.

The woes over the cities: read Matt 11. 20-25; Luke 10. 13-15, 21. Note that these cities have not only been reduced to ruins, but that even their site has been a matter of dispute.

As to Jesus' wanderings, read Mark 7. 24-31; Matt 15. 21-28.

As to Jesus and the Gentiles, read Matt 8. 5-13; Luke 17. 11-19; Matt 12. 41, 42; Luke 4. 25-27; 10. 30-35.

As to the confession at Cæsarea Philippi, read Mark 8. 27-38; Matt 16. 13-20.

Read the story of the feeding of the multitudes given in Mark 8. 1-9. Compare with that of Mark 6. 30-44. Note points of resemblance and contrast. Some scholars consider these stories doublets, describing the same event with such changes as might easily come from oral tradition. Give reasons for or against this view. Would the disciples have asked the question of Mark 8. 4 if the feeding of the five thousand had occurred but a little while before?

CHAPTER XVII

FACING JERUSALEM

The third turning point   Two events were noted in the last chapter that formed turning points in Jesus' work—his turning from Galilee and his acceptance of the title of Messiah. To these there is now joined a third: Jesus decides to go to Jerusalem and foretells his suffering and death. "He began to teach them, that the Son of man must suffer many things, and be rejected by the elders, and the chief priests, and the scribes, and be killed, and after three days rise again. And he spake the saying openly" (Mark 8. 31, 32).

Why Jesus turned to Jerusalem   We do not know when Jesus formed this resolution to go to Jerusalem. He saw it apparently as the will of his Father, which he read in the course that his life had taken. Other doors were closed to him. In Galilee, where his work had begun with such promise, there were now the conspiring Pharisees and Herodians, and a people that had turned from him. To go to Gentile lands was to give up his mission. Only the way to Jerusalem was open. There he would make the last appeal to his people. The issue of that appeal, however, he clearly foresaw, and for that he had to prepare his disciples. The spirit that had opposed him in Galilee was far stronger in the city. He had met its emissaries, who had come down to censure and oppose (Mark 7. 1). With them he would find the priestly party, with whom he had as little in common as with the Pharisees. He knew that his journey meant death.

Jesus true to his principles   The journey, though perhaps a change in his plans, was not a change in his spirit or method. Here, again, the story of the temptation outlines his later life. The finger of God pointed to Jerusalem, it was his to go. His duty was not to save himself, but to trust God; not to find his own way, but to obey. If God's way led to Jerusalem and death, then suffering and death were a part of God's plan and of his work. His death, then, was to accomplish what his life had failed to do. Some glimpse of the greatness of his spirit comes to us as we look at this step. There is his independence of thought. His spiritual insight is his own; it is not dependent upon others. Neither the Old Testament nor the teachers of his day knew anything of a suffering Messiah. Yet at the moment when he takes his place before his disciples as Messiah he begins to declare that he is a Messiah that must serve and suffer and die.

Though the traditional thought of the Messiah did not help him here, he seems to have found guidance from other sources. He had seen what had happened to John and read in it his own end (Matt 17. 9-13). That had been the fate of faithful messengers in the past, as he told them later at Jerusalem (Matt 23. 29-36). He was not to escape it. It is not unlikely too that he found light and help in the great words of the writer of the second part of the book of Isaiah. He had gained inspiration from this source before. In this book were the words that he had read in the synagogue at Nazareth and had made the program of his life (Isa 61. 1, 2); and another verse from this writer echoes in the answer that he sent back to John (Isa 58. 6; see Luke 4. 18, 19; 7. 22). In this same book is the wonderful passage about the suffering servant. From the very beginning it was applied to Jesus by the church. He himself seems to have found in it light upon the strange path that he was now to take. That it was not regarded as a Messianic passage by the Jews would have made no difference to him. Two of its great thoughts reappear in his words in these days. First, he called himself a servant. "The Son of man came not to be ministered unto, but to minister" (Mark 10. 45; Isa 52. 13). "I am in the midst of you as he that serveth" (Luke 22. 27). Second, he declared that he was to "give his life a ransom for many" (Mark 10. 45). The same thought appears in the prophet;

Suggestions from John and Isaiah

in some way the suffering of the servant is to be for the healing and forgiveness of men: "He was wounded for our transgressions, he was bruised for our iniquities; the chastisement of our peace was upon him; and with his stripes we are healed" (Isa 53. 5).

The transfiguration meant a preparation   The story of the transfiguration seems to come immediately after the confession at Cæsarea Philippi and before the journey toward Jerusalem. It was Jesus' own preparation for the hard days that were before him, and it has a certain correspondence with the experience at the baptism and in the wilderness. In this case, as then, he was passing through a period of conflict. What he had settled then in principle he was now to put to its last application. The way of obedience and trust and service was to become the way of death. It was an hour of struggle, and, as was his custom, he went apart to pray, taking with him Peter and James and John. What that hour of prayer meant, how he won his victory, and how the strength came to him from his Father we do not know, except that here too a voice came to him, and he knew that this course that he had chosen was his Father's will. But even the dulled disciples, heavy with sleep, awoke at last and knew that God was in the place. And so Jesus gathered strength, as in the wilderness and the garden, for the days that lay before him (Mark 9. 2-8; Matt 17. 1-8; Luke 9. 28-36).

Jesus prepares his disciples   At no place do we see so clearly the work that Jesus wrought with his disciples. He did not simply tell them that he must go to Jerusalem and die. He began patiently a course of instruction. We do not know how long a time elapsed from this declaration until their actual arrival at Jerusalem. It seems to have been deferred long enough to give opportunity for their training and to insure his presence there at the time of the great feast of the passover. It was no easy test to which he subjected them. They had followed him on his wanderings after the tide had turned against him. That was hard enough. That he accepted the role of Messiah must have stirred a tumult of hope and ardent imagination in their hearts. Now he declared that his Messiahship meant suffering and death. No wonder that Peter protested. Jesus' answer is significant: "Get thee behind me, Satan; for thou mindest not the things of God, but the things of men" (Mark 8. 33). We might translate the words, "You are not thinking God's way, but man's way." There is a certain passion in Jesus' response that suggests a deeply stirred soul. It seems to reveal the struggle through which he had just passed. Jesus saw, indeed, in the suggestion of Peter that he should turn from all this, the same subtle tempting spirit of evil that he had faced in the forty days of temptation. Here, as there, Jesus perceived the real issue. It was no indifferent matter of ways and means. The whole principle of life was at stake. That principle he now set forth in sharp and paradoxical phrase: "Whosoever would save his life shall lose it; and whosoever shall lose his life for my sake and the gospel's shall save it" (Mark 8. 35).

The disciples stood the test. They followed him when he turned toward Jerusalem. And yet he had to return to his theme again and again, now to set forth his great principle of giving and serving, again to declare what it was to mean for his own life. They did not understand how such a fate could happen to the Messiah (Mark 9. 30-32). Since Jesus had declared himself as Messiah, the old popular dreams and hopes seemed to revive in them. They began disputing as to the relative positions they were to hold in his kingdom (Mark 9. 33-37). Two of them, James and John, boldly took the matter into their own hands and went to him, asking that he should promise them first and second places in the new realm (Mark 10. 35-45). All this he patiently met by his teaching. He called the twelve and put a child in the midst, teaching the lesson of humility. He laid down again his great life principle: "If any man would be first, he shall be last of all, and servant of all" (Mark

The principle of service and sacrifice

9. 35; Matt 18. 1-5). There is more sorrow than anger in his rebuke of the sons of Zebedee. He points to his own example: "Which is greater, he that sitteth at meat, or he that serveth? is not he that sitteth at meat? but I am in the midst of you as he that serveth" (Luke 22. 27).

The journey
to Jerusalem

There is little definite knowledge of the events of the last journey to Jerusalem. Here, as elsewhere, it is not certain except in a few cases, that the materials grouped together by the evangelists are in the right order of time. Luke gives us the picture of the Master leading on, fearless and with fixed purpose: "When the days were well-nigh come that he should be received up, he steadfastly set his face to go to Jerusalem" (Luke 9. 51). And Mark gives us the picture of the disciples: "And Jesus was going before them: and they were amazed; and they that followed were afraid" (Mark 10. 32).

The
demand of
discipleship

Jesus' teaching during this period concerned not only the law of service and its meaning for his own life in the suffering and death that awaited him; he also pointed out what the demand of discipleship was. Most of the sayings in which he demands the supreme surrender, the whole-hearted decision for himself and God, come within this period. His disciples were to be like men on their way to execution carrying their own cross; they were to come to him with their lives in their hands, ready to live the life or give it as might seem necessary (Mark 8. 34). Only so would they really find their life. And what else mattered in comparison with life. Better to lose all else, the right eye even, or the right hand, than to lose life itself (Mark 9. 43-48). And from his immediate followers he demanded absolute decision. There was no time for them to be making farewells or burying the dead. He wanted no men who tried to plow while looking back at the same time (Luke 9. 57-62). It was probably on this journey that he met the rich young ruler and asked him to give up his riches and join their company (Mark 10. 17-22).

Two incidents are given us connected with Jesus' passing The healing
at Jericho through Jericho on this last trip to Jerusalem. One is the story of the healing of the blind beggar, Bartimæus, that is, son of Timæus. It is the last deed of healing which is described to us. It happened probably as they were leaving Jericho, though Luke sets it at their entrance. There was an accompanying crowd from the city. Learning the meaning of the excitement, the beggar raised his voice and called upon Jesus: "Thou son of David, have mercy on me." It was the cry to which Jesus was wont to respond, the cry of faith and need, a cry which rang only the louder when they tried to stop him. And Jesus healed him (Mark 10. 46-52).

The other incident is that of Zacchæus, a chief publican Jesus and
the publican and rich (Luke 19. 1-10). What Jesus saw was not the publican but the man, the man who could forget his wealth and station and dignity in his eagerness to see Jesus. That Jesus read his spirit aright is seen by the issue. To Jesus the publican declares: "The half of my goods I give to the poor; and if I have wrongfully exacted aught of any man, I restore fourfold." It was but another instance of Jesus' open eye and ready welcome for that humility and earnest desire which were the open door to the kingdom. And though he was almost at the door of Jerusalem, with all its narrowness and watchful enmity, he did not hesitate to go in and lodge with this publican and sinner. Indeed, it is probable that he spent the Sabbath day with him, as his entrance into Jerusalem seems to have been on Sunday.

DIRECTIONS FOR READING AND STUDY

As to the impending suffering and death and its meaning, read Matt 17. 9-13; 23. 29-39; Isa 52. 13 to 53. 12.

As to the transfiguration: Mark 9. 2-8; Matt 17. 1-8; Luke 9. 28-36.

As to the principle of service and sacrifice: Mark 9. 33-37; 10. 35-45; Luke 22. 24-27.

The predictions of suffering and death: Mark 8. 31-38; 9. 30-32; 10. 32-34.

The Jericho incidents: Mark 10. 46-52; Luke 19. 1-10.

CHAPTER XVIII

CLOSING DAYS

The accounts of the last week WE have noted in our study how fragmentary the records of Jesus' life are. The opening events are reported quite fully, perhaps because they occurred at Capernaum, the home of Peter and other disciples. For the long period of his wanderings after leaving Galilee there is little that can be definitely placed. Now, in the last week of his life, the accounts suddenly become very full again. In the four Gospels about one third of the space is given to these events, inclusive of the resurrection stories. There are several reasons for this. The events took place in a great city before many eyes. The city was the home of John Mark, probably the first writer of a complete gospel story. More important, however, is the fact that these were days of intensest interest to the disciples, and these events became central for the faith of the church. What happened at this time sank deep into their hearts. Moreover, the days were crowded with teaching and incident.

Three features Three outstanding features mark Jesus' work: First, he asserts quietly but unmistakably his Messianic claim. Second, he speaks a final and urgent message of warning. Third, he openly enters into conflict with the leaders of the people, scribes, Pharisees, and priests. By the first and third steps in this course, instead of shunning the danger, he himself helps to hasten the end.

Jericho to Bethany The journey from Jericho was probably made in the early morning before the heat of the day came on. It was a steep road, rising some thirty-five hundred feet in the fifteen miles of distance. There must have been a score or more in Jesus' company. Besides the twelve there were a number of women (Luke 8. 1-3; Matt 20. 20); and there

118

were probably other disciples accompanying. Jerusalem was
not a strange city to Jesus. Whatever may be the case as
to the ministry in Jerusalem, recorded by the fourth Gospel, as a loyal Jew Jesus would have made at least an an-
nual trip thither to one of the feasts, such a trip as that
taken when he was twelve years of age. A couple of
miles outside the city lay the village of Bethany. According to John 11. 1, it was here that Mary and Martha
lived, and at their house the company probably now
waited till preparations could be made for the entry into
the city.

There is a passage in Zech. 9. 9 which describes the
entry of the Messianic King into Jerusalem: "Rejoice
greatly, O daughter of Zion; shout, O daughter of Jerusalem: behold, thy king cometh unto thee; he is just, and
having salvation; lowly, and riding upon an ass, even upon
a colt the foal of an ass." With evident purpose Jesus
sends to a nearby village and has brought to him an ass.
On this a coat is spread and, mounting it, he rides into the
city. For those who might understand, it was the first
public assertion of his Messiahship. At the same time it
set forth the manner of Messiah that he was, coming humble,
unarmed, upon a lowly beast. *The meaning of the entry*

How far the multitudes perceived this we do not know.
John says (12. 16) that even the disciples did not understand this at first. So much at least they understood, that
this was their Master's entrance into the city of which he
was to be King. Meanwhile the people that filled the city
in thronging crowds at the passover time, coming not only
from Judæa and Galilee but from parts far beyond, had
heard of Jesus' presence and came out to meet him. Whatever else was present, the dominant note was enthusiasm.
They joined the disciples in spreading garments and
branches in the way, and raising the cry: "Hosanna;
Blessed is he that cometh in the name of the Lord: Blessed
is the kingdom that cometh, the kingdom of our father *The reception by the multitude*

David: Hosanna in the highest" (Mark 11. 1-11). Before
this he had charged with silence any who would have
greeted him as Messiah. Now he had no word to say, except to respond to the displeasure of the Pharisees at this
demonstration by declaring, "If these shall hold their peace,
the stones will cry out" (Luke 19. 39, 40).

Cleansing the temple   Unwilling as yet to trust himself to his foes, Jesus with-
drew for the night to the quiet and safety of Bethany. Ap-
parently, his first visit on the next day was to the temple.
Here he saw again what had probably often stirred his
soul. His work now brought him into contact with the
priestly party, and the opposition is as sharp as with the
Pharisees. If religion was a matter of form and pride with
the Pharisees, it was a matter of position and power and
profit with the priests. To retain its place, the priestly
party had shown itself quite ready to enter into bargains
with the Romans. One of their sources of profit was
the cause of what now met Jesus' eyes. In kindly
consideration for the poor, the law provided that a pair
of doves would be acceptable as an offering from these
(Lev 5. 5-10). The temple party found this a chance for
profitable traffic. Still another chance came with the required payment of the temple tax. For this only the
coins were accepted that Israel herself had once minted, and
Roman money had to be exchanged for these. So the
temple courts were filled with the money-changers and
sellers of doves, all this being a monopoly of the priests.
Stirred with anger, Jesus drove them out. "Is it not written," he said, "My house shall be called a house of prayer
for all nations? But ye have made it a den for robbers"
(Mark 11. 17). Apparently, his righteous anger joined
to the approval of the multitudes left them no desire for
resistance, nor did they dare to call the temple officers.
"They could not find what they might do; for the people
all hung upon him, listening" (Luke 19. 47, 48; Mark 11.
15-19).

The second aspect of these last days of Jesus' ministry is the note of warning. It appears in the double lament over Jerusalem. The first of these Luke gives us as spoken by Jesus at the time of the triumphal entry. As he drew nigh the city, he wept over it. He was about to make his last appeal, but the city did not recognize its day of visitation. Soon the day of warfare would come, and its foes would overthrow it (Luke 19. 41-44). The other is placed by Matthew after the woes against the Pharisees. Its beautiful words show his distress for the city and his confidence as to his ultimate triumph: "O, Jerusalem, Jerusalem, that killeth the prophets, and stoneth them that are sent unto her! how often would I have gathered thy children together, even as a hen gathereth her chickens under her wings, and ye would not! Behold, your house is left unto you desolate! For I say unto you, ye shall not see me henceforth, till ye shall say, Blessed is he that cometh in the name of the Lord" (Matt 23. 37-39).

The same message is given in several parables. The first of these is placed by Luke on the last journey to Jerusalem (19. 11-27). Matthew's parable of the talents may be simply a variant of the same (25. 14-30). Luke's story of the nobleman who went to get his kingdom is the history of Archelaus. At his death Herod had bequeathed Judæa and Samaria to his son Archelaus. The latter had to go to Rome to have his title to the realm confirmed. There he was opposed by an embassy from Judæa, against whom, however, he was successful. All this Jesus uses to enforce his lesson of stewardship. He is the King who is to depart and leave the interests of the Kingdom in their trust. And they are to answer for the use they make of their pounds.

The parable of the fig tree is a similar warning, addressed not to the disciples but to the nation. Israel was the unfruitful fig tree having its last opportunity. "Let it alone this year also, till I shall dig about it and dung it; and if it

bear fruit thenceforth, well; but if not, thou shalt cut it
down" (Luke 13. 1-9). The story of the cursing of the
fig tree is nothing more than this same parable acted instead of spoken (Mark 11. 12-14, 20-23). Jesus sees a
fig tree in full leaf, but finds no fruit as he comes in search.
He pronounces a curse upon it, and they find it withered
as they pass the next day. As a mere act of petulance this
is inconceivable. Some have thought that the whole story
as found in Matthew and Mark grew out of Luke's parable
just noted. The other alternative would be to conceive it
as the same parable put into action, as the old prophets
were wont to do. The parable of the Lord's vineyard is
more a parable of judgment than of warning. The figure
was familiar (Isa 5. 1; Psa 80. 8). Israel was like a
vineyard intrusted by its master to the care of husbandmen
who were to make some return of its fruits. Jehovah had
been sending his servants, the prophets, and looking to
Israel for fruitage. Instead they had beaten and slain them.
Now he had sent his Son, and they would put him to
death. There could be but one end—that the vineyard
should be taken from them and given to others. Here again,
with the warning, is the assertion of Jesus' own Messiahship
(Mark 12. 1-12).

Days of conflict   The third outstanding aspect of these last days was Jesus'
open conflicts with his enemies. Again and again they
tried to entrap him. "By what authority doest thou these
things?" they asked him (Mark 11. 27-33). He met them
with another question: "The baptism of John, was it from
heaven, or from men?" His own authority, he felt, was
like that of John, from God himself. But they dared not
answer his simple question. To say from God was to condemn themselves, for they had not believed John; to say
from men would stir against them the people who held John
a prophet.

The tribute money   Their second question seemed more cleverly planned:
"Is it lawful to give tribute unto Cæsar or not?" (Mark 12.

13-17). To say yes would arouse the people; to say no would give them ground for lodging charges with the Romans. Jesus' action was as simple as it was unanswerable. He called for a coin and asked them what image it bore. They answered, "Cæsar's." "Render unto Cæsar the things that are Cæsar's, and unto God the things that are God's," was his reply. His answer was not an effort to divide matters between church and state, nor yet a mere clever device to confound them. They were quibbling; his whole passion was to have men yield to God the things that were God's.

The incident with the Sadducees shows how Jesus could take a trifling, absurd query and lift it to moral and spiritual heights (Mark 12. 18-27). They brought him the impossible and foolish case of a woman who, in accordance with the old law (Deut 25. 5-10), had been married in turn to seven brothers. "In the resurrection whose wife shall she be of them?" they asked. It was their effort to laugh out of court the doctrine of the resurrection, in which they did not believe. Jesus left their absurdities to one side. He simply replied: "You do not know the Scriptures or the power of God: and as to the life to come, have you not read the word, I am the God of Abraham, and the God of Isaac, and the God of Jacob? God is not the God of the dead, but of the living." *The question of the Sadducees*

The climax of his controversy was reached in the seven woes in which he denounced the Pharisees (Matt 23. 13-36). Matthew, who gives them most fully, is probably right in placing them here. Here, at the close of his ministry, he shows forth the inner spirit of that whole system of rules and formalism into which the religion of his people had degenerated. These words could have only one result—an open enmity that should end in his death. *The seven woes*

No passage in the Gospels is more difficult to interpret than the thirteenth chapter of Mark and its parallels. Jesus and his disciples were leaving the temple, the splendid *Jesus' teaching as to the future* building which was the pride of all the Jews. Deeply impressed, one of them said to him, "Teacher, behold, what manner of stones and what manner of building." Then Jesus made the startling answer which was the basis of one of the charges made against him in his trial: "There shall not be left here one stone upon another, which shall not be thrown down." A double thought was probably in Jesus' mind: first, that city and temple were doomed to destruction at the hands of Israel's enemies; second, that the temple and what it stood for was to make place for a truer faith. The natural question of the disciples was, "When shall these things be? and what shall be the sign when these things are all about to be accomplished?" Then follows a discourse, different from the customary direct and simple teachings of the Master, describing the woes that are to come and the strange signs that are to herald them.

Jewish apocalypses

The whole passage resembles strongly a class of writings well known among the Jews at this time, called apocalyptic. An apocalypse is an uncovering of secret things, especially of the future. The books of Daniel and Revelation are examples within our Bible. The minds of the people were filled with apocalyptic ideas at this time. The writings were generally marked by three features: (1) a certain circle of ideas including those of judgment, resurrection, the overthrow of the devil and his angels, the destruction of the earth, and the appearance of a new heaven and a new earth; (2) the discussion of times and seasons and the signs of these events; (3) imaginative descriptions of the glories of the new age.

Jesus and apocalyptic thought

If we are to judge Jesus' relation to all this, we must look at his teaching as a whole, remembering how easily in individual cases his teachings might be unconsciously changed by those who handed them down in the years before they were written out. In his clear and definite teaching he shows some agreement with this apocalyptic thought and some differences. (1) Jesus believed with these

writers that the rule of God was coming and that there was
to be a new earth. That was his teaching of the kingdom
of God. (2) Jesus believed that he was to come again,
and that he was to judge men. When he knew that
suffering and death were before him, he began at the same
time to declare that he should come in glory and that he
was to be the judge of men (Mark 8. 38; Matt 25. 31-46;
26. 64). (3) He believed that this coming was near at hand
(Matt 10. 23; Mark 9. 1). But (4) the whole spirit and
tone of Jesus' teaching was different. Although, like the
early church and Paul, he thought that the coming was near
at hand, yet he did not deal in figures and calculations.
"But of that day or that hour knoweth no one, not even the
angels in heaven, neither the Son, but the Father" (Mark
13. 32). (5) His interest was not in drawing pictures of
physical glories. A fragment from an ancient writer shows
us what some of these dreams were. In this Jesus is reported as having said: "The days will come in which vines
shall grow having each ten thousand branches, and in each
branch ten thousand twigs, and in each twig ten thousand
shoots, and in every one of the shoots ten thousand clusters,
and on every one of the clusters ten thousand grapes, and
every grape when pressed will give five and twenty metretes
of wine." Jesus did not talk of the future to bring such
visions to men, but to strengthen them against coming
trial and to call them to watchfulness and earnestness.

Many scholars believe that these words of Mark 13 belong only in part to Jesus. It may very well be that the
question of the disciples led Jesus to speak of the future,
to tell them of the days of trial that he foresaw, that he
might forewarn and prepare, as well as to declare his own
confidence in the future. With their own minds full of
these apocalyptic hopes, the changes may easily have crept
in, or even teachings have been added which they assumed
to represent his thought. In the end we must fall back
upon the body of Jesus' teachings and their unmistakable

Does this represent Jesus?

moral and spiritual emphasis, so different from the apocalyptic dreams that filled men's minds at that time.

The picture of judgment
It was probably at this time that Jesus drew the great
judgment scene given in Matt 25. 31-46. Here, as in the
other picture teaching of Jesus, it is a mistake to seek a
special meaning in every detail. Two great truths stand
out. The first is the fact of judgment. The second is the
principle of judgment. Here nothing is said of nation-
ality, Jewish or Greek, nothing of creeds or forms of practice; men are judged by the spirit of love and helpfulness,
and the service done to the needy Jesus accounts as a service rendered to himself.

DIRECTIONS FOR READING AND STUDY

The Messianic King. Read Mark 11. 1-11; Luke 19. 39, 40; Mark
11. 15-19.

Words of warning: Read Luke 19. 41-44; Matt 23. 37-39; Luke
19. 11-27; Matt 25. 14-30; Luke 13. 1-9; Mark 11. 12-14, 20-23;
Mark 12. 1-12.

Conflicts: Read Mark 11. 27-33; 12. 13-27; Matt 23. 1-36.

The future: Read Mark 13; Matt 25. 31-46.

State in your own language Jesus' charges against the Pharisees
as given in Matt 23. 1-36.

CHAPTER XIX

THE LAST HOURS

THE last hours were at hand. No one knew it better The plot than Jesus. The elements of power were arrayed against him: on the one side the priestly party, or Sadducees, whom his deed at the temple had angered; on the other the Pharisees, with their leaders, the scribes, who had opposed him from the beginning. The two parties were usually bitterly opposed to each other; now they were ready to join hands (Mark 14. 1, 2; Matt 26. 1-5). For the present they feared the people, the crowds of the pilgrims who were present for the passover and who favored Jesus; but they were waiting their chance. Jesus had been spending his days during this last week in the city, teaching in the courts of the temple where the people gathered. The first night he had gone to his friends in Bethany, after that apparently to some house upon the Mount of Olives (Mark 11. 11; Luke 21. 37, 38). The circumstances gave Judas his opportunity. A double motive probably prevailed with this disciple in the deed which has made his memory a shame. Like many others, he had been moved at first by the preaching of Jesus. But while the others of the twelve stood loyal, he could not meet the test when Jesus began to declare that his kingdom was not to mean earthly power and that suffering and death impended. It is likely that a certain angry resentment at Jesus' course made his natural avarice more ready to respond when the temptation came to gain a reward by taking Jesus' foes to this place of his retirement. And so he bargained with them for his thirty pieces of silver (Mark 14. 10, 11).

Mark and Matthew both give the incident of the anointing The anointing at this place (Mark 14. 3-9). It may have occurred that first day of Jesus' entry after he had returned to Bethany. John tells us that it was Mary of Bethany who brought the costly ointment and poured it over his head, breaking the bottle as though she would not have it subject after this to any common use. To the prosaic disciples it seemed a foolish, wasteful deed. Here, as so often, Jesus shows his appreciation of the finer aspects and deeper meanings of life as he rebukes them. For him it was a deed worthy to be told wherever his gospel was proclaimed. In this hour when he faced his great trial, such an act of tender and gracious love moved his heart. "She hath anointed my body beforehand for the burying."

The supper— was it the passover? The last crowded days must have left Jesus little time for his disciples. With the end drawing near he felt the need of such time both for fellowship and for instruction. "With desire I have desired to eat this passover with you before I suffer," Luke reports him saying (22. 15). All the Gospels report in detail the last supper which they ate together. It was held in the upper room of the house of some friend in the city (Matt 26. 17-19). Whether this supper was the passover, scholars are not agreed. The synoptic Gospels state this definitely, but there are strong reasons to the contrary. Had this been the night of the passover, the Jewish leaders would not have been abroad, but would all have been at their homes, according to strict custom. Neither could any trial have been held on the following day, for the day was holy like a Sabbath day. In this case the right tradition seems to be that of the fourth Gospel, which definitely fixes the following day as the passover (John 13. 1, 29; 18. 28). In the symbolism of the early church the Lord's Supper was looked upon as the Christian passover, and that is the probable ground for the tradition as to date which the synoptic Gospels follow.

Another warning There was one element of discord in the company that gathered about the table. No doubt Jesus had made more than one attempt to stem the change which he had seen

taking place in Judas in these last days. Now he saw that
it had been in vain. Perhaps he wished to make a last
appeal; possibly, failing of that, to remove Judas from the
company that he might have these hours in unmarred fellowship. The fourth Gospel states that Judas left during
the evening. In any case, Jesus warns his disciples once
more of the approaching danger by telling them that one
of their own company should betray him, one that was
taking food with him from the same dish.

Then followed another lesson, a parable which was to be **The new**
acted again and again in the long years to come (Mark 14. **covenant**
22-25; Matt 26. 26-29; Luke 22. 15-20). As so often in
the past, Jesus used a picture to set forth the truth, this
time, however, putting it in action. Taking a piece of bread
during the supper, he broke it and said, "This is my body."
And giving them in turn the cup of wine, he said, "This
is my blood of the new covenant, which is poured out for
many." The act and the simple words were full of meaning. Here was another word of warning to prepare his
disciples for his coming death. Here, again, was an interpretation of that death. Though the hatred and evil of
men might bring it about, Jesus knew that his death was
the will of the Father and for the saving of men. To the
words, "poured out for many," Matthew adds "unto remis-
sion of sins." Though the action of Jesus came so simply,
there was evident deep solemnity and consciousness of what
this meant. He spoke of a new covenant that he was establishing. Long years before Jeremiah had spoken of such
a day, when Jehovah was to write his law not upon tablets
of stone but in the hearts of men. Jesus knew that this
new day for men had come. The oldest record of these
events comes not from the Gospels but from the apostle
Paul, writing some twenty years after this time (1 Cor 11.
23-25).

From the upper room the little company started out for **A final**
the Mount of Olives where they had been spending the last **warning**

few nights. Jesus' thought was still with his disciples. One had already deserted him. Despite all efforts to prepare them, he foresaw how it would be with the others. You shall all be offended in me, he told them. Peter, ready as ever, insisted that he at least would be loyal. Jesus knew that the end was at hand. Before cock crow, he says to Peter, that is, before early morning, "Thou shalt deny me thrice" (Mark 14. 26-31).

The praying in the garden They had reached the Mount of Olives now and the place called Gethsemane. Jesus knew upon what errand Judas had gone. Flight would have been easy. His enemies did not care so much for his life as simply to be rid of him. But Jesus had settled long since where his path lay. Though there was no hesitation, there was, however, a shrinking and a deep anguish of spirit. It was not simply the horror of a terrible death. There was the deep concern for his disciples that had been weighing upon him, and for his people. For this hour he had prepared in the temptation. To this he had looked forward in that night of prayer on the mount of transfiguration. To these two great hours of struggle the third and hardest was now added. "My soul is exceeding sorrowful even unto death," he told the three disciples whom he had asked to watch with him. Prone on his face he prays. The passion of his soul trembles through his prayer: "If it be possible, let this cup pass away from me." Yet the deep undercurrent is the same as in that prayer which he taught his disciples. There is perfect confidence, and there is utter surrender to the will of God: "Abba, Father, . . . not what I will, but what thou wilt" (Mark 14. 32-42; Matt 26. 36-46; Luke 22. 39-46).

Arrest, desertion, and denial In the distance Jesus heard his enemies approaching. Worn out with the strain of the week, the disciples had slept while he prayed. While he was yet calling them, Judas came leading a band of soldiers and servants from the Pharisees and the priests. What Jesus foresaw took place; the disciples were panic-stricken. "They all left him and fled" (Mark 14. 43-52). Mark adds the curious incident of the young man who followed with only a linen cloth flung about him, and who fled naked when they tried to seize him. It is an interesting possibility that this was Mark himself, that the disciples had taken the Last Supper at his mother's home (see Acts 12. 12), and that the young man, awakening from sleep, had followed them. If so, then the suggestion is correct that we have in this anonymous reference "the monogram of the artist in a dark corner of the painting." Peter, a little braver than the rest, followed to the house of the high priest, where Jesus was first taken. Luke tells the story of his denial simply but vividly. Sitting in the light of the fire that had been kindled in the court, one after another of the servants, seeing Peter, charged him with being a follower of Jesus the Galilæan. Three times Peter uttered this denial. "And the Lord turned, and looked upon Peter. And Peter remembered the word of the Lord, how that he said unto him, Before the cock crow this day thou shalt deny me thrice. And he went out and wept bitterly" (Luke 22. 54-62).

DIRECTIONS FOR READING AND STUDY

The plot: Mark 14. 1, 2, 10, 11; read also Matt 27. 3-10.

The anointing: Mark 14. 3-9.

The Last Supper: Mark 14. 12-25; Luke 22. 15-20; compare 1 Cor 11. 23-25.

Warnings: Mark 14. 26-31; Luke 22. 35-38.

At Gethsemane: Mark 14. 32-52.

The denial: Mark 14. 66-72.

Write down the instances found in these passages of Jesus' attempt to prepare his disciples for the end.

CHAPTER XX

THE TRIAL AND CRUCIFIXION

The course
of the trial

THE accounts of the trial of Jesus do not wholly agree. According to Mark and Matthew, Jesus was at once taken to the house of the high priest and thus brought before the Sanhedrin while it was yet night. John may be right in stating that he was first taken to Annas, former high priest, father-in-law of Caiaphas and probably the real leader in the movement against Jesus. A night meeting would be irregular, but they were in great haste. The next day was the passover. The preparations for the feast began on this the preceding day and so the latter part of this day was sacred. They must not trench upon the sacred day, and they must run no risk of trouble being made by the people in Jesus' favor. At any cost Jesus must be brought before the Roman governor for judgment immediately. So the leaders may have been gathered at once, and the formal judgment not passed till morning, as Luke 22. 66 suggests.

The
conviction

Even now they were scrupulous about the formal rules of procedure. In their own minds the case was settled: Jesus had flouted sacred laws and customs. He had set their authority at naught in cleansing the temple. He had condemned them as faithless in his parables. But they must find a charge upon which they could condemn him to death and they must have two witnesses agree. In this they failed. Then at last the high priest challenged Jesus with the question, "Art thou the Christ?" Jesus had been silent. Now he must respond if he was to be true to himself; and there was confidence and courage in his answer: "I am: and ye shall see the Son of man sitting at the right hand of Power, and coming with the clouds of heaven." With

132

such assurance Jesus faced the end.   To them it was blasphemy, and they forthwith passed their sentence.

They next had to secure a sentence from Pilate. The **The accusation before Pilate**
Sanhedrin had large powers of local government, but not
that of the sentence of death.   Before Pilate Jesus' offense
had to be given a political turn.   Not blasphemy was the
charge, but that as Messiah he conspired to be king.   Pilate's
position in Jerusalem was not an easy one.   Rome had nowhere a people more difficult to handle.   It was apparent
to him from the first that there was no real treason here.
The poor peasant who stood before him must have seemed
to him only a harmless fanatic.   But these fierce leaders
of the Jews, insistent and stirring up the people, were by no
means harmless, and Jewish tumults were not to be courted.
So Pilate wavers between the desire to release Jesus and
the fear of consequences.

The court seems to have been held before the palace. **Pilate, Herod, and the people**
Pilate's first judgment was, "I find no fault in this man."
The priests then added another charge, that he was stirring
up the people from Galilee to Judæa to revolt.   Pilate
grasped at the word Galilee.   If this was a Galilæan the
case belonged to Herod, who was at the time in the city.   So
at last Jesus met that crafty, cruel ruler whom he had called
"that fox."   Before Herod's shallow curiosity, however,
Jesus kept silence, and Herod had no deeper interest.   So
back to Pilate Jesus went, and the governor sought again
to release him.   And now the people came into action.
Their favor had been short-lived; they had no room for
a Messiah who could not defend himself.   Pilate appealed
to them, offering to release Jesus according to a certain
custom; but the people, stirred up by the priests, called for
another prisoner and began to raise their cry against Jesus,
"Crucify, crucify."   Cowardly at heart, Pilate at last passed
sentence of death.

And now for the third time that morning Jesus suffers **The mocking of Jesus**
mockery and abuse.   This meek and silent figure in peasant's

garb, yet claiming to be the Messiah, had stirred his foes to
brutal ridicule. They had mocked him in the court of
Caiaphas, striking the blindfolded captive and bidding him
name the man who struck him. Herod's soldiers had put
on gorgeous garments in mockery. Now Pilate hands him
over to his men and, after the brutal custom of the time,
Jesus suffers the cruelty of scourging. The soldiers in play
give him crown and robe and a reed for scepter, and then
change their mock homage to blows and insult.

The way of
the cross

All this did not last long, for Mark says the crucifixion
took place at nine. The criminal himself was usually compelled to bear the heavy timber upon which he was later
hung. Jesus was evidently too weak for this. The name
of the man who bore the cross is probably remembered
as being later a disciple. Broken though he may have been,
Jesus still had a word for the few women who followed
him lamenting, and for the city whose end he saw.

The
crucifixion
The seven
words

Crucifixion was a mode of death made terrible by pro-
longed suffering, to which was added the shame of a
form of execution reserved for slaves and lowest criminals.
In the presence of the deeper agony of spirit the mere description of physical suffering is out of place. It was the
common place of execution to which Jesus was led, and
two robbers suffered the penalty at the same time. In few
words the Gospels have given us the picture: the hardened
soldiery gambling for his garments, his enemies jeering
at him, the crowds looking on, and the women who had followed him from the north sorrowing at a distance. The
four Gospels report seven words of Jesus spoken from the
cross. In only one case, however, do two of the Gospels
report the same word. Two words are reported as spoken
to others: one to the penitent thief, "Verily I say unto thee,
To-day shalt thou be with me in paradise"; and one given
by John, spoken to his mother and a disciple: "Woman,
behold, thy son," and "Behold, thy mother." Three words
of prayer are reported: "Father, forgive them; for they

know not what they do"; "My God, my God, why hast thou forsaken me?" "Father, into thy hands I commend my spirit." The fourth Gospel adds two other words: "I thirst," and "It is finished." The wine and myrrh, offered to deaden the senses and to lessen the pain, Jesus refused. He wished to keep his full consciousness to the last. Instead of the suffering which often lasted two or three days, Jesus' death came after but three hours, and then, apparently, suddenly. "Jesus cried again with a loud voice, and yielded up his spirit."

His death showed again how he had been able to bind men to him. From all the cruelty and brutality and indifference of that hour, there stands forth the devotion of the women from Galilee who watched the scene from afar. And to them must be joined Joseph of Arimathæa, evidently a man of wealth and prominence, probably a member of the Sanhedrin. Joseph had the courage to ask for the body from Pilate, and provided the tomb in which it was buried. *Friends in death*

As he had lived, so Jesus died, in the spirit of love for men for whose saving he counted this death, and in utter confidence and obedience toward God. One word seems to indicate that this confidence left him for at least a moment —the cry which Matthew and Mark report: "My God, my God, why hast thou forsaken me?" The inference is probably wrong. The story of the temptation shows how Jesus, in the days of struggle before his ministry, used the words of the Scriptures for guidance and strength. Here in his last trial, they come again to his lips. It is the twenty-second psalm that he is repeating. But the psalm, of which these evangelists repeat but the first verse, is a song of faith and not simply a cry of anguish: *The spirit of Jesus in death*

> Our fathers trusted in thee:
> They trusted, and thou didst deliver them.
> They cried unto thee, and were delivered:
> They trusted in thee, and were not put to shame.

The meaning of the cross

What Jesus hoped for from his death was not wanting. It did for men what his life alone had not accomplished. The cross, symbol of shame for that day like the guillotine or gallows for ours, became the center of the message of his disciples and the symbol of honor for the ages following. From the first men saw in his death, as did he, not a tragic accident or the triumph of his foes, but some great purpose of God. It wrought the sense of sin and the feeling of penitence which he had wished to call forth. It stood forth as the crowning deed of his love in which they saw the love and mercy of God. It fixed forever the ideal of his life as that of love and service, and the ideal of the Christian life for those who were to follow him.

DIRECTIONS FOR READING AND STUDY

Before the priests: Mark 14. 53-65; Luke 22. 63-71.
Before Pilate and Herod: Mark 15. 1-20; Luke 23. 1-25.
Crucifixion and burial: Mark 15. 21-47; Matt 27. 32-66; Luke 23. 26-56.

Write briefly in your own words the story of the trial, incorporating the items from the three synoptic Gospels.

PART III
THE JERUSALEM CHURCH

CHAPTER XXI

THE BEGINNINGS OF THE CHURCH

WHAT Jesus' enemies were concerned about was not simply to wreak vengeance upon an individual who had offended them. They wanted to put a stop to a movement that threatened to endanger their position as leaders. The simplest way was to kill the Master. His disciples, a group of enthusiasts without training or standing, could very well be disregarded. None of them were, therefore, molested. When they had gibbeted the leader they felt the matter was disposed of. *The plan of Jesus' foes*

So, indeed, it seemed. Nothing is more certain than the fact that the disciples were utterly perplexed and disheartened by the sudden events of the day. Face to face with the terrible reality, Jesus' warnings had little effect. A Messiah seized by his foes, humiliated, scourged, bound to a cross—how could such a thing be? They could not think of him as the Messiah now, but as "a prophet mighty in deed and word before God and all the people." They had "hoped that it was he who should redeem Israel," but their dream was over (Luke 24. 13-21). *Disheartened disciples*

Just as certain, however, is the fact that almost at once a radical change took place. The scattered company gathered together. The perplexity was gone. Instead there were men with a clear and confident conviction. The fear had vanished. In the city in which their Master was killed, before the people that had seen his shameful death, they were ready to speak their faith in him. And it was not simply an old faith regained; there was a courage and a joy that surpassed the old days. They were not mere followers now, they were leaders. And all this was not a passing enthusiasm. Under these men as leaders a great *The sudden change*

139

movement began which in a couple of generations spread throughout the whole empire. What was the cause of this transformation?

The resurrection

The first cause was the conviction that Jesus was living. That was the center and foundation of all else. From all the New Testament writings that touch this period we hear the same word: Jesus rose from the dead on the third day and appeared to his disciples. The earliest and most important record is that of Paul in his first letter to the Corinthians, written some twenty years after Jesus' death. Paul undoubtedly received this word directly from Peter, whom he visited at Jerusalem only a few years after Jesus' death (Gal 1. 18). He declares to the Corinthians that what he preached to them was the common faith of the church as he himself had received it—"that Christ died for our sins according to the Scriptures; and that he was buried; and that he hath been raised the third day according to the Scriptures; and that he appeared to Cephas; then to the twelve; then he appeared to above five hundred brethren at once, of whom the greater part remain until now, but some are fallen asleep; then he appeared to James; then to all the apostles; and last of all, as to the child untimely born, he appeared to me also" (1 Cor 15. 3-8). The other reports are found in the book of Acts and the four Gospels.

Differences in the records

When we come to a closer study of these records we are met by two questions: How are we to reconcile the apparent differences in these accounts; and, How are we to conceive the manner of the resurrection and of these appearances? It may be stated at the very first that only by violence can these accounts be harmonized in their details. Matthew gives the appearances in Galilee, Luke in Jerusalem, while the last part of Mark's Gospel has been unfortunately lost to us, as the note given in our American Standard Revised Edition indicates. There have been differences of interpretation likewise as to the manner of the resurrection and the appearances. Our oldest witness, Paul, lays no stress upon the physical. He believes, of course, in a bodily resurrection, but he will not dogmatize about the nature of that body. He seems to put Jesus' resurrection in line with the resurrection of the saints, of which he says: "It is sown a natural body; it is raised a spiritual body" (1 Cor 15. 20-53). In the same way Paul classes Jesus' appearance to him on the way to Damascus with that to the disciples after his resurrection. Luke, on the other hand, emphasizes the physical, even to the extent of picturing Jesus as eating (Luke 24. 39-43).

To the first question we may answer: While it is not possible to reconcile these differences now, neither is it necessary. In the years that elapsed between these events and the writing of the Gospels, it was inevitable that such discrepancies should arise. The fundamental fact, however, is clearly held by all these writers. The very discrepancies emphasize the central agreement. Nor is it important to be able to answer the second question. The actual issue is whether we believe in the reality of the spiritual world. If the physical is all there is of life, then these stories are mere hallucinations. But if the real life be the personal and spiritual, then the manner of these appearances is not vital, and to attempt to decide is simply to try to answer the unanswerable. The one clear fact, without which the wonderful story of early Christianity is a mere riddle, is the fact that these disciples were following a living Lord, and not a dead and defeated leader. *The central question*

What this conviction meant that Jesus was living we cannot overestimate. If he were living, then he was the Messiah, then his death was part of the will and plan of God. Then too Jesus would come again and establish his Kingdom upon the earth. It is this confidence in the second appearing of Jesus and in his final triumph, that fills the whole early church with hope and joy. The Christians are those who wait for the appearing of their Lord. *What the faith meant*

What is the relation of these narratives of the resurrection to Christian faith to-day? Are they not its foundation? And if so, are not these discrepancies a serious hindrance? To this we must answer: The conviction of the living Christ is central for Christian faith to-day. But the foundation of that conviction is not primarily the story of the appearances. It is, rather, the personality of Christ itself; it is this life that shines forth in the Gospels, convincing us of its reality and of the God whom it shows forth, and proving its reality by what it did for the early church and for the generations since, and by what it will do to-day for those who surrender to it. The real foundation is not a historical argument or proof; it is this personal moral conviction and experience.

Next to their conviction of the living Christ, there is another great fact that stands at the beginning of the Christian church and accounts for the transformation of these men. That was the gift of the Spirit. These disciples believed that their Lord would some time return in glory, but their religion was not simply one of waiting. Their Master was the exalted Christ at the right hand of God and he had given to them the Holy Spirit. The Spirit of God was in their midst and in their hearts now. God was not a doctrine, he was a presence. Religion was not a mere duty, it was a life which they already possessed. There is a spirit of enthusiasm that fills these pages of Acts, a spirit of joy and a sense of power. "And day by day, continuing steadfastly with one accord in the temple, and breaking bread at home, they took their food with gladness and singleness of heart, praising God, and having favor with all the people. And they were all filled with the Holy Spirit, and they spake the word of God with boldness. And the multitudes of them that believed were of one heart and soul: and not one of them said that aught of the things which he possessed was his own; but they had all things in common. And with great power gave the apostles their

witness of the resurrection of the Lord Jesus: and great
grace was upon them all" (Acts 2. 43, 46, 47; 4. 31-33).

This full measure of enthusiasm and power had not **Pentecost**
been granted the disciples at once. Nor did they begin
their public work immediately after the assurance that
Jesus was risen. They were to wait together in Jerusalem
in prayer until they were prepared for the great task. "Ye
shall receive power, when the Holy Spirit is come upon
you: and ye shall be my witnesses both in Jerusalem, and in
all Judæa and Samaria, and unto the uttermost part of the
earth" (Acts 1. 8). This was the word of the risen Christ
to them. Luke describes how he was seen by the disciples for the last time and then taken from them (Acts 1.
6-11; Luke 24. 51). The idea of an ascension distinct from
the resurrection appears only with Luke, not being mentioned by Paul or in the other Gospels. Obedient to the
word, the disciples gathered together daily in prayer in
Jerusalem, one hundred and twenty of them in number.
Pentecost was the name given by Greek-speaking Jews, or
Hellenists, to the feast that came on the fiftieth day after
the passover. The climax of their waiting came on that
day. "And when the day of Pentecost was now come, they
were all together in one place. And suddenly there came
from heaven a sound as of the rushing of a mighty wind,
and it filled all the house where they were sitting. And
there appeared unto them tongues parting asunder, as of
fire; and it sat upon each one of them. And they were
all filled with the Holy Spirit, and began to speak with
other tongues, as the Spirit gave them utterance" (Acts
2. 1-4).

For Christian thought the word "Pentecost" means now **The two**
not a Jewish but a Christian festival. The name commonly **great facts**
used in English is Whitsunday. The day has been called the
birthday of the Christian Church. That is going too far.
That day might be fixed at the time when Peter and the
others first confessed Jesus as the Christ. But Pentecost

was the beginning of Christianity as a militant and conquering fellowship. The conviction that Jesus was living and the gift of the Spirit go together as the two great facts that explain the being and power of the early church. The first named gave the church its great hope; the second added to the hope for the future an actual possession for the present. While they still looked forward, they were nevertheless conscious of a rule and presence of God in the world and in their life. Religion was a possession, not a mere hope.

When was the Spirit given? Two questions arise in connection with Luke's description. According to the accounts in Acts, the Spirit had not been given to the disciples before. This is not the uniform New Testament conception. The fourth Gospel declares that on the very first day of the resurrection Jesus breathed upon his disciples and said, "Receive ye the Holy Spirit" (John 20. 22). More important is the word that Jesus spoke to Peter after his confession at Cæsarea Philippi: "Flesh and blood hath not revealed it unto thee, but thy Father who is in heaven" (Matt 16. 17). It was God's Spirit who had shown this to Peter. All true life in men is due to the Spirit of God. In this case it was simply an unusual experience under unusual conditions, marking the beginning of a new epoch.

The gift of tongues The gift of tongues of which Luke speaks is one that we find mentioned elsewhere, especially in Paul's letters. Luke conceives it as the ability to speak in foreign languages. Visiting Jews in Jerusalem, coming from many countries, were attracted by what had happened here in Pentecost, and as they came together Luke declares they heard the disciples speaking the varied tongues which these visitors represented. Paul's description of the gift of tongues is quite different (1 Cor 14. 1-33). It was a rapt ecstatic utterance, coming from men under strong spiritual excitement. Of themselves these utterances did not convey any meaning, either to Christians or to others. Outsiders coming in and listening would naturally think these people mad; and while Paul believed it to be the work of the Spirit, he rated it below that earnest but ordered and intelligible speaking which he called prophesying.

If there is any contradiction here, we must give Paul the preference. He is a witness at first hand, writing of what he himself has seen and known. Luke, in these first chapters, is using material that has been handed down to him. Even in Luke's narrative there are some things that suggest that what occurred is not different from what we find with Paul. If these visitors had heard the disciples speaking in foreign languages, they would not have charged them with drunkenness (Acts 2. 13). Peter, replying to this charge, makes no reference to the foreign speech at all. No one can say that such a miracle could not have occurred. Within Christian writings, however, miracles must be judged by the principles of the Christian faith and according to their moral meaning and spiritual value. Such a gift of foreign speech would have had two possible meanings, one to convince these outsiders, the other to aid the disciples in later foreign missionary work. It failed to do the first and we find no reference anywhere to the latter. It was not the foreign speech, but the preaching from a heart filled with the Spirit like Peter's, that won the many that were added that day. *Was it speech in foreign languages?*

Peter's speech shows that the early church saw in this experience the fulfillment of the prophecies, found not only with Joel 2. 28, 29 but elsewhere, which set forth the gift of the Spirit as the mark of the Messianic age. For many years Israel had felt herself without the living voice of a prophet. God was far away. Men had only his laws. In the new age it was to be different; God was to speak again with men and dwell with them. It was not merely, then, that they had seen their risen Lord and that they rejoiced in the hope of his coming; they had with them day by day this witness and inspiration of God's presence. *The Spirit and the new age*

DIRECTIONS FOR READING AND STUDY

As to the resurrection, read for general statements 1 Cor. 15. 3-8; Acts 1. 1-11.

Appearances in Jerusalem: Matt 28. 1-10; Luke 24. 1-53.

Appearances in Galilee: Matt 28. 16-20.

The gift of the Holy Spirit: Acts 1. 12-14; 2. 1-21.

Compare 1 Cor 14. 1-33 as to the speaking with tongues; note the points of likeness and difference between this and the picture in Acts 2.

CHAPTER XXII

THE FAITH AND THE MESSAGE

THE book of Acts is the principal source of our knowledge of this earliest period, a work written some fifty years after the death of Christ. As with most of the New Testament writings outside the Epistles, the book itself does not give the name of the author; but early tradition assigns this and the third Gospel to Luke, a physician and for some time companion of Paul on his journeys. As in the Gospel, the author uses various sources at his command. Only a small part of the material comes from direct personal observation. This latter is included in what are called the "we sections," such as the journey to Rome, where the pronoun "we" is constantly used. These parts are vivid, full of detail, and of the greatest value. The earlier portions are of a more general character, and show a tendency to idealize which is very natural with one who looked back with reverence to those first days.

The book shows a definite plan and much skill in composi- tion. Its purpose is to show how the gospel, rejected by all but a small number of the Jews, spread throughout the Roman world from Antioch to Rome. It is not a general history of the church, nor is it described correctly by the name that the church has given it, "The Acts of the Apostles." There were other apostles that worked besides Peter and Paul, but their work did not bear upon the plan of the author, and so he passes them by. No doubt he was governed in this also by the materials that he had at hand. Whatever the reason, it must be constantly remembered that this book gives us only scenes from the early church, not a full history. We know nothing of the beginnings in Galilee or in Rome, nothing of how the great church in

Africa arose. We can see that such a man as Barnabas had a long life of active service, but we know only a fragment of his work, and then merely because he touches Paul. Even of Paul himself, there is less than a decade of his life for which we have anything like a full record.

The disciples remain Jews

The conviction that their Master was living was what brought together the scattered disciples. But the little company that gathered thus did not think of themselves as forming a new church or beginning a new religion. In their own mind they were still good and loyal Jews. They did not give up any of their old faith or separate themselves from their own people. They went to the temple at the hour of prayer. They spoke in the temple about Jesus to those who would listen. They kept the laws of the old religion as they had always done. Peter was shocked at the suggestion that he should eat meat that was not ceremonially clean. They were astonished when the report was brought back that uncircumcised Gentiles (that is, Gentiles who were not even proselytes to the Jewish faith) had believed and received the Holy Spirit. It is clear that these first disciples had not yet grasped the full meaning of what had come to them.

What was new: Jesus

What, then, was new in their faith and their message? We may answer in a word: Jesus the Christ. "Jesus of Nazareth, a man approved of God unto you by mighty works and wonders, him, being delivered up by the determinate counsel and foreknowledge of God, ye did crucify and slay. The things which God foreshadowed by the mouth of all the prophets, he thus fulfilled. This Jesus did God raise up. God hath made him both Lord and Christ. Being by the right hand of God exalted, and having received of the Father the promise of the Holy Spirit, he hath poured forth this, which ye see and hear. Repent that your sins may be blotted out; that he may send the Christ, who hath been appointed for you, even Jesus; whom the heaven must receive until the times of the restoration of all things."

These words are taken from the reports of Peter's speeches (Acts 2. 14-40; 3. 12-26). They give us in substance the faith of this early church—the message which they preached, and the answer to the taunts of their foes who mocked at the idea of a Messiah that had been crucified. We may state this faith as follows: (1) Jesus lives; God has raised him from the grave. (2) The resurrection is the evidence that Jesus is the Messiah; God has made him Christ and Saviour by raising him from the dead. (3) His sufferings and death were no accident or defeat, but according to the purpose of God and the word of the Scriptures; his death was for the sins of men. (4) This Jesus is coming again as the Messiah, when he shall judge men and shall set up his kingdom; repent, therefore, and make ready. (5) Those who repent and believe shall receive forgiveness of their sins and the gift of the Holy Spirit; this gift, bestowed by Jesus, is the second evidence that he is the Messiah.

All these conceptions center in Jesus. Jesus lives; Jesus is the Messiah; Jesus died for men; Jesus is coming again; Jesus gives the Spirit. Jesus is the creed of the early church. His personality and his mastery of these disciples explain all else. The resurrection is important, but only as the resurrection of this Jesus whom they had known. He fills the whole horizon of their thought and faith. He determines their thought of God: God is one whose spirit is like that of Jesus; he is "the God and Father of our Lord Jesus Christ." He determines their hope of the future, the hope that filled the early church with confidence and joy; Jesus was to come and bring the new heaven and the new earth. He determines their thought of religion. It is true they still go to the temple and keep the old laws. But that was the outer form of their life. His spirit and his teachings rule them; and we see this in the life of the new community: its reverence and joy, its spirit of brotherhood and good will.

What the
Gospels show

There are other writings besides Acts which throw light upon the thought and faith of the first community; these are the first three Gospels. Our present Gospels were not written during this time, but the beginnings reach back to these first years. They show us how deeply the disciples appreciated the living memory of Jesus of Nazareth. They did not simply think of a risen Christ or dream of his return. They cherished his word. They recalled the stories of his deeds of mercy and love. They kept alive his spirit.

The oral
gospel

At the beginning there were no written Gospels. Everything was passed on by word of mouth. The Oriental has always had a marvelous memory for words. We do not have it because we do not need it in this day of books. There were present in the first community not only the twelve but others who had been witnesses "concerning all that Jesus began both to do and to teach." The living testimony of these men would naturally be prized above any writings. For the future there was no concern, since they thought the return of the Lord so near at hand.

The interest
of the
disciples

The first interest of these disciples would be in telling the story of Jesus' life and deeds. Their preaching to others would naturally begin with this, just as Peter does at the house of Cornelius: "Jesus of Nazareth, how God anointed him with the Holy Spirit and with power: who went about doing good, and healing all that were oppressed of the devil; for God was with him" (Acts 10. 38). We can see here what points were emphasized: the anointing with the Spirit at his baptism, his deeds of healing, especially with the demoniacs, and whatever else showed his power and so indicated that he was the Messiah. The story would naturally end with his death, which was for the salvation of men, and his resurrection, which proved him to be the Messiah of God. The words of Jesus would be just as carefully preserved as the story of his deeds. But while the story of his life was used in the preaching and winning of converts, the words of Jesus were used especially in the teaching of the disciples who had been won.   Such a word would always be decisive so far as faith and duty were concerned.

These stories of Jesus' deeds and collections of his words are what appear a generation later in our Gospels.   They show us more than anything else how the personality of Jesus stamped itself upon these disciples.   The narrative is so simple that it is easy to miss its unique value and meaning.   The Gospels nowhere try to describe or analyze or define.   They are simply witnesses.   They let Jesus speak to us and walk before us.   And so they bring us what no description and no definition of any creed could bring: the living Christ himself.   It makes little difference just how long it was before these oral traditions were set down in writing, or how they were combined in our present Gospels; these words and this picture carry in themselves the conviction of their reality. *The sources of the Gospels*

We must read these Gospels to understand what the early church was thinking of, and not merely Paul's letters and the book of Acts.   They were telling men not simply of the resurrection, but how Jesus had mercy upon the demoniacs, how he fed the hungry and blessed little children, and how he said to men, "Your sins are forgiven."   These disciples may have kept the old law, but we must remember that it was they who gathered the sayings like those of the Sermon on the Mount and handed them down.   They told one another the story of the good Samaritan, of the righteousness that was more than that of the Pharisees, of the poor in spirit and the meek and merciful who were to inherit the earth, and of the love that was to be like God's love and go out to the evil and the good.   No one of the stories of Acts tells us so much of the real spirit of the first disciples as this. *The witness to the early faith*

DIRECTIONS FOR READING AND STUDY

Read Peter's speeches, Acts 2. 14-40; 3. 11-26; and the prayer of the disciples, Acts 4. 23-31.

Make a list of the names or descriptive titles used in referring to Jesus in these passages.

Read Psa 22 and 69, and Isa 52. 13 to 53. 12.

From these passages select such verses as might have seemed to the early church to describe and foretell the sufferings and death of Jesus, or give any reason for the same.

CHAPTER XXIII

THE LIFE OF THE FIRST COMMUNITY

WHAT impresses us most in the life of the first com- **Fellowship**
munity is its spirit of fellowship. It is the picture of a
family that meets us here. "The multitude of them that
believed were of one heart and soul. And they continued
steadfastly in the apostles' teaching and fellowship, in the
breaking of bread and the prayers." They called each
other brother and sister. They greeted one another with a
kiss. In larger or smaller groups they took frequent, if
not daily, meals together. It was a fellowship of life as well
as faith and worship. They cared for the poor. "Not one
of them said that aught of the things which he possessed
was his own. Neither was there among them any that
lacked."

Some of the phrases which Luke uses in this narrative **Not**
have led certain students to believe that this was a case of **communism**
strict community of goods, or communism. He says: "All
that believed were together, and had all things in common;
and they sold their possessions and goods, and parted them
to all, according as any man had need" (Acts 2. 44, 45).
A little scrutiny will show that Luke is generalizing here
from particular instances, and that there was no fixed rule.
John Mark's mother, evidently a prominent member of the
community, retained her home (Acts 12. 12). Peter definitely tells Ananias that he was under no necessity of selling
his property. What we have here is not a formal order,
but a great spiritual impulse, a movement of spontaneous
love and devotion which impelled men to share what they
had with all that were in need. Probably the feeling that
the coming of the Lord was near at hand had its influence
also. One man is noted especially, because he sold a piece

153

of ground and gave over the proceeds. It was this that was the undoing of two other disciples. They saw the esteem and honor that came to Barnabas through his generous deed and coveted it for themselves. So they sold their property too. They could not, however, bear to give over all the proceeds. They wanted to have the applause for generosity and yet keep some of the money. Their sudden and tragic end made a deep impression.

The care for the poor

Whatever there was of communism here disappeared very soon, and we do not hear of it elsewhere. But the churches elsewhere followed this first example in the care of the poor. Everywhere this same spirit of love appeared. Back of the need of the individual believer there stood always the resources of the whole community. At Jerusalem there seemed to be special occasion for such help. Part of it may have been due to the fact that the disciples that came from Galilee would have lost their regular means of support. At any rate, it is one of Paul's special tasks later on to send gifts to the mother church.

Gatherings for worship

Of formal services of worship we read nothing. The disciples participated in the worship of the temple. Their own gatherings were in their homes. We read that they "continued steadfastly in the apostles' teaching and fellowship, in the breaking of bread and the prayers." This suggests the nature of their gatherings. The teaching would concern the words and deeds of Jesus, including the vision of the risen Lord, and the exposition of Old Testament passages which foretold all this. Then, as they were moved by the Spirit, there would be prayer and exhortation.

The worship free

All the worship of the early church must be thought of as wholly free and spontaneous. These disciples were Jews, and so accustomed to the worship of the synagogue. That worship was informal and democratic, giving opportunity for any one to speak who had a message, and laying special stress upon the reading of Scriptures and teaching. Besides this, there was in the early church the belief in the gift of the Spirit as belonging to all disciples. It was not office or education that determined whether one should speak or pray, but the impulse of the Spirit.

The words "breaking of bread" have a religious meaning **The Lord's** here, as is indicated by their connection with prayers. The **Supper** reference is to the Lord's Supper, as in Acts 20. 7, 11. How the Lord's Supper was celebrated we do not know. It seems that here, as later at Corinth (1 Cor 11. 20-22), the Lord's Supper was a part of a common meal which was taken together. Apparently, the disciples met together for such meals quite frequently. The exact form of ceremony we cannot tell. If we follow the suggestion of Paul's words written but a score of years later (1 Cor 11. 23-25), the leader at some place in the meal took a loaf of bread and broke it, repeating the words: "The Lord Jesus in the night in which he was betrayed took bread; and when he had given thanks, he brake it, and said, This is my body, which is for you: this do in remembrance of me." The broken bread was then distributed to be eaten by those present. Then the leader would take a cup of wine and add: "In like manner also the cup, after supper, saying, This cup is the new covenant in my blood: this do, as often as ye drink it, in remembrance of me." Perhaps at first they used the simpler words of the earliest gospel: with the bread, "Take ye: this is my body"; and with the wine, "This is my blood of the covenant, which is poured out for many."

Besides this simple service, one other form was in use **Baptism** from the beginning, that of baptism. It marked the reception of new members into the fellowship. The simple form used at first was into the name, or upon the name, of Jesus. It was not till later that the church used the form in Matt 28. 19, "In the name of the Father and of the Son and of the Holy Spirit." The baptism into the name of Jesus meant that the believer confessed himself as belonging to the risen Lord.

How was the early church organized? Was it episco- **Organization** palian or congregational? Such questions do not apply at this period. There was no formal organization at all. There was a company of disciples, and they had their leaders, as any such company will have. The leaders in this case were very naturally the twelve. The later church has usually called them simply the apostles, but there were other apostles besides them. Strictly speaking, the apostles were the men who gave their time wholly to missionary work; as such they were the founders of Christian communities. Paul is one of them, though he was not one of the twelve. In 1 Cor 15. 5, 7, he mentions first the twelve and then the apostles as though these two did not mean the same. Barnabas too is an apostle (Acts 14. 14). The twelve were, of course, of the number of the apostles, for Jesus had chosen them not only to be with him but to carry his message.

The Twelve

This seems to have been the distinct function of the twelve at Jerusalem. They were witnesses, teachers. When one was to be selected in Judas's place, the requirement is put forward that he is to be one of those who had been associated with Jesus and so could be a witness (Acts 1. 21, 22). But the apostles did not choose him. It was the church that came together and decided as to the choice by means of lot. The twelve, of course, exercised other leadership besides that of teaching. They had supervision at first of the poor relief, but it was the church, and not the twelve, that selected the men to take their place in this. They were to give themselves to prayer and teaching (Acts 6. 4). From their association with Jesus and selection by him, the twelve would naturally be the leaders and spokesmen of the community in general matters.

The seven and the brothers of Jesus

Besides the twelve there were "the seven," who were chosen to look after the daily meals for the poor. Perhaps this daily ministration, for which the phrase "serve tables" is also used, may have had to do with the arranging of the daily common meals for the whole company. The seven are not called deacons, and were perhaps only a provisional

committee. One other name becomes more and more prominent as time passes—James, the brother of Jesus. The
brothers of Jesus had not believed on him from the first.
Indeed, they even considered him beside himself. Paul
tells us that Jesus appeared to his brother James after the
resurrection, and the brothers of Jesus are found in the
early church almost from the beginning. Their relation to
Jesus would naturally win for them special regard. With
James, however, there must have been in addition a strong
gift of leadership. Later church writers speak of him as
the first bishop of Jerusalem, but we read nothing of any
bishop at Jerusalem or of the election of James to this or
any other office.

It has been a common conception that these first disciples
after the resurrection met together and organized the Christian Church. By some it has been held that supreme
authority was given to Peter or to the twelve, or that during
the days before his ascension Jesus gave to his disciples a
divine plan of organization. What has just been noted shows
nothing of this kind. Strictly speaking, there was no separate
church at first, only a community of disciples, who felt
themselves one, but still counted themselves a part of the
Jewish people. The twelve were not church officials, and
neither Peter alone nor they all together exercised any supreme authority. They were teachers and witnesses because
they had been with Jesus. When a step of importance had
to be taken, the body of disciples took it, as in filling Judas's
place or appointing the seven. There was no plan of bishops
and elders and deacons which they knew of as a law for
the church. What Paul says later describes the even simpler
life of these first days: "Ye are the body of Christ, and
severally members thereof. And God hath set some in the
church, first apostles, second prophets, thirdly teachers, then
miracles, then gifts of healings, helps, governments, divers
kinds of tongues" (1 Cor 12. 28). This is not a list of
offices to be found in every church. These disciples formed

A brother-
hood not an
organization

a brotherhood, one body of Christ with one Spirit in them all, and in the life of that brotherhood they all took part each as he was led by this Spirit. The careful organization of the church was to come later.

DIRECTIONS FOR READING AND STUDY

Read Acts 1. 15-26; 2. 41-47; 4. 23 to 5. 11; 6. 1-6.

CHAPTER XXIV

FROM JEWISH SECT TO CHRISTIAN CHURCH

THE most interesting question in New Testament history is, How did the Jewish sect become the Christian Church? Here at the beginning stands the little Christian community at Jerusalem. Its members are loyal Jews. They have a hope and a life which other Jews have not; but still they think of themselves as Jews, and they keep the rules of the religion of their people. They would have welcomed Gentiles that might have come to them, just as the Jews welcomed such converts. But they would have expected such converts to keep the Jewish laws of religion as they did; in other words, first to become Jews. In a brief generation the change takes place. The community at Jerusalem gives place to the church of the empire. Christianity is being preached, not as a Jewish hope, but as good news for all men. Nothing is said about being a Jew or keeping Jewish rules, but only about faith in Christ, and about living a new life of love in the Spirit of God. It is Christianity as a universal and spiritual religion. *Jewish sect at first*

This is the greatest crisis in the life of Christianity. The change did not take place without a struggle. Two great forces were at work to bring it about. The first was the pressure of outward events, the persecutions of the Jews, which showed the disciples that the new was really different from the old. The second was the inner force of the spirit of the new religion itself. This was the main cause in the change. It was this spirit, working through men like Stephen and Barnabas and Paul, that made the new faith a world faith. *The forces working change*

The first years of the Christian community at Jerusalem were, on the whole, a period of peace. Luke reports only *A time of peace* two cases of persecution. The first instance occurred in connection with the healing of a lame man at the temple by Peter and John. Attracted by the event, the people gathered together and were addressed by the apostles, who called them in the name of Jesus to repent and look forward to the coming of Jesus as Messiah to restore all things. Upon this the temple guards arrested them for making a disturbance and the next day they were brought before the Sanhedrin. It is not the Pharisees, the old foes of Jesus, that are proceeding against the disciples here, but the Sadducees. Worldly and at heart religiously indifferent, the Sadducees probably cared very little about the disciples preaching the resurrection. They did fear the results that might come from the development of such a movement, to which they thought they had put an end with the death of Jesus (Acts 3. 1-26).

Gamaliel

Despite the warning given the apostles, the movement continued to grow. A second time the Sadducees, or temple party, laid hold upon the leaders and put them in jail. At this juncture, Luke tells us, it was the counsel of Gamaliel that saved them: "Refrain from these men, and let them alone: for if this counsel or this work be of men, it will be overthrown: but if it is of God, ye will not be able to overthrow them; lest haply ye be found even to be fighting against God." Gamaliel was a rabbi of highest standing, and his advice was followed (Acts 5. 12-42).

The reason for peace

These cases, after all, were but incidents. The Christian community had relative peace and so a good opportunity for that rapid growth of which Luke speaks. The Sadducees came to look upon them as harmless enthusiasts, or else were deterred from action against them by their growing favor with the people. The Pharisees, who had been so bitter against Jesus, showed no hostility. The reason for this is not far to seek. These disciples offered no criticisms, but kept the law as good Jews, went to the temple, and observed hours of prayer and rules of purity.

But a change was taking place within the church itself. **The Hellenists** Among the many new members that came to it were included Greek-speaking Jews, or Hellenists. We hear of them in connection with the appointment of the seven. They were newer members of the community and their widows were being neglected in the distribution of relief. A majority of the seven then appointed were probably Hellenists, and Stephen is usually reckoned with them. These Hellenists were Jews who had lived abroad but had returned to Jerusalem. This return indicated their devotion to their country and its faith. At the same time their life in other lands and their use of the Greek tongue would tend to make them more open-minded. Among these men we can reckon probably Philip, who carried the gospel to Samaria; Barnabas, whose name is put before that of Paul in the account of the first mission across the sea; and Stephen, the first martyr.

It was Stephen who brought on the crisis. What he **Stephen's teaching** taught we cannot definitely know. We have only the accusations of his enemies and Luke's report of his speech, which at best is fragmentary, being broken off at the point where he was beginning to set forth his own position. Stephen did not anticipate Paul's teaching. He did not oppose the law by saying that men were saved by grace alone through faith, and not by keeping the law. He spoke of the law as "living oracles." But he aroused their enmity at two points. (1) The temple, he declared, was only temporary and not really necessary. God did not dwell in houses made with hands. Probably Stephen went back here to the word of Jesus about the destruction of the temple. Now, as then, it aroused their fury. The temple and its inviolability were at the heart of their faith. Jeremiah had made such an attack once and suffered for it (Jer 7. 1-15; 26. 8, 9). At this point perhaps his opponents interrupted him with fierce accusations: He was speaking against the holy place and against the law. Stephen may well have had Jeremiah in mind when he answered, and still further stirred their hostility. (2) "You charge me with opposing the law. It is you that oppose it. You are like your fathers, always resisting God when he spoke through the prophets, receiving the law but never keeping it" (Acts 6. 8 to 7. 53).

The charges

This last charge also reminds us of Jesus' teaching in his attack upon the Pharisees and in the higher righteousness which he demanded. Both these points are reflected in the charges which they preferred when they brought him before the council: "This man ceaseth not to speak words against this holy place, and the law: for we have heard him say, that this Jesus of Nazareth shall destroy this place, and shall change the customs which Moses delivered unto us" (Acts 6. 13, 14).

The attack upon the temple had stirred the Sadducees; what he had said about the law aroused the Pharisees. The trial had been before a formal session of the council. Now, apparently, the session broke up in confusion. To their minds he had himself confirmed the charge of blasphemy made against him. Whether with Roman consent or not, we do not know, but they hurried him forth and inflicted the penalty provided by their law, death by stoning. Luke shows us the spirit of this first disciple who sealed his witness with his death: "And they stoned Stephen, calling upon the Lord, and saying, Lord Jesus, receive my spirit. And he kneeled down, and cried with a loud voice, Lord, lay not this sin to their charge" (Acts 7. 54-60).

What Stephen wrought

Stephen wrought more by his death than by his teaching in life. He brought to a close the day when Christianity could live on undisturbed as a harmless Jewish sect. In their formal charges the witnesses may have been false, as Luke suggests. In the main point they were right: this new movement meant an end to the temple and to the customs of Moses. What was more important, Stephen helped not merely their enemies but the church herself to see the meaning of the faith. In the first place came the fact of persecution. It did not matter that most of the disciples had not shared in the insight of Stephen or held his views. They found themselves driven forth on account of the temple and the law, though they reverenced both. They had to face the question: What is our real faith, Jesus the Messiah and the hope of his coming, or Moses and the temple and the laws? And they saw how clearly Christ and the hope of the Kingdom and the new fellowship stood first, and how much they meant. In the second place, Stephen initiated the first missionary period. True, there was no such clear purpose in their minds as when Paul set forth. But an ardent living faith drives to utterance. "They therefore that were scattered abroad went about preaching the word" (Acts 8. 1-4).

The period of persecution and expansion thus went hand in hand. The driving force back of the persecution was the Pharisees, and the leader in the movement was a young man named Saul, who had been present at the stoning of Stephen. The apostles apparently remained in Jerusalem in hiding. Many of the disciples scattered throughout Judæa and Galilee and Samaria, some probably going farther. There must have been little groups of disciples beyond these limits even before this time; we read of disciples at Joppa, Lydda, Cæsarea, Damascus, and Antioch. The real work of expansion did not come through formally appointed missionaries or through the apostles. For the most part, it was done by common men and women, speaking as they had opportunity to those whom they met in their ordinary work of life. It was a great lay movement, and such, indeed, Christianity remained for the first century. *Persecution and expansion*

A few figures, however, stand forth. The first is Philip, not one of the twelve but one of the seven, for the twelve were in Jerusalem. His first mission was to Samaria, his next southward as far as Gaza (Acts 8. 5-40). Only two incidents are given from these journeys. Near Gaza Philip *Philip* met an Ethiopian, a man of high official position at home, and a proselyte, who was just returning from Jerusalem. The reference to Isaiah shows us how the early Christians were already interpreting the Old Testament in relation to Christ. The story of Simon Magus gives us a side-light upon conditions at that time. It was a day of many religions and much superstition throughout the empire. There were all manner of priests and prophets and charlatans, and people were ready to believe almost any magic or mystery. Simon was but one of many who fed on this spirit, which was for him a source of livelihood. In Philip he recognized a superior power, and even more so in Peter and John when these came down from Jerusalem. To be able to give the Holy Spirit by the laying on of hands seemed to him just another profitable device, and he was willing to pay well for the secret. All this was not so much a sign of great wickedness as a picture of what religion meant to many in that day—not faith and righteousness, but magical rites and mysteries of all kinds. Similar cases are met later in Paul's work: Elymas, the sorcerer, and the soothsaying girl (Acts 13. 6; 16. 16).

Barnabas and Antioch

The question of Peter's relation to this expansion must be considered later on. Luke shows us clearly that this new movement in the church was a lay movement. The spread of the gospel was not through appointed ministers and missionaries, but simply through those "that were scattered abroad." These went as far as Phœnicia and the coast near by, the great city of Antioch to the north, and the island of Cyprus. Of all this work we have but one definite item. At Antioch these disciples preached not only to Jews but to Gentiles also. Their success here was so great, and their preaching to the Gentiles such an innovation, that the church at Jerusalem had to take notice of it. Fortunately, it was Barnabas whom they sent down, himself a Hellenist from the island of Cyprus that lay off this coast. "He was a good man, and full of the Holy

Spirit and of faith." Even greater success followed his
coming until the burden and the opportunity drove him to
look for aid. And so he took a step which helps to usher
in another period. "He went forth to Tarsus to seek for Saul;
and when he had found him, he brought him unto Antioch.
And it came to pass, that even for a whole year they were
together with the church, and taught much people; and
that the disciples were called Christians first in Antioch"
(Acts 11. 19-26).

DIRECTIONS FOR READING AND STUDY

As to Peter and John, read Acts 3. 1-26; 5. 12-42.

As to Stephen: Acts 6. 8 to 7. 60. Compare Jer 7. 1-15; 26. 8, 9.

As to Philip: Acts 8. 1-40.

As to Antioch, read Acts 11. 19-26.

Locate the following places upon the map and note the enlarg-
ing circle: Samaria (city), Gaza, Lydda, Joppa, Cæsarea, Damascus, Antioch, Cyprus.

The Ethiopian was reading the Scriptures in the Greek, that is,
the Septuagint version. Compare Acts 8. 32, 33 with Isa 53. 7, 8,
and note the difference in the versions.

PART IV
PAUL AND THE CHURCH OF
THE EMPIRE

ST. PAUL'S JOURNEYS AND THE EARLY CHRISTIAN CHURCH, 40-100 A.D.

Copyright 1906 and 1912, by Charles Foster Kent.

Scale of Miles
0 20 40 60 80 100
KENT AND MADSEN
HISTORICAL MAPS
SHEET VI

CHAPTER XXV

THE MAN AND HIS TASK

In the story of the beginnings of Christianity there is one man who claims a larger space than all others of that first century put together. Some have looked upon him as the one true interpreter of Jesus, others as the man who turned the new faith aside from the simple teaching of Jesus, yet no one has disputed his importance. In any history of New Testament times his thought and work fill the main place after the study of Jesus. What makes this more remarkable is certain facts about this man. He was not one of the twelve. He had no such standing as belonged to one who had associated with Jesus. He had been, indeed, a persecutor of the new way. He began his work on his own account. The mother church at Jerusalem gave him no credentials. There were times, in fact, when the recognized leaders of the church, Peter and James, were opposed to him.

There are two reasons why this special attention is given to Paul. In the first place, we are in better position to know him than any other figure of the New Testament. The picture of Jesus, it is true, stands out clear and definite. And yet our oldest Gospels were written a full generation after his death, they give us his words in Greek, while he spoke Aramaic, and of his life they report but a few months or years. Of his followers almost all, even of the leaders like the twelve, are but names to us. Paul is the exception. It is true that most of our knowledge of his life is limited to a period of seven years. And yet there is probably no man of antiquity who is better known to us. It is not simply that so large a part of the book of Acts is given to him, nor yet the fact that we possess writings from his own hand. It is the character of these writings. This man was not writing for a public press, nor for unknown readers, nor for posterity. He was not producing "literature," or thinking of style or of the impression he would make. We see a soul of deep passion, of strong conviction, and transparent sincerity pouring forth its thought and feeling. And this man's thought is never mere thought, no theoretic theology; it is his faith and his experience. Not the *Confessions* of Augustine, nor the letters of Luther, nor the *Journal Intime* of Amiel reflect so truly or transparently the man.

His
importance

The second reason for the space given to Paul is the importance of the man. It was this man, not one of the twelve, who saw the meaning of Christianity as a universal religion and freed it from Judaism, who saw it as a spiritual faith and freed it from Jewish rule and law. It was he who carried it out into the great Roman world and established it province by province about the Mediterranean. When in his last years he was looking toward Rome and Spain, he could speak of those things "which Christ wrought through me, for the obedience of the Gentiles, by word and deed, in the power of signs and wonders, in the power of the Holy Spirit; so that from Jerusalem, and round about even unto Illyricum, I have fully preached the gospel of Christ" (Rom 15. 18, 19).

The Jew

Our first question about such a man is, Where did he come from, and what was his preparation for such a work? Scattered here and there we find not a few references that help us answer these queries. Three times Paul speaks of his race (Rom 11. 1; 2 Cor 11. 22; Phil 3. 5). To say that Paul was a Jew means as little for that time as it does now. There were Jews then, as now, loyal to every tradition of their faith. There were Jews, especially in the dispersion, who were of a more liberal cast, as well as some who had turned from the faith of their fathers. Though Paul's home was in the dispersion, in Tarsus of Cilicia, he belonged in the first class. "A Hebrew of the Hebrews" he calls himself. In such a home the native Aramaic tongue was spoken, which was not the rule with the Jews dwelling abroad. The Pharisaic standard prevailed, the strictest observance of the law. As to his own life, he could appeal to those who knew him at Tarsus and at Jerusalem (Acts 26. 4, 5). He had completed his education at Jerusalem under the noted teacher Gamaliel, perhaps at the home of an elder sister (Acts 22. 3; 23. 16).

Paul was a Hellenist, a Greek Jew. However strict the home might have been, the fact remains that he spoke Greek as well as Hebrew, that his early life was passed in a great city, and that he had a knowledge of the world of his day and its thought that none of the twelve could have had. A language is never a lifeless vehicle; it always involves a certain direct contact with another life and knowledge of it. The Greek tongue was the channel through which there poured the rich life of that old world. True Paul was not a student of Greek rhetoric or literature. He did not attend the great university at Tarsus, which could be mentioned with the schools at Athens and Alexandria. But this language that he knew was still open door and open window for the thought of the wide Roman world. When Paul went out to preach the gospel it was more than a mere language that he possessed.

The Greek

Paul was a Roman. Like many Jews he had two names. It is interesting to note that it is not by his Hebrew name Saul, but his Roman name Paul, that he is best known. Far more important than the name is the fact that Paul was a Roman citizen, and was one by birth. How the family had obtained this privilege we do not know. It suggests a family not only of standing but of some means. Roman citizenship was by no means so common yet in the empire. For Paul it meant more than a welcome protection in his work. It had its effect upon his spirit and character. He is not simply a Hebrew of Hebrews; he is a man of Tarsus, "a citizen of no mean city." It gives him an imperial outlook. The world of the twelve is Palestine; Paul's world

The Roman

is the empire, and it is the empire that he plans to take for Christ.

All this means an unusual equipment for a great task. The soil from which Christianity sprang was Judaism. No Greek or Roman could have been its interpreter. For that a Jew was needed, and Paul was more of a Jew than were the twelve. But it needed not only a Jew, but a Jew who had found out where Judaism failed. Here again Paul's experience fitted him. His very strictness as a Pharisee made him see the failure of the law, and saved him from such half-way positions as James and Peter could take. At the same time Paul's life as Hellenist and as Roman fitted him for the task that was waiting: to take this religion freed from Judaism, to interpret it to the world of Greek thought, and to plant it in communities throughout the great world of Roman life. The fruits of his toil show his fitness for the task. Besides all this there was his personal charater, an unusual combination of strong traits. He had the strength of will that could stand alone and that never knew defeat. He had a deep religious nature that enabled him to speak the new message from his own heart. He had the insight into the meaning of the new faith and the ability to state it. He had the master mind to plan the planting of a church throughout the empire, and the patience and skill and tact to carry out that plan.

DIRECTIONS FOR READING AND STUDY

As to Paul the Jew: 2 Cor 11. 22; Rom 11. 1; Phil 3. 5; Acts 22. 3; 23. 16; 26. 4, 5; Gal 1. 14; Rom 8. 2; 9. 1-5.

As to Paul the Hellenist: Acts 17. 16-34. Paul meets these Greeks as a Palestinian Jew could not have done. Note his tact and courtesy, and his skill in finding a point of contact for his message.

As to Paul the Roman: Acts 16. 36-39; 21. 39; 22. 25-29; 25. 10-12.

CHAPTER XXVI

CONVERSION AND CALL

FOR some men life unfolds in a simple and direct prog- A twice-born man ress from beginning to end. These have been called the once-born men. There are others whose life is marked by a great break, a revolution through which at last they find their true selves. These are the twice-born men, and such was Paul. His whole life falls into two distinct parts, divided by his conversion. Neither his thought nor his work can be understood without reference to that experience. Through that experience Paul won his message, for his burning message is, first of all, something that he himself lived and achieved; and in that same experience he obtained his call.

Paul was a young man at the time of Stephen's death. **The opponent** It seems that his residence was then in Jerusalem, and that he had remained there after finishing his course under Gamaliel. If so, he was in Jerusalem during the time of Jesus' public ministry. In any case, so devoted a Jew would have been at the passover, whether living in Jerusalem or at Tarsus. All this makes it probable that Paul had seen Jesus and was in the city at the time of his death. He knew the first Christian community and its teachings. So strong a nature as his could not take a passive attitude. He opposed the new movement with all his might, and for two reasons. In the first place, it was a delusion. It believed in a dead Messiah. Its Messiah was one that the law called accursed because he had been put to death upon a tree (Deut 21. 22, 23). In the second place, these Nazarenes were setting up something beside the law and above it. Stephen's teaching made that clear, and Paul consented to his death.

How did the change come in Paul's faith? That it was

sudden does not imply that there was no preparation for
it. There was, first of all, a negative preparation. Paul
had found out that his religion of the law was a failure.
It is true he was very zealous: "I advanced in the Jews'
religion beyond many of mine age among my countrymen,
being more exceedingly zealous for the traditions of my
fathers" (Gal 1. 14). But it has often been noted that men
may be most intolerant of others when they have become
uncertain of their own position. They are fighting enemies
both within and without. Of this fight in Paul's case we
have a picture from his own hand in Rom 7. It is hard
to put ourselves back into this chapter. The law was for
this young man the special gift with which God had distin-
guished his people, raising them by its possession far above
the nations. That law was his religion. To keep it was
the way of life. Because of such obedience the Messiah
and the new kingdom were to come. In sober fact, however, the law had brought him not life but death. Paul
was too honest and too deeply in earnest to deceive himself. The law, in the first place, stirred up his evil desires. The very commandments became simply occasions
for his sinning, just as too many rules in a schoolroom will
provoke boys to the opposite (Rom 7. 7-11). In the second
place, the law served to make plain his hopelessness. It
showed him that there was another law in him, a law
of selfishness and impurity and sin. His conscience told
him that the law was right and good, but his own life
followed another law. "I consent unto the law that it is
good. But I am carnal, sold under sin. The good which
I would I do not: but the evil which I would not, that I
practice" (Rom 7. 14-23). And this brought him face to
face with the third fact: the law is good, but it has no
power. It can stand above me commanding and condemn-
ing, but it cannot help me. What I need is a new law
within me, such as that of which Jeremiah spoke. "Wretched
man that I am! who shall deliver me out of the body of

this death?" (Rom 7. 24). This is Paul's interpretation
of his old life. Paul is not merely theorizing here. There
are years of earnest effort and bitter disappointment back
of these words.

The second preparation for the change was positive. Paul *The positive*
probably knew Jesus and certainly knew the first disciples. *preparation*
Paul was not the kind of man to carry on such a campaign of
persecution without a study of this movement which he
opposed, and without adjusting himself to its claims. Further, he had seen these men. Earnest, but restless and dissatisfied, he saw the enthusiasm and joy and peace of
these disciples. He saw Stephen full of joy and peace in
the very moment of his death. With a man of his deep
religious nature such impressions would register themselves deeply. These men possessed what he had been striv-
ing for in vain.

With all the preparation, the change came not gradually *The*
but with a sudden crisis. There are five notable references *experience*
to this event in his letters—Gal 1. 15-17; 1 Cor 9. 1; 15. 8;
2 Cor 4. 6. And three accounts are given in the book of Acts:
9. 1-19; 22. 4-21; 26. 9-18. These accounts differ in details.
They agree in the main. In his persecution of these Nazarenes he had taken a commission from the Sanhedrin and was
on his way to Damascus. On the road he had a vision of the
risen Christ. Luke speaks of a voice, but the vision is the
central fact and the one to which he himself refers. He saw
the Lord. Luke says that Paul began at once to preach
Christ in Damascus (Acts 9. 20). Paul declares that he first
went away into Arabia. The latter was undoubtedly the
case. A new experience had come to him that was to
change his faith and his life. It was like Paul, both as
man of thought and man of action, that he should look
its meaning full in the face and shape his life accordingly.
For such thought he goes into Arabia.

The vision of the risen Christ meant even more to Paul *The changed*
than it did to the disciples at Jerusalem. Jesus is not dead *thought*
of Christ

but living. He is not the deluded and defeated leader; he is the Messiah, "declared to be the Son of God with power, according to the spirit of holiness, by the resurrection from the dead" (Rom 1. 4). The vision thus removed from Paul's path his first stumbling-block. The cross was the second stone of stumbling, as Paul found it later with his countrymen when he preached to them. He who died upon the tree was accursed. Now, however, he saw that the curse was borne for men. The death was not God's condemnation of this man, but God's love for all men, that men might be saved from their sins. Hence the death on the cross, which had been his stumbling-block, was to become the center of his message. For him it was to be the unsurpassed measure of God's love, the supreme deed by which God sought to win men to himself.

The changed idea of religion But all this had a decisive meaning for Paul's own religious life. It was not simply that he had been mistaken in persecuting the Messiah. His whole life and effort had been wrong. No wonder he spent his three days at Damascus without food and drink. He saw his whole life as a failure. He had thought of religion simply as something to be done. With all his heart he wanted to be righteous, but the righteousness was to be his own doing. And he had thought that by such doing and such righteousness his people might bring in the Kingdom and cause the Messiah to come. All that was changed. The Messiah was already here. God had sent his Son, not because they had earned it, but just because of his own love and mercy. That was the great difference—the changed thought of God. Paul had come here to Jesus' thought of God as the loving Father. What had been for Jesus the simple expression of direct faith, Paul had gained through this struggle and by the vision of the cross: God is not the giver of laws justifying men only as they have kept all his commands. He is the God of mercy, the Father. He sent his Son into the world that he might reconcile men

to himself. The righteousness that men cannot earn he
gives.

No man knew better than Paul himself how decisive that What the
change meant
change was. What he had prized before, he now put aside:
his Hebrew lineage, his zeal for the law, his strict Pharisaic life. In place of the old pride is a new spirit. There
is the humility and reverence of one who takes the great
gift of God's forgiveness and love, which no effort of his
had been able to earn. And there is the joy and confidence
of one who has found the meaning of life, its treasure and
its strength. He sets forth the contrast and the change in
his life in a fine passage: "We are the circumcision, who
worship by the Spirit of God, and glory in Christ Jesus,
and have no confidence in the flesh. Though I might also
have confidence in the flesh. If any other man thinketh
that he hath whereof he might trust in the flesh, I more:
circumcised the eighth day, of the stock of Israel, of the
tribe of Benjamin, a Hebrew of the Hebrews; as touching the law, a Pharisee; concerning zeal, persecuting the
church; touching the righteousness which is in the law,
blameless. But what things were gain to me, those I counted
loss for Christ. Yea doubtless, and I count all things but
loss for the excellency of the knowledge of Christ Jesus
my Lord: for whom I have suffered the loss of all things,
and do count them but dung, that I may win Christ, and
be found in him, not having mine own righteousness, which
is of the law, but that which is through the faith of Christ,
the righteousness which is of God by faith: that I may
know him, and the power of his resurrection, and the fellowship of his sufferings, being made conformable unto his
death; if by any means I might attain unto the resurrection of the dead. Not as though I had already attained,
either were already perfect: but I follow after, if that I
may apprehend that for which also I am apprehended of
Christ Jesus. Brethren, I count not myself to have apprehended: but this one thing I do, forgetting those things

which are behind, and reaching forth unto those things which are before, I press toward the mark for the prize of the high calling of God in Christ Jesus" (Phil 3. 3-14).

Paul finds his lifework

In this experience Paul found not only the answer to his own needs, but his lifework as well. He was not a man who did anything by halves. His religion had been his chief interest up to this time, despite the struggle and dissatisfaction of his life. There was far greater reason why he should give himself absolutely to the cause of this new faith. Here was the answer to his own needs, and he wanted others to have it. But his call was not simply to preach; it was to preach to the Gentiles. The twelve were at Jerusalem; that was not his place. He saw what they had not discerned: this faith was a world faith, not a Jewish faith. Judaism with its laws and ceremonies belonged to the past. This was a message of the God and Father who loved all men, and who asked of men only that they should put their trust in him. He had found not simply the Messiah to whom the Jews had looked forward, but the Saviour who belonged to the world. They at Jerusalem had not seen it; let them preach to the Jews. It was his task, laid on him by direct command of God himself, to take this message into the world. No one among all his fellows had been a more zealous and devoted Jew than he. Now, however, he says, "It was the good pleasure of God, who separated me, even from my mother's womb, and called me through his grace, to reveal his Son in me, that I might preach him among the Gentiles" (Gal 1. 14, 15). That did not mean that he was not to preach to Jews. It did mean that he was to go out into the Roman world and not to stay in the land of his fathers.

Conversion and call

The work of the great apostle cannot be understood until we appreciate his profound conviction as to the direct commission that he had from God. To this call he goes back again and again. When some of the Jewish Christians from Jerusalem attack his authority, and insinuate that he is an upstart and an innovator without credentials from the mother church or recognition from the real apostles, he begins his letter of defense by writing himself as "Paul, an apostle (not from men, neither through man, but through Jesus Christ, and God the Father, who raised him from the dead)" (Gal 1. 1). He tells the story of that call before King Agrippa in defense of his life, and sums up the passion and devotion of his whole life in the phrase: "Wherefore, O King Agrippa, I was not disobedient to the heavenly vision" (Acts 26. 16-20). The call was like a compelling power, not a choice of his own: "Necessity is laid upon me; for woe is unto me, if I preach not the gospel" (1 Cor 9. 16). And this was his strength in the midst of terrible obstacles and persecutions which were a constant accompaniment of his work. Back of all these was the consciousness that he was an apostle sent forth of God (1 Cor 4. 9-13). An apostle was one who had seen Christ, and who had received from him the commission to bear his gospel. The vision and the commission had come to him, and with all his personal humility he set that commission proudly side by side with those of Peter and James and John (Gal 2. 7-9).

DIRECTIONS FOR READING AND STUDY

Paul's life as a Jew under the law: Rom 7.

The three accounts of the conversion in Acts: 9. 1-19; 22. 4-21; 26. 9-18.

Paul's own references to the same: Gal 1. 15-17; 1 Cor 9. 1; 15. 8; 2 Cor 4. 6; Phil 3. 3-14.

Compare the four accounts of the conversion and Paul's course immediately thereafter as given in Acts and Galatians. Note the agreement and the differences. The preference naturally is to be given to Paul's own account in Galatians.

Read Gal 1. 1-17; 1 Cor 4. 9-13.

CHAPTER XXVII

DAMASCUS, SYRIA, AND CILICIA

The periods of the life PAUL'S life falls naturally into four periods: (1) The years before the conversion; (2) seventeen years of quiet labor in Damascus, Syria, and Cilicia; (3) seven years of world mission; (4) five years of imprisonment. These last years may have been followed by a brief period of liberty and a second imprisonment, but of this we cannot be certain. The third period is the only one of which we have any detailed knowledge. Fortunately, these are the years of Paul's great achievements, where it is most important for us to know.

The sources We have two sources of knowledge for our study of Paul's work—his letters and the book of Acts. These accounts supplement each other. Acts gives an outline of Paul's life, and connects this with the growth of the church as a whole. But we learn very little from Acts about the real life of the Pauline churches. Because Luke is describing the spread of the church, he tells simply how the churches were founded. The letters, on the other hand, tell us how these churches grew, what their life was, and how the new religion met the many questions that confronted it in the Roman world. Where Luke and Paul differ, we must follow the latter; for Paul writes of what he knows at first hand, while Luke is largely dependent upon others and writes at a much later period. There are three places in which such differences may appear: (1) Luke emphasizes the part played by the Jerusalem church, and her authority and supervision. Paul's letters show how the great Gentile church grew up apart from the founding or direction of the Jerusalem leaders. (2) Luke is inclined to emphasize the idea of harmony. The letters reveal the conflict that shook the church in the first generation: whether Christianity was to be a world faith and a religion of the spirit, or a Jewish sect and a religion of the law. (3) Occasionally there seems to be a difference in order of events. Paul, for example, declares that he went up to Jerusalem at the close of the fourteen years in Syria and Cilicia, and that he had his conference with the apostles at this time. Luke places this conference after the first missionary journey.

The first three years of this period Paul spent in Damascus. Through Ananias, he came in touch with the disciples there and probably began preaching at once. His work ends with a persecution, the first in the long list that he was to suffer. Instigated by the Jews, the governor tried to seize him, and Paul escaped only by sudden and secret flight (2 Cor 11. 32, 33; Acts 9. 23-25). Damascus

Then follows Paul's first visit to Jerusalem since his conversion (Gal 1. 18-23). Despite Acts 9. 26-30, we must accept Paul's statement here, that he did not take up any public work or come before the church as a whole. He spent two weeks in quiet with Peter, meeting only James in addition. Beyond doubt he laid before Peter his own work and his conception of the gospel, and this can hardly have been without influence upon the latter. Peter had something to give Paul in return. True, Paul emphatically asserts his independence of the Jerusalem apostles so far as his gospel is concerned; but that does not mean that Paul would not welcome eagerly what Peter could tell him as to the life of Jesus, and especially his teachings. Paul's gospel was not dependent upon such details, but his letters show that he was not indifferent to them. The story of the suffering and death of Jesus would be of especial interest, and this he used in his preaching (Gal 3. 1). He mentions other facts about the life of Jesus in his letters. Probably in his preaching to Gentiles in particular he would narrate the outline of Jesus' life. More important than The first visit to Jerusalem this is the remarkable insight into the inner spirit of Jesus, his love and patience and humility, which Paul shows even in passages where the name of Jesus is not mentioned, such as 1 Cor 13. Besides this Paul would be interested in the teachings of Jesus. A word of Jesus stood for Paul beside the Old Testament as a word of authority. He must have welcomed, therefore, all that Peter could tell him from his rich memories of personal intercourse with Jesus.

Syria and Cilicia

Fourteen years follow of which we know equally little. During all this time Paul tells us that he kept away from Jerusalem, working in Syria and Cilicia. The latter was his home province and it was natural that he should go back to Tarsus to begin. The center of the Syrian territory was Antioch. It was a great city, ranking next to Rome and Alexandria in importance. Here East and West met and all nations were found mingled together, including many Jews. It was a commercial center of first rank. In these respects it resembled Corinth and Ephesus, like them joining to its wealth great luxury and profligacy. It is significant for Paul's work, that just as Antioch became his center now, so for the last period of his work Corinth and Ephesus were his headquarters. To Antioch Paul comes upon invitation of Barnabas.

The work

Paul's plan of work during these fourteen years was probably not very different from that of the seven years that follow. He did not simply remain in the cities, but, making Tarsus and Antioch his centers, traveled up and down the coast and through the surrounding regions. We have one passage from his own hand which probably refers at least in part to this period. In it he gives a moving picture of his life of unremitting toil, of hardship and constant danger, as he goes from place to place planting his little communities of disciples and watching over them. The experiences of sea and shipwreck may well have come in this time, as much of his travel would naturally be by vessel. "Are they ministers of Christ? (I speak as one beside himself) I more; in labors more abundantly, in prisons more abundantly, in stripes above measure, in deaths oft. Of the Jews five times received I forty stripes save one. Thrice was I beaten with rods, once was I stoned, thrice I suffered shipwreck, a night and a day have I been in the deep; in journeyings often, in perils of rivers, in perils of robbers, in perils from my countrymen, in perils from the Gentiles, in perils in the city, in perils in the wilderness, in perils in the sea, in perils among false brethren; in labor and travail, in watchings often, in hunger and thirst, in fastings often, in cold and nakedness. Besides those things that are without, there is that which presseth upon me daily, anxiety for all the churches. Who is weak, and I am not weak? who is caused to stumble, and I burn not?" (2 Cor 11. 23-29).

We have called these years the time of quiet labor. They were, however, by no means lacking in importance. In two respects they were of the greatest significance for Paul's work. (1) Paul himself was being trained for his great position of responsibility and leadership. He was a young man when he began; he was a tried veteran when he concluded. These years of work and thought showed him the wealth of the Christian religion, and ripened in him those thoughts with which his later letters are filled. (2) Paul was firmly establishing a strong Gentile church, and was doing this on a basis of freedom from the Jewish law. When he went up to Jerusalem at the end of these years the Gentile church was already a fact, and the mother church could do no less than recognize it. *Significance of this period*

A chronological outline of Paul's life may be added here. These dates are only approximate, and vary somewhat with different scholars. Paul was probably born about the same time as Jesus, and was converted from two to five years after Jesus' death. *Chronological outline*

I.   Period of youth and preparation.
II. Seventeen years of quiet work, 35 to 52.

  (1) At Damascus, three years.
  (2) In Cilicia and Syria, with headquarters at Tarsus and Antioch, fourteen years.
III. The missionary journeys, 52 to 59.
  (1) A brief journey through Cyprus and Galatia.
  (2) Work in Macedonia and Achaia, with headquarters at Corinth for one and a half years.
  (3) Work in Asia with headquarters at Ephesus for two years.
IV. The years of imprisonment, 59 to 64.
  (1) At Cæsarea, two years.
  (2) On the way to Rome, one year.
  (3) In Rome, two years.

DIRECTIONS FOR READING AND STUDY

Read Gal 1. 15-23; Acts 11. 19-26; 2 Cor 11. 23-29.

Trace upon the map the journeys so far referred to: Jerusalem to Damascus and return, Jerusalem to Tarsus, Tarsus to Antioch.

CHAPTER XXVIII

GENTILE AND JEWISH CHRISTIANS

SOME twenty years had now elapsed since the death of Jesus. The church was well established through two large districts. The first district had for its center Jerusalem, and included the churches of Judæa, Samaria, Galilee, and the cities of the adjoining coast lands such as Cæsarea and Joppa. These churches were predominantly Jewish. The second district was to the north, and included Syria and Cilicia. These churches were predominantly Gentile. At the head of the former work were James and Peter. At the head of the latter was Paul.

These two divisions of the church were not merely geo- graphical. Nor were they racial, a matter of Jew and Gentile. The real question at issue was: What is Christianity? The immediate question, however, was that of the Jewish law. The life of the faithful Jew was regulated by innumerable laws. Besides the religious feasts and ceremonies, there were endless restrictions about what was clean and unclean applying to food and places and persons. To these rules the Jew was accustomed from his childhood. They were looked upon as sacred and unchanging, as given by God through Moses. What should the Christian do about these rules?

The first disciples probably thought nothing about the matter. The rules were more or less a habit of life, and they continued them. It was another matter when the gospel spread to the Gentiles. Here two serious questions arose: (1) Must the Gentiles be circumcised and keep the Jewish laws in order to be Christians? (2) If the Gentile converts do not keep the law, how can the Jewish Christians who keep the law associate with them? For the great object of the law was to keep ceremonially clean; to associate with those who did not keep the law would render a man unclean in the same way as if he did not keep the law himself.

Peter and Cornelius

These questions the church had not fairly faced and settled. Luke, it is true, tells us that this whole matter was met by Peter. He gives us the story in Acts 10. 1 to 11. 18. There he tells how Peter, in obedience to a vision, goes to Cæsarea and preaches the gospel to a Gentile, a Roman centurion named Cornelius. The latter is called "a devout man," that is, a Jewish proselyte, though apparently not circumcised. Peter goes in to this man, and baptizes him and his household, though such association meant ceremonial impurity to a Jew. On his return he is remonstrated with by the brethren at Jerusalem. In reply he tells of the vision that he had of the clean and unclean meat, and the words that came to him, "What God hath cleansed, make not thou common." The church then acquiesces in this position. As a matter of fact, however, this was the whole cause of Paul's conflict. If the church did take this position at this time, they did not maintain it. It seems quite likely that Luke has put this story concerning Peter at an earlier date than where it really belongs.

The situation at Antioch

The real crisis came at Antioch at the close of this period of Paul's work. So long as he was not disturbed from without, Paul had felt no need of raising the question. He had preached his gospel of faith to the Gentiles without asking them to keep the law. He had probably allowed Jewish Christians to take their own course. There was no harm in his eyes in keeping the law so long as men saw clearly that they were not saved by this, but by their trust in Christ, and so long as these Jewish Christians were ready to associate with their Gentile brethren. The church at Antioch was mainly Gentile and the Jewish Christians did not hesitate to sit down with these Gentiles at the Christian meals which they ate together. This was the "liberty in Christ Jesus" which Paul preached and which the Jewish brethren accepted.

It was men from the Jerusalem church that brought about the crisis. The church there, it seems, had been moving backward toward Judaism rather than away from it. Among the new converts were not a few Pharisees, and there was an increasing element that stood for strict observance of the law (Acts 15. 5). They had at least the example of James, if not his leadership. This party sent representatives down to Antioch to find out what the practice there really was. Paul calls them false brethren, "who came in privily to spy out our liberty which we have in Christ Jesus, that they might bring us into bondage" (Gal 2. 4; Acts 15. 2). These men began teaching Paul's converts that they could not expect to be saved if they did not keep the law, putting circumcision as the sign and test of the whole (Acts 15. 1). They probably attacked Paul's authority at the same time, declaring that he was no genuine apostle, but that the true apostles were at Jerusalem, and that these kept the law. *Judaizers from Jerusalem*

Paul decided to act at once and went up to Jerusalem. He had a threefold reason for going. (1) The immediate reason was that he saw his work in danger, and he wanted to secure freedom for carrying on that work among the Gentiles. He did not ask for authority, for he believed that his authority came direct from God. He simply wanted recognition of the fact that his right to proclaim this gospel was on a par with theirs. (2) Paul wanted to maintain fellowship with the mother church for the sake of his Gentile converts. That church was the living link with a great past. They represented a heritage of which Paul the Christian was as proud as Paul the Jew had been: the whole story of Jehovah's dealings with his people, the words of prophet and psalmist, and all the rest of the Scripture. The Christian Church was but the continuation of that history, the true Israel. The Old Testament was its Sacred Scripture. *Why Paul went to Jerusalem*

The mother church joined these pagan converts to that past. (3) And, finally, Paul believed in the one church and the one fellowship of Christian believers. By this he did not mean one organization or one central authority. He never submitted his churches to direction from Jerusalem or elsewhere. The unity was that of the Spirit and of fellowship. Then, as later, he did all that he could to maintain it. The body of Christ was one. The disciples were all brothers and members one of another.

The Jerusalem conference: the agreement

Luke gives us some interesting material in his account of the Jerusalem meeting (Acts 15), but we must turn to Paul to get the real meaning of that occasion. Of the details we cannot be sure. It seems that there were two gatherings. Paul and Barnabas reported their work before the church as a whole. The Judaizing disciples raised their demand that Gentile converts should keep the law. Paul had with him a Greek convert, Titus, who was not circumcised. Their request that Titus should submit to the rite Paul flatly refused. Then, however, Paul lays the matter before Peter and James and John in private conference. From them he asks the recognition of his right to preach the gospel to the Gentiles, and that there should be fellowship between the Gentile churches and Jerusalem. Face to face with the story of his great work, these men cannot say no. They see the Spirit of God in what Paul is doing and they give him the hand of fellowship. They will preach, as before, to the Jews; he to the Gentiles. Paul has won his first great point, freedom to carry on his work. In return he promises to remember the poor at Jerusalem, a promise that he loyally carried out.

The decree

Luke relates, in addition to this, that the church issued a formal decree requiring that the Gentile Christians should "abstain from the pollutions of idols [that is, from meat that had been offered to idols], and from fornication, and from what is strangled, and from blood" (Acts 15. 20). If such a decree was given at this time, it does not appear to have had any particular effect. Certainly, it did not solve the problem of the relations of Jews and Gentiles. Paul does not mention this in speaking of the conference, nor does he refer to it later when he takes up, with the Corinthian church for example, one of the matters here referred to. The decree as such seems to have had no authority for him. It is quite possible that such a decree was issued later and sent to the churches of Syria and Cilicia. It was certainly not carried by Paul west of the Taurus.

The agreement at the Jerusalem conference was really a compromise, not a solution. How insufficient it was soon appeared. Peter in the course of his work came to Antioch, where the Jewish Christians had associated freely with their Gentile brothers. When Peter came down he did the same. Into this scene of fellowship there came some of the Judaizing Christians from Jerusalem. Paul says they came from James. What they said we do not know. They may have admitted that the Gentiles could be Christians without keeping the law. But they insisted that a good Jew must keep the law and dare not associate with such Gentiles. What right had he to throw over the sacred law of Moses? Why should he give up the heritage of the fathers that had set Israel apart, and put himself on a plane with the Gentiles? With such arguments they not only swept Peter off his feet, but the rest of the Jewish Christians, and even Paul's old friend, Barnabas. *The new conflict at Antioch*

Here, at last, the real issue appears, and it is Paul that brings it out. The real question is not that of dividing territory, Jewish and Gentile, or recognizing each other's work. The question is, What is Christianity? Or, as Paul puts it, How shall a man be justified? Paul does not simply take the defensive. He attacks Peter. Peter is dissembling, playing a part. Peter believes as truly as Paul that he is saved not by keeping rules, but by faith in Christ; by the mercy of God, and not by what he earns through keeping the law. But if Peter expects to be saved by this, why does *The real issue* he try to compel these Gentiles to keep the law? (Gal 2. 14-16).

Two results Just what the issue of the matter was at Antioch we do not know. Two results are plain. (1) The Jerusalem agreement turned Paul definitely toward the larger Gentile world. The final and greatest period of his ministry now begins. From Antioch he moves on to Galatia, from Galatia to Macedonia, Achaia, and Asia, while beyond these his eyes rest upon Rome and distant Spain. (2) The conflicts with the Judaizers continue, and form Paul's severest trial. But there is never any doubt in Paul's mind as to his right or as to the final issue. History justifies him. The gospel which moves through the Roman world is a gospel that is free from Judaism and Jewish law. And Christianity ceases to be a Jewish faith and becomes a world religion.

DIRECTIONS FOR READING AND STUDY

Read Gal 2; Acts 15. 1-35.

Compare carefully these two accounts. Some scholars hold that Luke is following the common custom of writers of his day in composing the speeches that are assigned to Peter and James, either using materials that he had on hand or setting forth what he assumed to be their position.

CHAPTER XXIX

PAUL THE MISSIONARY

Now there begin the seven years of work which mark the crown of Paul's ministry. Into these seven years is crowded an achievement beyond what many great men have wrought in a lifetime. One province after another Paul lays claim to in the name of Christ. With restless energy he carries the message, assisted by a group of workers. Nor is he content to be a mere wandering preacher. As he goes he establishes Christian communities, and over these he keeps watch, dispatching one or the other of his assistants, or sending letters like those which have come down to us under his name. **Seven great years**

Beneath all these varied activities there lay a definite plan, which comes to the surface again and again. Paul did not strike out at random into the Gentile world. His plan was nothing less than to win the whole empire, and to do this by planting the church in order in the Roman provinces that surrounded the Mediterranean. In an interesting passage, written to the Romans about the close of this period, he tells of these plans. "God sent me," he says, "to be a minister to the Gentiles. This mission I have fulfilled from Jerusalem around as far as Illyricum. I have one last task here, to take to Jerusalem the money that I have collected for the church there. This done, I shall start for Spain, stopping on the way at Rome to see you as I have long wished to do" (Rom 15. 14-33). This imperial plan appears in the way in which Paul refers to his work. As a rule, he does not mention the cities where he works, but speaks, rather, of the provinces. He refers to Asia, not to Ephesus, to Macedonia and Achaia, not to Corinth and Philippi (Rom 16. 5; 1 Thess 1. 7). **The conquest of an empire**

Paul saw the meaning of Christianity

It was a great conception, this winning of an empire for the new faith. Paul has been called a second Alexander, moving westward instead of eastward in this march of conquest. More than anything else it brings to light the difference between him and the Jerusalem leaders, and the significance of Paul's idea of the gospel. With the exception of Peter, it seemed that they were content to remain at Jerusalem, praying and waiting for the heavens to open again and Christ to return. Paul saw the wealth and the meaning of the new faith as they did not, a religion of life and power for all men and not alone the Jews. That conception was back of the mission: "I am not ashamed of the gospel: for it is the power of God unto salvation to every one that believeth; to the Jew first, and also to the Greek." That was why he felt himself sent to all the Gentiles and counted himself "debtor both to Greeks and to Barbarians" (Rom 1. 13-17).

Certain limits

This general plan had certain limits. (1) Paul would not go where others had laid the foundation (Rom 15. 20). That is why he makes it plain to the Roman church that he is simply stopping off to see them on his way to Spain (Rom 15. 24). (2) Paul would not work in Jewish territory. This may help answer the question sometimes raised, Why did not Paul, who swept around the circle of the sea from Jerusalem to Spain, go south to Egypt, especially to Alexandria? The reason may be that Alexandria was so much of a Jewish city. It had a large and prosperous Jewish population, which had its separate quarter, even having its own city walls inclosing it. (3) One other element enters into Paul's plans. He felt that the return of the Lord was near. The time was short. He had to give his message and start the work and care for it from a distance as well as he could. But he could not remain, he must hurry on.

Missionaries in the Roman world

The missionary was not a strange figure in that age. It was a day of religious ferment. The old national religions

were passing away. New cults were coming in, especially
the mystery religions from the east. Traveling merchants
and soldiers were often zealous propagators of such faiths.
There were also traveling teachers of rhetoric and philosophy. The Jewish missionaries were probably the most
active. Jesus spoke of the Pharisees as compassing sea
and land to make one proselyte. The bitterness of the Jews
against Paul was caused largely by his success in making
converts and in drawing away the proselytes whom they
had won.

Paul's first act in coming to a city would be to find quarters **Paul's**
for himself. Ordinarily, he planned to stay for some period **principle of**
and so sought a place where he could carry on his trade of **self-support**
tent-maker. For to his many burdens he added this other,
that of self-support. From only one church, that at Philippi,
was he willing to take aid. He believed in the right to such
support for Christian apostles. He defended the principle
and his own right to this later on. But for himself he
would not assert this claim. "We bear all things, that we
may cause no hindrance to the gospel of Christ" (1 Cor 9.
1-18). Paul probably had a double reason. He did not
want to be confounded with traveling rhetoricians who
talked simply for hire, and he wanted to remove all ground
for misunderstanding and criticism of his motives on the
part of his Jewish enemies.

Paul's next task was to find a way of approach for his **Paul and the**
message. That led him naturally to the synagogue. He **synagogue**
did not consider this a violation of his agreement to go to
the Gentiles. Apparently, that meant to Paul simply that
he was to keep away from Jewish territory. But here, where
none of the apostles from Jerusalem came, there was no
reason why he should not speak to the Jews. This, however,
was not the main reason for his presence in the synagogue.
Jewish missionary work had been carried on for years, and
while the Jews were hated by many, there were others who
were attracted by their lofty moral and religious teachings.

These adherents or sympathizers afforded some of Paul's
first and best converts.

After the
synagogue
In the free worship of the synagogue there was always
opportunity for such a visitor to speak. Naturally, Paul
could not continue his preaching permanently in the synagogue. Some Jews he won, but the major part would
refuse his message. Often they followed him from one city
to the other and turned the Jews against him. But he had
found interesting hearers among the proselytes, and now
through these he could meet other Gentiles. So his work
was continued usually in the house of some well-to-do convert. Thus in Philippi he was guest of Lydia, at Thessalonica he used the house of Jason, and at Corinth that of
Titus Justus (Acts 16. 15; 17. 7; 18. 7). In Ephesus we
read that he continued in the synagogue three months.
Apparently, Paul's success there demanded a larger room
than a private house could afford, and so he spoke in a
public hall, "the school of Tyrannus" (Acts 19. 8, 9). One
of the oldest manuscripts of Acts adds to these verses the
words "from the fifth to the tenth hour," that is, from eleven
to four. Paul, it would seem, rented for this part of the
day a hall which was given to other uses as well.

Paul as
speaker
Judged by the common standards of his day, Paul was
not a great speaker. It was a day when rhetoric and oratory
were carefully cultivated, and of these things Paul made no
pretense. His enemies said that he was rude of speech, that
his speech was of no account and his bodily presence weak
(2 Cor 11. 6; 10. 10). Paul makes no denial. He says
to the Corinthians: "I was with you in weakness, and in
fear, and in much trembling. And my speech and my
preaching were not in persuasive words of wisdom" (1 Cor
2. 3, 4). At Athens they called him a babbler (Acts 17. 18).
It is a fair question, however, whether the fault did not lie
in the artificial standards of the time rather than with Paul
himself. Simple, direct, unpolished, even rude, his speech
probably was. But it met the final test: he stirred men's

hearts and swept them off their feet. He carried the council of Jerusalem, though he stood there almost alone. And how many a later company, Jew and Gentile, cultured and pagan, was borne down by the earnestness and sincerity and moral power of his address. Earnestness and spiritual power were the mark of Paul's speech. The man was wholly lost in his message. Men did not listen to fine phrases, they heard a man, and a man aflame with his thought. Some might call him mad, but others trembled (Acts 26. 24; 24. 25). With this earnestness went a power of will that made Paul commanding when he spoke as when he acted. Back of all else was the utter devotion of his soul and his utter dependence upon God. Men felt that God was speaking through this man, and he could call the Corinthians to witness that though in weakness, yet his speech was "in the demonstration of the Spirit and of power."

But though Paul's speech was plain and direct, with no *His eloquence* regard for niceties of style, there were times when it must have risen to heights of real eloquence. We are justified here in drawing conclusions from his letters; for these were spoken, not written, being dictated by him. Even with the limitation of slow dictation, Paul's letters show us passages where his soul, kindling at the great truths he is considering, rises to speech of beauty as well as power. Such is the simple but beautiful song of love that lifts itself above the controversies of the Corinthian church (1 Cor 13). Such are the passages which interrupt again and again his argument in the letter to the Romans. "Who shall separate us from the love of Christ? shall tribulation, or anguish, or persecution, or famine, or nakedness, or peril, or sword? Even as it is written,

> For thy sake we are killed all the day long;
> We were accounted as sheep for the slaughter.

Nay, in all these things we are more than conquerors through him that loved us. For I am persuaded, that neither

death, nor life, nor angels, nor principalities, nor things
present, nor things to come, nor powers, nor height, nor
depth, nor any other creature, shall be able to separate us
from the love of God, which is in Jesus Christ our Lord"
(Rom 8. 35-39).

What Paul said in his sermons we cannot know with
certainty. Not one of them lies before us. His letters are
not sermons. He writes in these to companies of Christians,
discussing special questions of faith and life. We find
theology in them and practical maxims, but this is quite
different from what he would bring to a group of Gentiles
to whom he was preaching the gospel for the first time.
And yet we are not left without some real knowledge. Brief
as it is, such a summary as that given us in Acts of the
sermon at Athens is suggestive of Paul's method in a particular situation. And of much more importance are some
of his references and passages in the epistles (1 Thess 1. 9,
10; Acts 14. 15-17; Rom 1. 18 to 2. 16; 1 Cor 15. 1-11).

Paul's
message

The passages just noted suggest what his preaching to the
Gentiles was. We may distinguish certain parts in this
message: (1) Paul proclaimed to them the living God. He
probably did not say much about idol-worship. He did not
need to. That was a dying faith. It was enough to bring
to them the word of that God who had made the world and
ruled in history; who had sent his prophets and in these
latter days had sent his Son to show forth his mercy, whom
also he had raised from the dead. (2) He preached to
their conscience. With searching words he set forth their
sin. It was not mere sin of ignorance. God had not left
himself without a witness. There was an inner law that he
had written in their hearts. But they had darkened this light
by their disobedience, and had turned to their sinful desires.
All this God had passed over, but now he was calling men
to repent; the day of judgment for men's sins was at hand.
(3) He preached Jesus Christ. However Paul began, his
sermon always tended to this. Here was his real message.

All else was preparation. "We are ambassadors therefore," he says, "on behalf of Christ, as though God were entreating by us: we beseech you on behalf of Christ, be ye reconciled to God. Him who knew no sin he made to be sin on our behalf; that we might become the righteousness of God in him" (2 Cor 5. 20, 21).

Here Paul had reached the heart of his message—"Christ, and him crucified." For him this was no mere phrase or formal doctrine as it is so often to-day. It was a gift of life that he was bringing to men, and of life here and now. That was what it had meant to him. It had changed his whole life. He probably did not dwell upon Jesus' words and deeds as man. He told how God had sent his Son to men, of his death, and how God had raised him from the dead. Then he set forth the meaning of all this. It was God's love for men. God had done this to win men to himself. This God in his mercy was willing to receive them all as his children, to give them forgiveness and life. He asked only faith in return, that men should trust him and give themselves to him. That life was theirs here and now: forgiveness, and peace, and the Spirit of God in their hearts. But besides this there was a hope: very soon this Jesus was to return and set up his final and full kingdom upon the earth. *Christ crucified* (margin)

There is no indication that men responded to this message in the mass. In 1 Cor 1. 18-31 is given a picture of the failure and success of Paul's appeal. Paul declares that his message of the crucified Christ was a stumbling-block to the Jews. They wanted signs, that is, indications of power. How could they accept a Messiah who, instead of overthrowing Israel's enemies, had himself suffered death? The Greeks, he said, thought his preaching foolishness. They wanted wisdom, fine rhetoric, and philosophical speculation, or strange mysteries such as the new religions from the East afforded. Paul brought them a simple message of a God who showed his love to men and called them to repent. *Failures* (margin)

And others would draw back at this moral demand, the call to leave sin, to live a new life of righteousness.

Success

But there were others that were won: some of them by the ethical appeal, smitten in their conscience by his searching words; many of them by his message of the living God, the God of love and power who could save them from their sins and from death. It was a day when the old faiths were breaking down, and especially upon the common folks the burdens and misery of life rested heavily. What men wanted from religion was help, redemption from these ills. That was what Paul promised: Christ the power of God and the wisdom of God.

Lower classes won

Paul tells us that most of these converts, at least in Corinth, were from the poorer classes. Early Christianity, as a whole, was a lower and middle-class movement. "Not many wise after the flesh, not many mighty, not many noble" responded. Every great and permanent religious movement has followed this order. It has never filtered down from an upper few, but has had its origin in the great masses in which the real strength of any generation lies.

The brotherhood

The little bands of converts Paul gathered together. Among them were a few of wealth and station. Such a convert would offer his house as a meeting place for the little brotherhood. Over these circles Paul watched. To them he sent his messages, rebuking, exhorting, comforting, teaching, encouraging. And these little communities, with their spirit of love for each other, with the evident joy and peace of their new faith, formed in turn an attractive power that drew others from without. At the same time their members became themselves missionaries to propagate the new religion with zeal and enthusiasm. And when they moved to other places they kindled new fires. It was not Paul and Peter and Barnabas alone that spread Christianity. They were but leaders of a great company. The new religion was a great lay movement. Jesus was a layman. Paul was a layman, who never asked ordination from anybody. And the great work of spreading the faith in the first generation was done by men and women whose names have long since been lost to us, but whose work remains to this day.

DIRECTIONS FOR READING AND STUDY

Read Rom 15. 14-33. Locate upon the map the provinces of Syria, Cilicia, Galatia, Macedonia, Illyricum, Achaia, Asia. Illyricum lay along the eastern shore of the Adriatic, extending north to Italy. The region is marked Dalmatia upon our map. We have no record of Paul's work there.

As to Paul's trade and support of self, read Acts 18. 1-4; 1 Cor 9. 1-18.

For a typical synagogue experience, read Acts 13. 13-16, 42-52.

Concerning Paul as a speaker, read 1 Cor 2. Read Rom 8. 35-39 as illustration of what he may have meant by 1 Cor 2. 6, 12.

As to Paul's message, read 1 Thess 1. 9, 10; Acts 14. 15-17; Rom 1. 18 to 2. 16; 1 Cor 15. 1-11.

Read 1 Cor 1. 18-31.

CHAPTER XXX

GALATIA

Paul's method

THE seven years of Paul's world mission have usually been divided into three missionary "journeys." This, however, is misleading. It leads us to think of Paul as wandering from place to place, stopping a few days or weeks, preaching a few sermons, then passing on, and at the end of each tour coming back to Antioch. Such was not his method. Paul's plan was, rather, to take the great Roman provinces one at a time, and to stay long enough in each to firmly establish the work, leaving it then in charge of others though retaining a general supervision. It is true his stay was often cut short by opposition. But he spent a year and a half in Achaia with his headquarters at Corinth, and twice that time in Ephesus. He probably spent some months in Macedonia, mainly at Philippi. Antioch practically ceased to be his headquarters during this period. It is a better plan of study to take up the provinces one at a time, studying in turn Galatia, Macedonia, Achaia, and Asia.

First journey: the company

We need not suppose that Paul mapped out from the very first his whole plan of campaign. It is to Cyprus, the old home of Barnabas, that they turn first, and their attendant is John Mark, the cousin of Barnabas. John Mark, the traditional author of our second Gospel, may also have come originally from Cyprus. But it has been noted that his home was in Jerusalem, where his mother's house was a meeting place for the disciples. Barnabas had for years been a leader. He was a man of broad and unselfish spirit. That is shown by the sale of his field, the money for which he gave to the Jerusalem church, and by the way in which he yielded later to the leadership of his companion in this journey.

The little band of three was sent forth by the Antioch Cyprus
church with prayer and benediction. From Seleucia, the
port of Antioch, to Salamis of Cyprus, where they landed,
was about one hundred and twenty-five miles. There were
a good many Jews in the island and here at Salamis they
preached in the synagogues. They traversed the island from
east to west, probably something over a hundred miles of
journey. Luke has but one incident of their whole stay, the
story of the magician, Bar-Jesus, a Jew who was in the
company of the proconsul, Sergius Paulus. He makes no
note of conversions, and we learn nothing more of Cyprus
beyond the fact that Barnabas and Mark made a return
visit some time later (Acts 13. 1-12).

"Now Paul and his company set sail from Paphos, and Paul as
came to Perga in Pamphylia: and John departed from them leader
and returned to Jerusalem" (Acts 13. 13). In these words
Luke marks the change that now comes; Paul is taking
the leadership and is moving on to wholly new fields. Barnabas goes with him. John Mark, perhaps dissatisfied that
Paul should take his cousin's place, possibly unwilling to
face the hardships of this new field, turns back again. From
this time on there is no question of leadership. Paul's company changes; he has many helpers through this period, but
there is only one directing spirit.

Paul had now reached the mainland with his face toward In Galatia
that West which he was to win for Christ. For the present,
however, it is not so large a circuit that they make. They
do not stop in Perga, where they land, but press on to
Antioch of Pisidia, lying straight to the north, about a
hundred miles inland. Iconium, Lystra, and Derbe, to which
they go next, lie to the east and south and rather close
together. Through these four cities they then retrace their
steps, stopping, however, this time at Perga. They set sail
not from Perga but from Attalia near by, and so return to
Antioch.

We must not, however, measure the length of their stay

in Galatia by Luke's brief record. The apostles must have
spent some months at least in this visit. We read of their
work in Antioch, that "the word of the Lord was spread
abroad throughout all the region" (Acts 13. 49). Luke
reports that they stayed a long time at Iconium, and that
they preached not only in Lystra and Derbe but in the
country round about (Acts 14. 3, 6). In the main centers
Paul turned first to the synagogue, as usual, for here in
Galatia also there were Jews to be found in the larger cities;
in Antioch and Iconium the synagogues are specially mentioned. But his main interest was in the Gentiles, and when
he went into the "region round about," it was Gentile
mission work.

One incident of this contact with paganism Luke gives us.
At Lystra Paul healed a lame man. When the people saw
what Paul had done, they began shouting, "The gods are
come down to us in the likeness of men." The old myths
abounded in tales of gods appearing among men, and it was
in such remote places that the old faiths were strongest.
Here at Lystra they cultivated especially the worship of
Jupiter. As the people used their native tongue, the disciples
could not understand their cries, and before they knew what
was happening the priest of Jupiter was present with his
garlands and his oxen ready to make a sacrifice. To such
people Paul had to bring his message. The words that Luke
reports in this connection may well have been his common
mode of approach in speaking to pagan hearers. They show
his skill and tact, and the broad sympathy that enabled him
to come into contact with men upon whom the Jew, proud
of his faith, would commonly have looked with utter scorn.
"We bring you good tidings, that ye should turn from these
vain things unto a living God, who made the heaven and the
earth and the sea, and all that in them is: who in the generations gone by suffered all the nations to walk in their own
ways. And yet he left not himself without witness, in that
he did good and gave you from heaven rains and fruitful

seasons, filling your hearts with food and gladness" (Acts 14. 15-17).

Traveling through such a country involved great hardship, heightened by Paul's efforts to support himself. Here, as later, Paul met the opposition of the Jews. Once his life was endangered. After the brief enthusiasm at Lystra, the Jews from Antioch and Iconium stirred up the people against him and he was stoned and left for dead. It was enough for Paul, however, that in all these places he was able to gather his groups of converts. His devotion to them is seen in the fact that when he reaches Derbe in the East, he does not push on to Tarsus and home. Despite hardship and the treatment he has received, he retraces his course, that he may comfort and build up these little companies. They in turn were devotedly attached to him. How they had received him is indicated by Gal 4. 12-20. He intimates there that he had had plans which would have taken him farther, and was detained in Galatia because of health. Perhaps it was a trouble with his eyes. In any case, he calls to their mind how they received him "as an angel of God, even as Christ Jesus," and that so far from despising him because of his illness, they were ready to pluck out their eyes and give them to him. As for him, he counts them his little children, whom he has brought forth in toil and pain.

It seems quite certain that it was to these churches that the epistle to the Galatians was written. We have already studied the first two chapters of this letter in connection with the Jerusalem conference. We do not know when it was written, probably not long after the founding of the churches, for Paul reproaches them with removing so quickly from his gospel (Gal 1. 6). The thought of the letter is not always easy to follow. We are not concerned to-day about Jewish laws and rules and their relation to Christianity, and the letter at first does not seem of interest. But it is different when we appreciate the importance of

Hardship and recompense

The letter to the Galatians

the fight that Paul is waging here. It was not the question
of a few churches in Asia Minor, but whether Christianity
was to be a universal and spiritual religion or a Jewish sect.
And our interest increases as we catch the earnestness and
passion of the man, which make these words live for us
despite nineteen centuries that lie between. The gospel that
he preached and the churches that he had founded with toil
and danger of life he now saw imperiled by men who disregarded the Jerusalem agreement and invaded his territory. He throws every resource into this fight. Logic,
Scripture, sarcasm, bitter denunciation, tender appeal—he
uses them all in this effort.

**The
opposition**

His enemies were not Jews but Judaizing Christians,
bitterly opposed to Paul because he did not ask his converts
to keep the law. Their argument seems to have been this:
This man Paul is not a genuine apostle. The real pillar
apostles are at Jerusalem, and they keep the law. Jesus is
the Jewish Messiah, foretold in the Jewish Scriptures. You
Gentiles may believe on him, but if you want the full gospel,
if you want to be real sons of Abraham, you must keep the
sacred law; and, first of all, you must be circumcised. To
this Paul makes reply in his letter, pouring forth a stream
of passionate declaration and entreaty, with no concern
for order or phrase. It falls, however, into three main
parts.

**The answer:
a gospel
from God**

1. Paul's assertion of his independent apostleship: "My
gospel did not come from men but from God, and there is
no other gospel. I never took instruction or authority from
the other apostles at Jerusalem. But they have recognized
my apostleship to the Gentiles and have given me the hand
of fellowship" (Chs. 1 and 2).

**Salvation
by faith**

2. "The Christian is saved by faith, not by the law:
When you were converted you received the Spirit. It was
the sign of your new life; but you received it because you
trusted, not because you had kept the law. Why not continue the same way? The men of faith are the real sons of

Abraham, not the men of the law. The law by itself means simply a curse, for it condemns every man unless he keeps every letter of it; and that no man can do. There is only one thing to do, to trust in the love of God as he comes in Jesus Christ. The Christian is not a servant keeping a law; he is a son living with his Father. You are all sons of God, through faith in Christ Jesus. Do not let anyone make a slave of you again. The Christian life is not circumcision or uncircumcision; it is faith working through love" (3. 1 to 5. 12).

3. The last part of Paul's letters is always given to practical advice. It is so here. He has said that Christianity was not a sum of laws but a life of freedom and a new spirit, the spirit of sonship. That freedom, he declares, does not mean license. It is simply an inner life that we live, instead of a set of rules imposed from without. But we must live out that inner life, we must walk by the Spirit. "The fruit of the Spirit is love, joy, peace, long-suffering, kindness, goodness, faithfulness, meekness, self-control" (5. 13 to 6. 18). *The life of sons*

Characteristic of this letter is its close. So possessed is Paul with the great question at issue that he comes back to it again. The last words, from 6. 11 on, were added by his own hand. The rest of the letter had been dictated, as was his custom. If the sickness to which he refers in this letter was a trouble with his eyes, it would explain his using an amanuensis, and making large letters when he himself wrote (6. 11).

DIRECTIONS FOR READING AND STUDY

Read Acts 13 and 14.

Follow carefully upon the map the line of journey. Using the scale of miles make an estimate of the total distance traveled.

Name in order the Galatian cities visited, and one or two incidents in connection with each.

Give a brief outline of Paul's life as he reports it in Gal 1 and 2.

Give the outline of Paul's argument in the second section, Gal 3. 1 to 5. 12, by means of five or ten key verses selected from this passage.

In the last section, 5. 13 to 6. 18, select five or six individual verses which seem to you best to sum up Paul's idea of the Christian life.

CHAPTER XXXI

MACEDONIA

MACEDONIA forms the next stage in Paul's campaign. Galatia was but one of a number of provinces in Asia Minor. The westernmost of these was called Asia, and held a number of cities besides its great center, Ephesus. But Luke tells us that Paul on his journey through Asia Minor felt himself under a definite guidance of the Spirit which led him past one district after another upon his way to Macedonia.

Of the journey toward Macedonia we know little. After Paul's return to Antioch from Galatia, he proposed to Barnabas that they start out to revisit the churches they had established. Barnabas was willing but wished to take John Mark along. Paul demurred to this, since Mark had failed them on the previous trip. So they parted company, Luke says, after "a sharp contention." Barnabas and Mark went to Cyprus. Paul started out with Silas. This time he went by land. First they visited the churches of his old field, Syria and Cilicia. From Tarsus they pressed on over the Taurus range to the little communities which he had just founded in Galatia, and which lay not far beyond. At Derbe he secured another companion for his journey, Timothy, a convert of his previous visit, the loyal and affectionate companion and helper of his remaining journeys.

So Paul came at last to Troas and to the Hellespont. Though he had felt himself under compulsion of the Spirit, we need not assume that it was a blind leadership for Paul. He saw that his journey was tending to Europe. Macedonia and Achaia were the Roman provinces into which the Grecian land was divided, and these now lay before him. He was beginning a new period in his life. His labors till then had not led him far afield. Cilicia was the province of his native city Tarsus. Syria lay between Tarsus and Jerusalem, no doubt often traversed by the young man on his way to Jerusalem and back. Cyprus could be seen in clear weather from Antioch. Derbe, in the eastern end of Galatia, was not more than one hundred and fifty miles' journey from Tarsus. He had never gotten far from this little corner of the Mediterranean, near whose angle Tarsus and Antioch lay. Now he was facing not only new provinces but a new continent. He was beginning not only a new epoch in his life but a new epoch for Christianity. Born in the Orient, the new faith was to have its fullest expression in the West. Here it was to shape mighty organizations, to mold new institutions of government and society, and centuries later to start out again from this new center upon a conquest of the world. To-day the cradle of Christianity has little to show. The eastern lands of Syria, Asia Minor, and Egypt, where first she had her strength, now show either the rule of the Moslem or a Christianity of a distinctly inferior type. We cannot but ask the question: What if there had been no Paul with his companions to carry the new faith westward in that early day of its enthusiasm and power?

The need of the Greek also   Paul himself could make no such forecast of history. What did he think of as he looked out for the first time upon the famed Ægean Sea and upon the circle of historic lands that surrounded it? Did he think of Troy, but a few miles distant, immortalized by Homer's song? Or did he recall the time when East and West had met here in one of the crises of history, when Xerxes had marshaled his millions which the nobler, bolder life of the West had driven back again? Or did he think of Socrates and Plato and Aristotle? Deeply as Paul realized the importance of the new step, it was not these thoughts that filled his mind. What he saw was a people whom all their art and philosophy and noble history had not been able to save from superstition and moral degradation. He faced them, as later on toward Rome itself, his heart filled with the courage and enthusiasms of a great message, his spirit burdened with the sense of a high obligation. These lands of light needed exactly what the rude folks of Galatia did, whom he had just left behind. "I am debtor both to Greeks and to Barbarians, both to the wise and the foolish. So much as in me lies I am ready to preach the gospel to you also. . . . For I am not ashamed of the gospel: for it is the power of God unto salvation to every one that believeth; to the Jew first, and also to the Greek" (Rom 1. 14-16).

Such thoughts must have prepared him for the vision that came by night, the man of Macedonia who stood before him saying, "Come over and help us." The vision at least found him ready. At once he sought a ship for Macedonia, sailed from Troas by way of the island of Samothrace, and on the following day landed at Neapolis. It seems likely that Luke joined the little company at Troas, and some have held that he was the "man of Macedonia." In any case, we note that at this period there suddenly begin the so-called "we" portions of the book of Acts (Acts 16. 10). *The vision and the call*

In various ways the Macedonian churches occupied a special place in Paul's work. The people themselves were of a sturdier, simpler life than Paul found in such centers as Corinth and Ephesus. At the same time, though there was full share of hardship and danger, Paul's enemies, the Judaizers, seem largely to have left him alone in this field. There was a solidity about this work, and it grew without great disturbance or crisis. Above all, there was a closeness of personal relation between the churches and the apostle which does not appear elsewhere in such measure. Luke tells us of only three cities where Paul stopped on this tour: Philippi, Thessalonica, and Berea. It was prob- *The Macedonian churches* ably on a later occasion that Paul pressed farther north and west to Illyricum.

Philippi was Paul's first stopping place. Apparently, he arrived the first part of the week, and so was there some days before the Sabbath. The Jews, because they were few in number, had no synagogue here but only a place of prayer, whose location at the riverside was for convenience in the matter of the ceremonial washings. Here the disciples met a number of women and opened conversation with them, and here Paul's first convert in Europe was won—Lydia, a seller of purple. Under the compulsion of her generous hospitality, Paul broke his rule, gave up his lodging and his work, and was entertained with his party in Lydia's house. So began the relation of special friendship which sets Philippi apart from Paul's other churches. This was the only church from which Paul took gifts. So sure was he of their friendship that he knew there would be no misunderstanding. They sent him gifts more than once during his stay at Thessalonica which followed; and a little later at Corinth they helped him again (Phil 4. 15, 16; 2 Cor 11. 8, 9). One of the last pictures that we have of Paul shows him a prisoner at Rome receiving Epaphroditus, a member of the Philippian church, who brings him again their love and their bounty; and the letter which he writes them in acknowledgment is one of the most attractive of his epistles. There is little additional that we know of the Philippian church. Paul visited it later on several occasions. We know the names of some of its members. Lydia must have been a woman of some means to be able to entertain the disciples as well as have meetings of the church in her house. Besides her we know Epaphroditus, who brought the gifts to Rome; Synzygus, whose name is translated "yokefellow," but whom Paul is probably addressing as his "true Synzygos" with a play upon the name; two women, Euodia and Syntyche; and Clement (Phil 2. 25; 4. 1-3).

To establish such close relations there must have been a stay of some months. Luke, according to his custom, tells only of the beginning of the work and of the way in which it was brought to a close. The latter was not due to trouble from the Jews, but to a conflict with superstition and greed. There was a young woman in the city, a servant or slave, who had the power of ventriloquism. This, as we learn from Plutarch, was what was meant by calling a person a python, which is the Greek word used here. The people thought that the girl was demon-possessed and had the power of soothsaying. The girl herself was probably unbalanced and thought the same. At any rate, her masters used her misfortune to make money. When Paul by his commanding word healed her, her masters found their source of profit gone and in revenge brought charges against the disciples. Paul and the soothsaying girl

The charge was that of bringing in new and unlawful customs, and probably referred to their teaching a religion that was not allowed. Philippi was a Roman colony with consequent special privileges, and was exceedingly proud of the fact. On such a serious charge Paul and Silas were sent by the inferior judges to the highest magistrates, who in a Roman colony were the prætors. These, without process of trial, and probably without even giving Paul the chance to assert his Roman citizenship, caused them to be beaten and flung into jail. Luke does not seem to have been with them at this time, the "we" portions ending just before this. He gives us, however, the graphic story of how the earthquake shook the prison and loosed the stocks in which Paul and Silas had been held, opening the prison doors, and of the jailor's attempted suicide and subsequent conversion. Charges and imprisonment

Meanwhile the prætors had had time to reflect upon their summary and illegal action, and in the morning they sent the lictors to the jailor with word to let the prisoners go. But Paul knew too well what his right of citizenship Release and departure involved. The prætors had committed a double illegality: first, in proceeding without a trial; second, in beating a Roman citizen, who by special law would be exempt from such dishonoring punishment in any case. Rome had a long arm and a regard for law, as these officials well knew. So there was nothing for the proud prætors to do but themselves to come to the prison, upon Paul's demand, in person to lead out the prisoners, and to beseech the scorned Jews, whom they had but yesterday treated so contemptuously, to leave the city. And so the disciples left; not in haste, however, for they first went to the home of Lydia, where a farewell meeting of the little church was arranged.

Thessalonica From Philippi Paul goes to Thessalonica, passing by, for some reason not known to us, the cities of Amphipolis and Apollonia. Here there was a synagogue, and for three weeks Paul was permitted to speak each Sabbath to the Jews gathered there. After that he probably worked some time longer in the city among the Gentiles. His converts numbered only a few Jews, but included a large number of proselytes, "devout Greeks," as Luke calls them, and a number of "chief women." The mission was a notable triumph. Here again it was Judaism that prepared the soil for Paul, and we need not wonder that the Jews who did not believe were stirred to anger against him. He was winning away the Greeks who gathered about them, and so they resorted to active measures. Not wishing to appear alone, they succeeded in stirring up a rabble which proceeded to the house of one Jason, where Paul and Silas lodged. Not finding these, they took Jason and some other disciples before the magistrates. Their charge was that the Christians proclaimed Jesus as king, which showed disloyalty to Cæsar. The charge was dismissed, the magistrates simply requiring Jason to give bond; but the disciples felt that the danger was not past and so sent Paul and Silas away by night.

Two letters written to the Thessalonians have been preserved for us. They are of greatest interest because they are probably the oldest writings that we possess from Paul's hand, as well as the oldest Christian writings of any kind. At this time the letter to the Galatians had not yet been penned, and the earliest of our Gospels was not written till at least fifteen years later. The first letter is so intimate, so personal, so direct and practical, that it gives us a fine insight into the apostle's own spirit and the method of his work. All the circumstances add to the interest. Paul had left the Thessalonians suddenly, without even the chance for farewell as at Philippi. His stay with them had not been long. He had not had much time to instruct them in the new faith, and most of them were Gentiles. Moreover, they were even then facing persecution. And so these questions filled Paul's soul: Would they stand fast? Would they hold to the simple truth? Would they lead the life that belonged to the Christian faith? He had tried to return for a visit but failed. When he reached Athens he could endure it no longer, and sent Timothy back to them. He himself pushed on to Corinth, and to Corinth Timothy came at last. His news filled Paul's heart with joy. True, there were problems; they could hardly be wanting in a church like this. But the church was standing fast. Paul writes his letter at once, a letter full of joy, of tenderness as of a mother toward her children, and of appreciation of their faith and love and loyalty. Not all the narratives of Acts can give us the insight into Paul's heart that a single chapter here affords.

More than half of the letter is taken up with personal reminiscence and suggestion, which is the more remarkable when we realize how anxious Paul was "to perfect that which was lacking in their faith." The opening words show the fine tact and courtesy which this man of deep passion and stern will could show. "I always thank God for you in my prayer," he begins, "remembering your faith and love and patience. The other churches in Macedonia and

Achaia have all heard of how the gospel came to you in power, of how you turned from idols to the living God, and how you have stood faithful. And you know what my life was with you. There was no flattery, no greed for money or honor. We came not to assert authority, but to love and serve. We were like a nurse with her babes, like a father with his children, loving you, working day and night, that we might not burden you, faithful in our teaching, unblameable in our lives. And you took our word not as man's word, but as God's word. And you proved your faith by suffering, just as your brethren in Judæa" (1 Thess 1. 1 to 2. 16).

Good news "We were deeply bereaved in leaving you, and I Paul tried more than once to come to you again. So we finally sent Timothy from Athens to encourage you. You remember that we had forewarned you of such trials. But when Timothy came just now with the good news, we were comforted by your faith. For now we live, if you stand fast. You are our glory and our joy. How can we thank God for all the joy that we have in you? May God bring us to you again. May he make your hearts abound in love, and may he establish you in holiness until our Lord Jesus shall appear with the saints" (2. 17 to 3. 13).

instruction and advice The second part of the letter, chs. 4 and 5, Paul devotes to instruction and practical direction. He speaks first of the sin of social impurity, which the Greeks took so lightly: "God called us not in uncleanness, but in sanctification." Then he takes up the question of the second coming. This teaching had evidently stirred up great interest. Some were inclined to neglect their work: What need of toil if the end be so near? Paul admonishes these to be quiet, and attend to their business, and to work with their hands, that they may thus commend the new faith to those without. Others were concerned about their friends who might die in the interval before the end. Would they not be excluded from the Kingdom when Jesus came? Paul said no, for the dead in Christ were to rise first. Others were eagerly discussing the time of his coming. To these Paul says: "The time no one knows. It is enough for us to watch and be sober, trusting in him 'who died for us, that, whether we wake or sleep, we should live together with him.'" And then in short, strong words he crowds together the many things he would say to them: "Be at peace, admonish the disorderly, encourage the faint-hearted, support the weak, render to no one evil for evil, follow after that which is good, rejoice always, pray without ceasing, in everything give thanks."

It is not hard to see why such a faith should spread. **A conquering faith** Here was the dynamic of a great enthusiasm, a spirit of faith, devotion, and brotherhood. And joined to this was a sober, earnest life with the noblest moral ideals. And these two things the Roman world needed—a living faith and moral power. What Paul did here he did everywhere: he showed that these were inseparable in the Christian faith. The second letter to the Thessalonians must have followed after a very brief interval, as it shows substantially the same situation.

Berea, to which Paul went directly from Thessalonica, **Berea** is the only other Macedonian church of which we know. Berea was a much smaller place, and it is likely that Paul stopped there in order to be near to Thessalonica, hoping to be able to return. Paul's stay could not have been very long, for the Thessalonian Jews could easily follow him. Here at Berea he had a larger success with the Jews. They were more open minded, and tested Paul's teaching of Jesus as the promised Messiah by a study of their Scriptures. As usual, Paul won converts from among the proselytes, both men and women. In all such cases it must be remembered that these were not necessarily close adherents, but that under this term we include many who were but loosely attached, though their minds had been prepared by some knowledge of the purer Jewish faith.

DIRECTIONS FOR READING AND STUDY

Read Acts 15. 36 to 17. 15.

Read First Thessalonians.

Note upon the map Paul's fields of labor up to this time and their location relative to Tarsus.

Trace the route of Paul's journey to Macedonia; note the provinces in Asia Minor which he passed by; locate Philippi, Thessalonica, and Berea.

Write a synopsis of First Thessalonians, summing up each paragraph of the letter in a sentence or two.

CHAPTER XXXII

ACHAIA

BEREA was Paul's last stopping place in the northern Paul at Athens province of Macedonia. He left it accompanied by some of the newly won disciples, Silas and Timothy not being with him. Turning at first toward the sea, they went finally to Athens, and here, for a time at least, Paul seems to have been left alone. What stirred him most in this great city was not its far-famed works of art, whose broken fragments still move our wonder to-day, nor yet its traditions of a noble philosophy. Of that noble philosophy not much was left. The Epicureans whom Paul met, though they counseled moderation and virtue, found the meaning of life in pleasure. Stoicism was the self-centered philosophy of a few strong souls. It had no message of service to fellow men and no word of help from God. For the Athenians as a whole, however, these questions of truth or faith had become simply matters for fine speech and interesting debate. They "spent their time in nothing else, but either to tell or to hear some new thing." What moved this Jew of pure faith most was the scene of shrines and temples and statues, "the city full of idols."

Here at Athens also there were Jews, and Paul met them The Areopagus speech and "the devout persons," or proselytes, at the synagogue. Athens, however, gave him a freer opportunity to speak to the people. The central market place was where they were accustomed to congregate, and here the apostle spoke with all that would listen. Luke reports to us a special address that Paul gave. Scholars are not agreed whether the Areopagus was a hill to which Paul was taken, Mars' Hill, or whether it means a council, or court, which was to pass upon Paul's teaching. Probably it was the latter.

The few words that Luke gives are at most a fragment or a summary. But even so they are very suggestive. With fine tact Paul finds a point of contact, the altar to the unknown God. He tells them of the God of all nature and all life, who is not shut up in temples. This brings him to his message of Jesus, through whom the word of righteousness and repentance comes now to men, and whom God has approved by his resurrection.

The response　What we have is really the introduction to Paul's true message. It may be that he was interrupted. In any case, Paul seems to have found no large response. A few converts are spoken of, but we learn nothing at this time or later of a church at Athens. There is no reason to be surprised at this. Paul's message demanded moral earnestness and humility. Jesus himself had set these as the gateway to life in such passages as the Beatitudes: the meek were to inherit the earth, and those that hungered and thirsted after righteousness. To all this the Athenian spirit was in greatest contrast.

Corinth　From Athens Paul goes to Corinth. The way had not yet opened for him to go back to Thessalonica. It pointed clearly to Corinth, and yet Paul at the beginning seems to have contemplated only a brief stay in the great city. It was a special vision, such as that which called him to Macedonia, that now showed him that he was to remain a longer period in Achaia before going north again.

Here at Corinth Paul was again at one of the centers of the empire. Antioch, Corinth, Ephesus were the great cities that he touched before he reached Rome. From Athens to Corinth was a brief journey, but a great change. Athens was the quiet city of culture, proud of its past, the university town. Corinth was the busy metropolis. It had been destroyed, had lain in ruins for a century, and been rebuilt but a hundred years before. The old population was largely gone. It was a modern city. Roman colonists were here and Roman officials, for it was the capital of Achaia. It had its philosophers and rhetoricians, as well as Athens. It had a strategic position for trade, lying on the isthmus and commanding two harbors. Goods were commonly transhipped to avoid the dangerous journey around the coast. It was a great commercial center and had large wealth. Like all such cities of the time, it had its masses of the poor, vastly outnumbering all the rest. A writer somewhat earlier than this reports four hundred and sixty thousand slaves. It was upon such a pyramid of oppression and wretchedness that the wealth of the great Roman cities rested. And that wealth brought in its train profligacy and vice. Corinth had even more than her share. Her very name had become a byword: men who led lives of indulgence and vice were said to Corinthianize.

It was in a state of depression that Paul entered the city. His work in Macedonia had been broken off. He had not been able to get back to Thessalonica. He had had little result from his labor in Athens. "I was with you," he tells the Corinthians, "in weakness, and in fear, and in much trembling" (1 Cor 2. 3). If he was stirred by the idolatry of Athens, he was deeply moved here by the shame and sin of the life about him. What could he do with his gospel of the cross, coming to these Greeks with their wisdom and their eloquence? And what could any gospel do with a city so sunken in sin? If such questions came to Paul in moments of depression, he had his answer. He may have distrusted himself, but he did not doubt his message. He could not compete with these Greeks in fine speaking; he had only what they would call the foolishness of the cross. But that message he would give simply, directly, "not in persuasive words of wisdom, but in demonstration of the Spirit and of power." "I determined not to know anything among you, save Jesus Christ, and him crucified." *Paul's mood and message*

The result justified the faith. What the fine rhetoric of the Corinthians could not do, or the philosophy of Athens, *The gospel of power* that his simple message accomplished. It seemed a message of weakness; it was, in fact, a message of power. It seemed foolishness; it had in it, in reality, the deep wisdom of God. Its great test was this, that it could meet the wickedness even of Corinth, and overcome it. All this Paul brings in the letter which he writes later on to the Corinthians. We understand his daring speech, his paradoxes, by remembering these circumstances. "For the word of the cross is to them that perish foolishness; but unto us who are saved it is the power of God. Hath not God made foolish the wisdom of the world? Jews ask for signs, and Greeks seek after wisdom: but we preach Christ crucified, unto Jews a stumbling-block, and unto Gentiles foolishness; but unto them that are called, both Jews and Greeks, Christ the power of God, and the wisdom of God" (1 Cor 1. 18-25; 2. 1-5). Corinth showed Paul the power of the new faith over against the worst conditions of the old world.

Paul's work   Paul's work began at Corinth much as elsewhere. He first sought a place in the Jewish quarter where he could carry on his trade. Here he found one Aquila with his wife, Priscilla. The emperor Claudius had driven the Jews from Rome but a short time before this, and these people had come from Rome to Corinth. Whether they were already Christians or not, we do not know. Paul's first reason for stopping with them was because they had the same trade. Gifts from Philippi supplemented what he thus earned. He did not win many of the Jews, for the church that we see later at Corinth was mainly Gentile. His work, when he left the synagogue, was carried on in the house of a proselyte who lived next to the synagogue, and the nearness probably helped to aggravate the anger of the Jews. Paul also won over Crispus, the ruler of the synagogue. With these he gained many converts among the Corinthians, and quickly established a strong church.

Before Gallio   The proconsul of the province at this time was Gallio, a brother of the noted Stoic philosopher Seneca. The hos-

tility of the Jews culminated at last in an effort to convict
Paul of serious charges before this Gallio. It is probable that here, as elsewhere, they tried to make it appear
that there was something politically dangerous in Paul.
To Gallio it was a quarrel among the Jews, and he drove
them out with scant patience. The Jews were never popular. In this case their discomfiture emboldened some of
the Corinthian bystanders, who improved the occasion by
beating up Sosthenes, who had been elected ruler of the
synagogue to succeed Crispus when the latter became
Christian.

DIRECTIONS FOR READING AND STUDY

Read Acts 17. 13 to 18. 18.
Write a paraphrase of Paul's speech at Athens.
Read 1 Cor 1 and 2.
Note what Paul has to say in praise and in criticism of the
Corinthians in these two chapters.
From what Paul says in these two chapters, try to determine
what his style of preaching was, and the qualities which it possessed
and which it lacked.

CHAPTER XXXIII

ASIA

Asia

ONE Roman province near at hand Paul had not yet touched, that of Asia. Paul uses this name always in the Roman sense, meaning the political province that occupied the western part of Asia Minor and included many cities besides its populous capital, Ephesus. He had passed by this province on the way to Macedonia. He had established his churches in Galatia to the east and in Greece to the west. Now he turned to this his last Eastern field.

Journeys in between

He did not, however, begin his work at once upon leaving Corinth. First he planned to go to Jerusalem and report to the apostles concerning his work. Ephesus was upon his way, and his friends Priscilla and Aquila accompanied him to that city. These remained in Ephesus, evidently locating for their business. Paul stopped long enough to speak in the synagogue and then pressed on, shipping from there to Cæsarea, from which place he went overland to Jerusalem. On the way back he stopped with his old friends at Antioch also, but the stay at both places must have been brief. His real work lay in his new fields, where he had had such marvelous success. First of all, he was anxious to see his Galatian converts. It had been several years since he had left them. During that time his enemies had been busy. His letter, which we studied, had been written to them probably from Corinth and but a short time before this. Now he visits them again and for the last time. His road was probably through Tarsus, as when he visited them on the way to Macedonia. On that journey he moved north when he reached Pisidian Antioch. This time, when he left them, he went directly west toward Ephesus (Acts 18. 18-23; 19. 1).

The work at Ephesus ranks in importance with that at Scanty sources
Corinth. Unfortunately, Paul has left us very little information concerning it. The letter marked in our Bible
"to the Ephesians" was probably not addressed to this
church. As the margin of our American Standard Revision indicates, the oldest manuscripts omit the phrase
"at Ephesus" from the first verse. In any case, the letter
throws no light upon the church at all, and lacks wholly
the local allusions, in which Paul's other letters abound.
When we consider that Ephesus was Paul's headquarters
for three years, the account in Acts is quite meager. The
Corinthian letters were written during these three years,
though not all from Ephesus, and give us some important
items.

To these scanty sources some scholars have added an- As to Romans 16
other writing. They hold that the last chapter of our
letter to the Romans has been added to this by mistake and
is really a note which Paul addressed to the Ephesian
church. The reasons for this can be readily seen. In this
chapter is a long list of names of persons to whom Paul
sends greetings. They are all known to him personally.
Would he have known that many in Rome, where he had
never been? With all the ease of travel in the Roman world
this would not be likely with the relatively small numbers
of a Christian community. Three of these names, moreover, point naturally to Ephesus. The first two are Prisca
(or Priscilla) and Aquila, who were with Paul in Ephesus. A third is Epænetus, "the first fruits of Asia," that is,
Paul's first convert in Asia, which with Paul means Ephesus.

What we have here, then, in Rom 16 is a writing dif- A letter of introduction
ferent in character from any other writing of the New
Testament. It is one of the "epistles of commendation"
to which Paul refers in 2 Cor 3. 1. These were very common
in the early church, especially a little later. Between the
little Christian communities men and women were constantly passing back and forth. These disciples were cared

for by the brothers of the church wherever they went, and would not think of stopping at a public inn. Among them would be leaders of the church, including apostles and disciples. The churches would help these on their way, as Paul expected help from the Roman church on the way to Spain. To prevent imposture, letters of commendation or introduction were written, and were either sent direct or given to the person whom they concerned, just as is done to-day. Paul's enemies in Corinth had probably brought such letters from Jerusalem. In a similar way Paul writes to commend Timothy and later on Titus to the Corinthian church, and letters from Ephesus paved the way for Apollos when he went to Corinth (Acts 18. 27). Phœbe was a prominent member of the church at Cenchreæ, one of the ports of Corinth. It may have been during Paul's last three months' visit at Corinth that she decided to go to Ephesus. Paul sends with her this letter of introduction. At the same time he takes opportunity to send greetings to his many friends there, naturally selecting those who were most prominent in the church or with whom he had close personal relations. Among the latter would be Rufus and his mother; Paul says, "his mother and mine." Probably Paul had lodged with her and received her motherly care. This brief note, as we shall see, has not a few suggestions as to Ephesus.

Synagogue and the school of Tyrannus

Paul sought his first opening at Ephesus, as usual, in the synagogue. For three months he used this as his place of teaching. He may have had some hope of winning the Jewish colony entire for the new faith. In any case, they gave him a ready hearing. Even at the end of this time he was not compelled to leave, and we hear nothing of open opposition from the Jews. In contrast with the situation elsewhere, it seems that during this whole period the converts simply met in the synagogue. When, however, a portion of the Jews refused his message, Paul separated the disciples and used the school of Tyrannus for his teaching. This use of a public hall was also unique. It fits in with the general picture that we have of a great success on Paul's part in this field.

Still another new feature in Paul's experience in Ephe- *Apollos and the disciples of John* sus was his meeting with certain men who had become Christians apparently without direct contact with either the Jerusalem teaching or his own. One of these was Apollos, whom Aquila and Priscilla had found and instructed in the Pauline gospel and sent on to Corinth before Paul arrived, but whom we find later there with Paul. Then there are twelve disciples whom Paul himself finds. These men, we are told, knew only the baptism of John. It seems probable that they knew of Jesus' life teaching; Apollos "taught accurately the things concerning Jesus." They did not, it would seem, know Paul's gospel—that Jesus died, that his death was for the sins of men, that he arose again, and that the new life of the Spirit was given to those who believed. They may have preached John's word of repentance and judgment, but not Paul's word of salvation by the grace of God.

Apollos represents a new type that was to have great *The Greek spirit in the church* influence in the church. He stands for the Greek spirit, with its eloquence, its rhetoric, and philosophy. In Alexandria, whence he came, this spirit had entered the Jewish circles. We may think of Apollos' thought and style as being somewhat like that of the letter to the Hebrews, finding in the Old Testament all manner of types and suggestions of the gospel and setting this forth in beautiful language. No wonder that he was popular with the men of the Greek spirit at Corinth, though we of to-day would prefer the "rude" speech of Paul (Acts 18. 24-28). The Christian message, then, even if in imperfect form, had reached such widely separated places as Ephesus and Alexandria apart from the work of Paul or the other apostles. It was spreading through the empire by many roads of which we know nothing to-day.

Two early
disciples

One other line we trace, which leads apparently to Jerusalem (Rom 16. 7). Paul speaks of Andronicus and Junias as fellow Jews, as men who had been in prison with him, as men who had been Christians before Paul was, and as apostles. These were probably of the original company of disciples at Jerusalem. They too may have represented Christianity in Ephesus before Paul. Now we find them working in hearty cooperation.

Success at
Ephesus

All this suggests a picture of harmony and peace, as well as of great success. Paul gathers about him not only many converts but a fine group of workers. These carry the message throughout the province. Epaphras is one of these, who bore the gospel to Colossæ, Laodicea, and Hierapolis, cities to which Paul sends messages later. Paul mentions others as his "fellow workers"—Priscilla and Aquila, Urbanus, women like Tryphæna, Tryphosa, and Persis (Rom 16. 3, 9, 12). Luke declares that "all they that dwelt in Asia heard the word of the Lord, both Jews and Greeks" (Acts 19. 10). As an illustration of Paul's success, he tells how the people who had been convinced by his message brought their books of magic and burned them, just as we read a few years ago of the great bonfires of pipes made by the Chinese who had given up opium. Luke declares that the value of these books was fifty thousand pieces of silver. What we gather from Paul's letters points to the same large results from the Ephesian labors. He declares that "a great door and effectual" was opened to him. Because of his labors he cannot at first go to Corinth himself. That he should stay three years at Ephesus is sufficient proof of the fruitful field that he found.

Opposition

But there are darker sides to the picture also. While we know little of detail, it is evident that Paul nowhere faced greater foes or was in greater personal danger than at Ephesus. It is not the Jews and their plots that trouble Paul here, for he seems to have met from these considerable response and little resistance. It is, rather, paganism and its

business interests. The pride of Ephesus was its magnificent
temple of Diana, or Artemis, whose foundations were some
three hundred and thirty feet long, which was surrounded
by a magnificent double row of columns, and boasted among
its adornments the work of such artists as Praxiteles. The
central treasure was the image of the goddess, supposed to
have fallen from heaven. Certain strange characters in-
scribed upon this image were held to have magic power.
The religions of Asia Minor were on a very low plane,
and Ephesus was a center of the immorality and superstition. This had its profitable side. A big business was
done in reproductions of the shrine, in copies of the magical
characters found upon it, and in other magical books and
articles. Paul's preaching had made inroads into this traffic.
It was not merely a question of his converts, but of the
popular influence he might exert as his teaching spread.
Demetrius the silversmith, who organized the mass meeting in protest, may have been the head of his guild for
that year. He and his friends secured the popular support by the appeal to religious passion and prejudice and
local pride. The local officials, however, seem to have
been distinctly favorable to Paul's position, aside from fear-
ing the results if such disorders should be reported to
Rome. Paul, however, was in no personal danger in this
case, the disciples and the local officials both persuading him
to remain away.

He himself reports far more serious dangers. He **Personal**
gives us no definite statement as to what the perils **dangers**
were, but it is evident that his very life was at stake.
He declares that Priscilla and Aquila "laid down their own
necks" for his life (Rom 16. 4). He writes the Corinthians
from Ephesus about standing in jeopardy every hour, and
adds: "If after the manner of men I fought with beasts
at Ephesus, what doth it profit me [that is, if the dead
are not raised]?" 1 Cor 15. 30-32). Later he says, "We
would not have you ignorant, brethren, concerning our af-

fliction which befell us in Asia, that we were weighed down exceedingly, beyond our power, insomuch that we despaired even of life: yea, we ourselves have had the sentence of death within ourselves, that we should not trust in ourselves, but in God who raiseth the dead: who delivered us out of so great a death" (2 Cor 1. 8-10). It seems, then, that Paul's life was more than once in danger, and he may even have fought with the wild beasts in the arena. In any case, here was a ministry upon a larger scale both of success and of danger than had marked Paul's work before.

The extent of the work
The Asian ministry thus marks another stage in Paul's career. His enemies declared that he had persuaded the people "not alone at Ephesus, but almost throughout all Asia." The interest of the Asiarchs, prominent provincial officials, showed that his influence had reached high quarters. Churches like those at Colossæ, Laodicea, and Hierapolis, founded by his helpers, looked to him as their apostle. The lower strata he reached also as in Corinth, for he refers to the slaves connected with two households, those of Aristobulus and Narcissus (Rom 16. 10, 11). As elsewhere, the church was divided into smaller groups which met in particular private houses. Thus Priscilla and Aquila had a "church in their house" (Rom 16. 3-5). When Paul speaks of "Asyncritus, Phlegon, Hermes, Patrobas, Hermas, and the brethren that are with them," it is not unlikely that here too he is speaking of groups that met in different houses and mentioning the leaders of five such circles. In any case, it was a large and strong church that he left behind. It is interesting to note the number of women here mentioned, remembering that the list is not one of members but of leaders in the church and special friends. Here, as usual, Priscilla is named before her husband Aquila. However conservative Paul may have been in principle, in practice it is evident he gave generous recognition to the noble women of his churches, and these women

played a large part in the church of the empire from the
beginning.

DIRECTIONS FOR READING AND STUDY

Acts 18. 18-23; 19. 1.   Trace Paul's journey from Corinth to
Jerusalem and back to Ephesus.   Note the former fields of labor
through which he passes.

Rom 16.   Of those to whom Paul sends greetings here, which
seem to be simply his personal friends?   State the total number
of names and the proportion of women.

Acts 18. 24 to 19. 41.   Tell the story of Demetrius and the mob.
This theater had a seating capacity of about twenty-five thousand.

CHAPTER XXXIV

THE LIFE OF AN EARLY CHURCH—I

Occasion of the Corinthian letters

Of no one of the early churches have we so full a knowledge as of the church at Corinth. We owe this to the preservation of the letters to this church which are contained in our New Testament. Paul was working at Ephesus soon after leaving Corinth. The two cities were joined by a great highway of the sea, with vessels constantly passing back and forth, and it was not hard for Paul to keep in touch with the church. Paul had received a letter from the Corinthians and had written one in return, both lost to us. A second letter was written him by the church, asking his judgment on various questions. About the same time Chloe, apparently a well-to-do Christian woman, sent some of her servants or slaves, also presumably Christians, and these informed Paul of serious conditions that had arisen in the life of the church. Later three other members of the church came, Stephanas, Fortunatus, and Achaiacus, the two last named being probably slaves of the first. Apollos too, who had been working at Corinth, came to Paul at Ephesus, and Paul, himself prevented from going by the importance of his new work at Ephesus, had sent Timothy as his personal representative. All this had taken place before Paul sat down to write the letter which we now have. It is a good instance of Paul's care of his churches and at the same time a picture of the freedom of travel which characterized the age.

The moral problem of the early church

More important than these incidents is the picture of the life of a Christian church in the Roman world, and the problems which the Christian religion faced in thus establishing itself. Christianity was a new way of living. Paul's first message to men concerned their relation to God: "We

beseech you on behalf of Christ, be ye reconciled to God"
(2 Cor 5. 20). But he did not stop with this. The new
religion was a life to be lived out among men. It meant
a new conduct and character. It was a moral revolution.
"If any man is in Christ, he is a new creature: the old
things are passed away; behold, they are become new"
(2 Cor 5. 17). Paul's greatest task was to show his converts what this new life meant. The old religions had little
to say about right living. Often their influence lay upon
the wrong side. The temple of Aphrodite at Corinth, for
example, had a thousand women attached to it who were
giving themselves to a life of shame as part of the service
of the goddess. The Corinthian converts had no trouble
in accepting the new doctrines and sacraments, but it was
not so easy to teach them that the new faith meant purity
and sobriety and uprightness. Nor was that all. Paul had
the further task of teaching them what the new spirit
meant in the thousand and one activities and relations of
life. These Christians had to live in the pagan world and
touch its life on every side. The political life, the social
life, the business life was pagan in spirit and practice. They
could not leave this world; how should they live the new
life in the midst of it?

In all these matters Paul shows a marvelous patience. **Paul's skill**
He knows he is dealing with children. They are still babes, **and faith**
and he does not expect everything at once. He is skillful
too. He holds up the highest principles, but he shows the
greatest tact and common sense in application. All fanatical
extremes are absent. More wonderful still is his faith. He
knows with what materials he has to deal in the Corinthian
church. In writing them he mentions a long list of those
who cannot enter the Kingdom of God—fornicators, idola-
ters, adulterers, effeminate, abusers of themselves with men,
thieves, covetous, drunkards, revilers, extortioners. And
then he adds, "And such were some of you" (1 Cor 6. 9-11).
Moreover, most of his converts were taken from the lower

social classes, from the great proletariat of Corinth. And yet before such folks Paul holds the highest ideals of Christianity, nor abates from them one whit. It is for these people that he sets forth his lofty ideal in the marvelous chapter on love (1 Cor 13). He believes that even such people can be made over in the spirit of Christ.

The problems that appear in the Corinthian letters may be taken up under two heads: (1) Moral problems; (2) Problems of church life. We shall take these up in the order noted.

Against impurity   The first problem that Paul had to handle was a peculiarly distressing one. Apparently the servants of Chloe informed him of this, that a member of the church had actually married his stepmother upon his father's death. And the church had permitted this without proceeding against this member. That does not mean that they defended such a deed. Individually they may have condemned it, but Paul demands that this man must be put out of their fellowship. With such men they might have to associate in the world without, but the Christian fellowship had a different meaning (1 Cor 5. 1-13). Back of this lay the broader question, the general matter of social immorality. Here was the prevalent sin of the Grecian world, for which Corinth was especially notorious. Paul's warnings do not imply that this sin had appeared in the church, but it shows how great a task Christianity had that the apostle should deem it necessary to solemnly warn the church upon this subject. "Be not deceived. The unrighteous shall not inherit the kingdom of God." It was an echo of the old prophetic message: Religion means righteousness. But Paul went further. The Christian was one who had received the Spirit of God. How could he dishonor the body in which that Spirit lived? "Know ye not that your body is a temple of the Holy Spirit which is in you, which ye have from God?" That was Christianity's first fight in the Roman world: it stood for purity of life (1 Cor 6. 9-20).

Paul's next question took him into the business world. He found his Corinthian converts indulging in sharp business practices, defrauding each other, and going to law. Has Christianity anything to say as to business? Paul did not go into the question in detail. He had no such occasion for this as we have now. But he made clear the principle: Religion has something to say about business. Brotherhood must be taken into business life. Neither fraud nor unrighteousness nor extortion has any place in the kingdom of God (1 Cor 6. 1-11).

Christianity had to meet the question of the family. The Corinthians had raised several questions as to marriage. There was an extreme party in the church, it appears, whose effort to be holy had carried them so far that they did not believe in marriage or in maintaining the relation of husband and wife. For them everything that had to do with the flesh was sinful. Paul denies this asceticism. Marriage is not sinful, though he feels that with the end so near at hand it would be better for Christians to remain unmarried, as he is. Others apparently thought that a Christian husband or wife whose partner was unconverted should take a divorce. This too Paul declares against (1 Cor 7. 1-40).

In the matter of womanhood Christianity also rendered a great service in setting up a new ideal. Social immorality in that day was widely prevalent, as we have seen. Divorce was common and on the increase. The father was not only the head of the household but the absolute master and ruler. Children and women had no rights. A woman had no standing before the law except as belonging to some man, father, husband, brother. In Greece education and freedom belonged only to the class of women called *hetairæ*, who purchased these privileges with their honor. In some points Paul was still the conservative Jew: The head of the woman is the man, he says, and the woman is the glory of the man as the man is the image and glory of God (1 Cor 11. 3, 8,

9). But Paul knows the deeper Christian truth—that every human personality is sacred: "There can be neither Jew nor Greek, there can be neither bond nor free, there can be no male and female; for ye all are one in Christ Jesus" (Gal 3. 28). Here lies in principle that position toward which woman has been moving since that day. For the woman, as for the child and the slave, Christianity meant emancipation. All were alike children of God, and the words "brother" and "sister" set them all upon the same plane.

Christianity and slavery

Slavery Paul touches upon with only a few words (1 Cor 7. 20-24). He bids the slave remain contented in his position. Christianity was not a political movement. It would have had short shrift in the Roman world had it been such. But it had a message that concerned slavery. (1) The slave knew himself as Christian to be a free man: "He that was called in the Lord being a bondservant, is the Lord's freedman." (2) Within the Christian Church the slave was a brother. The servants of Chloe and the slaves of Stephanas came to Paul not as mere letter-carriers, but as trusted Christian brothers. Within the church it was brother and sister, not master and servant. When Paul, later on, writes from Rome the charming letter to Philemon and sends back the runaway slave whom he has won to Christ, he sends him back "no longer as a servant [slave], but more than a servant, a brother beloved." It sometimes happened, indeed, in the early church that slaves held the highest office. (3) In these ideals Christianity set free the silent forces which were at last to make slavery impossible.

As to meat offered to idols

Paul's discussion of the question of the eating of meat that had been sacrificed to heathen gods shows how difficult the situation of the Christian was in the midst of the life of a pagan world. When an animal was sacrificed it was customary, after certain portions had been given to the priests, to use the rest for a feast which might be held in the temple or at home. Sometimes the meat was offered

for sale in the market. To such feasts the Christians would
be invited by their unbelieving friends, or they might un-
wittingly buy such meat in the markets. Was it wrong to
partake in either case?

Paul does not answer with a simple yes or no. He is not Paul's answer
giving rules; he is setting up principles of conduct. He
discusses these questions in two passages here (1 Cor 8.
1-13; 10. 14-33) and in Rom 14. He declares (1) that
idols are nothing at all. The meat offered to idols cannot
therefore be unclean. The Christian by his knowledge is
lifted above these things. When you go into a market to
buy meat, therefore, or when you are at the table of a
friend, you need not stop to inquire whether the meat offered
you has been sacrificed to an idol. (2) But there is something besides a man's own conscience, and that is his brother.
There are Christians who have not gained this knowledge.
To them eating meat that has been offered to idols seems
like falling back into the old idol-worship; and your eating
may lead them to do what would be against their own
conscience and so injure them. In such case the brother is
more important than the meat. The meat is a small matter.
"The kingdom of God is not eating and drinking, but
righteousness and peace and joy in the Holy Spirit." And
your knowledge is not the most important thing. There is
something greater than knowledge, and that is love. "Knowledge puffeth up, but love buildeth up." Therefore, says
Paul, "If meat causeth my brother to stumble, I will eat
no flesh for evermore, that I cause not my brother to
stumble." (3) But while an idol is nothing at all, and meat
offered to idols is not as such unclean, it is quite a different
matter for Christians to participate in the old idol feasts.
How should the Christian go from the Lord's Supper over
to some pagan festival, as though by accepting Christ
he had simply added another god and another feast?
Flee idolatry, Paul says; it is nothing but the worship of
demons.

DIRECTIONS FOR READING AND STUDY

As to social morality, read 1 Cor 5. 1-13; 6. 9-20.

As to marriage, read 1 Cor 7. 1-40.

As to slavery, read 1 Cor 7. 20-24.

As to pagan feast and meat offered to idols, read 1 Cor 8. 1-13; 10. 14-33; Rom 14.

CHAPTER XXXV

THE LIFE OF AN EARLY CHURCH—II

THE second class of problems that Paul met at Corinth were those that concerned the common church life. The new religion was not simply an individual life but a life in fellowship. Upon that fellowship Paul laid the greatest stress. In fighting the enemies of this fellowship he knew that he was fighting for Christianity itself. The Roman world of that day, like our own world, was strongly individualistic. The old bonds were breaking and men were seeking the life of individual freedom. That was especially true of the Greeks. Like our own age, they were inclined to underestimate religion as a social fact and Christianity as a fellowship. This fellowship Paul saw assailed by several dangers.

Problems of the church

There was the trouble that came from the "advanced" women of the congregation (1 Cor 11. 2-16; 14. 33-36). They had heard from Paul that Christianity meant not the bondage of rules but the freedom of the spirit. Why should they, then, submit to the old restrictions upon women, such as that which required them to wear a veil in public and forbade them taking part in open meetings? The question was, in fact, the same as that with the progressives who felt they could eat meat offered to idols. It was a purely individualistic point of view, which thought only of the individual conscience and liberty. What these women failed to consider was the effect upon others and upon the church as a whole. There was only one class of Corinthian women which appeared unveiled upon the street and spoke in public, and that was the *hetairæ*. For Christian women to do this meant not only to shock some of their Christian friends,

As to women

but to bring suspicion upon the Christian community. As a matter of fact, the Christians were often slandered simply because they were a mingled company of men and women meeting in private. Paul's argument, indeed, is not one that would appeal to us to-day. He argues more as a Jewish rabbi than as a Christian apostle. But his practical conclusion is both sane and Christian. The only mistake has been to try to make a permanent law for the church out of his practical counsel to the Corinthians.

Church suppers and the Lord's Supper

The same individualism appears in the troubles in connection with the church suppers. It was apparently the common Christian practice to meet in a fellowship supper, just as has been noted at Jerusalem. As a part of this supper or in connection with it, there was a memorial of the Last Supper of the Lord with his disciples, what we call the Lord's Supper, or the Holy Communion. There were probably prayers offered and at a given time such words were repeated as Paul gives here (1 Cor 11. 24, 25), and bread and wine were passed to all present. The Corinthian church was made up mostly of the poor. It had, however, some people of means. Some of these brought to these suppers their rich and abundant foods and wines, and feasted by themselves while the poor brethren looked on hungry and envious. They were simply turning the whole into such a pagan feast as they had long been accustomed to. It was pure selfish individualism without thought of the idea of fellowship or the feelings of their poor brethren. "This is not a mere feast," Paul says; "it is a supper with deep and solemn meaning. It is proclaiming the Lord's death; think of that and of your brethren. If you are hungry, eat at home" (1 Cor 11. 17-34).

As to spiritual gifts

The quarrel about "spiritual gifts" was simply another manifestation of the same spirit, joined to a certain pride and love of display which was characteristically Greek (1 Cor 12 and 14). In Paul's teaching, as with the Jerusalem apostles, the gift of the Spirit to believers was the great fact of the new life. Their religion was not simply a hope of what Jesus would do upon his second appearing; it was a great possession realized in this life. This gift was the source of that spirit which marked so strongly the early church, its joy amid all persecution, its peace and love and hope, and its inextinguishable enthusiasm. The possession of this Spirit manifested itself in different gifts, or forms of Christian activity and usefulness. Prophecy and speaking with tongues were two forms of these gifts which attracted especial attention in the Corinthian church. Prophecy was not prediction, but a form of earnest speech or exhortation upon spiritual themes to which the speaker felt himself driven as by a kind of inspiration. The speaking with tongues, as we have seen, was a kind of rapt, ecstatic utterance of an incoherent kind, whose meaning was understood neither by speaker nor listener.

Here was a great power in the early church; but here was also the possibility of serious danger. The enthusiasm might easily lead to fanaticism and disorder, and the spiritual gifts to spiritual pride. The test of true religion with Jesus was obedient trust in God and the loving service of men. In the new atmosphere these simple homely qualities were in danger of being lost. These conditions actually existed in the Corinthian church. Nothing shows Paul's sanity and moral insight better than the way in which he faced them. **The danger**

The Corinthians, it seems, were very proud of their gifts, especially of the speaking with tongues. To order and reverence they paid no attention in their meetings, nor did they care whether their prophesying and speaking with tongues was of any help to others. Each man thought that it was of first importance when he felt moved by the Spirit to make himself heard. Nor did one wait upon the other. Two or three of the men with tongues would be speaking their strange medley at the same time. It is easy to imagine what visitors thought when they came in, especially when **Pride and disorder** they saw women taking part in these disorders. With all this there was naturally a good deal of pride and contention.

Paul's principles Here, again, Paul does not simply give commands. He sets up great Christian principles. (1) True Christian gifts have their source in one Spirit, the Spirit of God. There should, therefore, be no conflict and no question of distinction of greater and less. Rather there should be perfect unity. The church is the body of Christ. As the body has different members—feet, hands, and the like—so the church needs different gifts. But all belong together and each must seek to serve the whole, not to live for himself. We are members one of another. (2) The purpose of the gifts is service. The test of their value is the good they do. This test shows the gift of tongues to be of very little value. The man himself may enjoy it, but it does not help others, since they do not understand; and it injures the church, since any visitors hearing it simply say, "These people are mad." But if these people hear a prophet (that is, a preacher or exhorter), then the truth strikes home to their conscience, and they declare, "God is among you indeed." (3) The final principle Paul illustrates in the thirteenth chapter, one of the most beautiful writings in all Christian literature. He calls it the most excellent way, the gift that is above all the other gifts of the Spirit, the spirit of love. For the Corinthians the presence of the Spirit meant the strange utterance and the striking accomplishment. For Paul it meant moral character and life, and these he sums up in the word which Jesus used, love. All your showy gifts, he declares, and all the knowledge of which you are so proud, is worth nothing without this spirit of love. And this love is very different from the spirit you have shown. It is patient and kindly; it has no jealousy or pride; it is modest and humble, full of hope and of faith in men. And when all your tongues and prophecies are done away, this love will last (1 Cor 13).

The last question that Paul takes up is that of the resurrection. He had learned that some among the Corinthians
were casting doubt upon the idea of a resurrection from the
dead. To the Greek mind it seemed absurd to talk of the
body being raised again when it had wasted away in the
earth. Here was the Greek spirit at work again, logical,
critical, speculative, setting up a philosophy of its own in
the place of Christianity. The issue for Paul was not a
matter of one form of doctrine as against another. It was
Christianity itself as a historical fact that was at stake:
was there a living Christ, and had God really come to men
in him? He brings forth three considerations. (1) What
I have preached to you, the Christ who died and rose again,
is the faith of the whole church, of the first disciples and
all. "Whether then it be I or they, so we preach, and so
ye believed" (1 Cor 15. 1-11). (2) We need not be
troubled about the physical body that decays or how it shall
be raised. It is not the natural body that is raised but a
spiritual body, such as it will please God to give (15. 35-
49). (3) Without this hope we have nothing. If there
be no resurrection, then there is no living Christ. And if
there be no living Christ, then our faith is empty. But now
the faith is ours with its glorious hope. "Death is swallowed
up in victory. O death, where is thy victory? O death,
where is thy sting? Thanks be to God, who giveth us the
victory through our Lord Jesus Christ" (15. 12-19, 29-32,
50-58).

Such were the dangers that confronted the early church
from without and within: persecution of enemies, the constant environment of a debased life with which they still
had to associate, the pull of the old habits, the peril of
fanaticism, and the great gulf between the lofty Christian
principles and these folks taken out of the lowest classes of
paganism. Why did not Christianity fail? Because it had
forces greater than all these. Deeper than the jealousy and
strife was the new spirit of brotherhood and love that bound

them together. Stronger than the lure of old evil in the world about or in their own hearts was the purifying and transforming power of the new Spirit. And not the least part of the answer to the question is the leadership of such a man as Paul, whose marvelous religious experience and power was joined to such wisdom in practical leadership.

The question of Second Corinthians We have little knowledge of the later history of the Corinthian church. The second letter, as we have it, is very hard to understand. The first nine chapters are very different from the last four. The former are full of a spirit of kindliness and confidence and suggest a perfect reconciliation between Paul and the church. The last four chapters take us into an atmosphere of strain and strife, where Paul is fighting for his apostleship. It seems probable that in later years, when Paul's writings were collected, two or three letters were joined together here. At that later time men did not care about the history of the church, but simply to have Paul's words.

The four letters Following out this idea, scholars have suggested that we probably have four letters from Paul represented in our two epistles. They would divide them as follows:

1. The first letter: 2 Cor 6. 14 to 7. 1. This is considered a fragment of the first letter that Paul wrote, it being his answer to a question from the church as to their relation to unbelievers as indicated in 1 Cor 5. 9-13. Note how these verses interrupt the order of thought; 7. 2 follows naturally upon 6. 13.

2. The second letter: our First Corinthians. As we have seen, this was written in answer to further questions from the church and because of information that Paul had received from messengers.

3. The third letter: 2 Cor 10 to 13. The Corinthians had not followed Paul's directions. Timothy had failed in his visit. The strife of the parties had continued and Paul's Judaizing enemies had come in and attacked his authority and his apostleship. Even when Paul visited them person-

ally from Ephesus he had met opposition, and from one man at least even insult. This third letter is Paul's defense and assertion of his authority. It is an impassioned appeal, and should be placed beside his letter to the Galatians. He appeals to his labors, exceeding those of all others (11. 16-33). He points to his experiences (12. 1-6). He calls to witness the wonderful work he had done among them (12. 11-13). He denounces his enemies in the sharpest terms (11. 13-15). He declares that he will come a third time to them, and that then he will not spare (13. 1-10).

4.   The fourth letter: 2 Cor 1 to 9, omitting the fragment of six verses marked above as the first letter. It seems that Paul had made his third visit, that his enemies gave way, that the church punished the offender referred to in 1 Cor 5, and the old relations were established. The echo of the past controversies, and the deep feelings they had stirred, may still be heard in these fine chapters; but the letter itself is full of Paul's usual spirit of joy and peace and confidence, with expressions of deep and tender affection. It has also some of his most beautiful expressions concerning his gospel and his ministry: "It is God, that said, Light shall shine out of darkness, who shined in our hearts, to give the light of the knowledge of the glory of God in the face of Jesus Christ" (2 Cor 4. 6). "Now the Lord [that is, Jesus] is the Spirit: and where the Spirit of the Lord is, there is liberty. But we all, with unveiled face beholding as in a mirror the glory of the Lord, are transformed into the same image from glory to glory, even as from the Lord the Spirit" (3. 17, 18). "God was in Christ reconciling the world unto himself" (5. 19). "And he died for all, that they that live should no longer live unto themselves, but unto him who for their sakes died and rose again" (5. 15).

Paul's work at Corinth was not in vain. The Corinthians formed one of the strongest, if not the strongest Pauline church. One of the earliest Christian writings that we have outside the New Testament is a letter written to the Corin-

The later church at Corinth

thians about fifty years after the founding of the church by one Clemens, writing for the church at Rome. Clemens speaks of the church in highest terms: "Who ever dwelt even for a short time among you, and did not find your faith to be as fruitful of virtue as it was firmly established? Who did not admire the sobriety and moderation of your godliness in Christ? And who did not rejoice over your perfect and well-grounded knowledge?" From his references it appears that Paul's name was held in highest esteem and his letters read in the church.

DIRECTIONS FOR READING AND STUDY

As to the position and conduct of women, read 1 Cor 11. 2-16; 14. 33-36.

As to the Lord's Supper and the church fellowship meals, read 1 Cor 11. 17-34.

As to spiritual gifts and the disorders in the church services, read 1 Cor 12, 13, and 14.

As to the resurrection, read 1 Cor 15.

Read the four chapter letter, 2 Cor 10 to 13; select from these chapters all that concerns Paul's life, experience, and person, and write this out in an ordered statement.

Read through the last letter, 2 Cor 1 to 9; select five or six verses aside from those quoted in this chapter, which reflect Paul's conception of his ministry and of the gospel.

CHAPTER XXXVI

PAUL AS PASTOR AND CHURCH ORGANIZER

PAUL was no mere wandering preacher moving from place to place, making a few converts and then passing on. Rather he was a great religious statesman; his aim was to plant Christianity throughout the empire. To this end he moves from province to province: Syria, Cilicia, Galatia, Macedonia, Achaia, Asia. For this reason he enters upon the great cities; we can mark the steps of his work by their names: Damascus, Tarsus, Antioch, Corinth, Ephesus, Rome. For this reason too we find Paul keeping his churches under most careful supervision. Paul is a great pastor and administrator. Acts shows us the preacher; the letters reveal the pastor. They give us a most lifelike picture of Paul's watchful care of his churches and of the constant thought and labor which this involved. Letters are passing back and forth; messengers are being received; one and another of Paul's helpers are sent on special missions; or Paul himself is planning to revisit the old fields. A single church like that at Corinth received at least four letters and three visits from Paul himself, besides sending letters and messengers again and again and being visited by Titus and Timothy.

There is no finer aspect to Paul's character than his pastoral spirit. Here, as so often, we must stop and marvel at the many-sidedness of the man. This great statesman founding an empire, this missionary of restless zeal, this profound thinker whose ideas have shaped the Christian thought of centuries, was at the same time the thoughtful pastor and friend, bearing upon his heart the care of all the little communities that he had established. His glowing words on love are no mere rhetoric (1 Cor 13). This love is the mainspring of his own life. The moving catalog of his hardships and sufferings he ends with these words: "Besides those things that are without, there is that which presseth upon me daily, anxiety for all the churches. Who is weak, and I am not weak? who is caused to stumble, and I burn not?" (2 Cor 11. 28, 29). The same spirit appears in another passage: "For though I was free from all men, I brought myself under bondage to all, that I might gain the more. And to the Jews I became a Jew, that I might gain the Jews; to them that are without law, as without law, . . . that I might gain them that are without law. I am become all things to all men, that I may by all means save some" (1 Cor 9. 19-22). Nothing reveals this spirit better, or shows the real Paul more clearly, than the words in which he bares his heart to the Thessalonians (1 Thess 2. 5-12).

Tact and kindliness

Next to the spirit of love, we must admire Paul's tact and kindliness in his relation to his churches. Paul understood "the gentle art of praising." He knows how effective praise is in the training of men. All his letters begin with words of generous recognition. "I thank my God upon all my remembrance of you," he writes the Philippians, "always in every supplication of mine on behalf of you all making my supplication with joy, for your fellowship in furtherance of the gospel from the first day until now" (Phil 1. 3-5). Even with the Corinthians, despite all he has to correct, he finds ground for such appreciation: "I thank God always concerning you, for the grace of God which was given you in Christ Jesus; that in everything ye were enriched in him, in all utterance and all knowledge; so that ye come behind in no gift" (1 Cor 1. 4-7). The same tact and skill is shown in the way in which he handles the matter of the collection for the poor at Jerusalem (2 Cor 8 and 9). He holds up the Macedonian churches to stir up emulation. He reminds the Corinthians that they had really been the leaders in this and praises their progress in other graces. He appeals

to the example of Jesus, to their love for him, to the praise
he has given them before others. But nowhere does he
rebuke them for their slowness after their first start, or
issue a blunt command.

To this tact and kindliness Paul adds courage and insight. He never draws back from any needed rebuke, Courage and insight
whether the quarrelsomeness of his dear Philippian friends
(Phil 4. 1, 2) or the disorders and immorality of the Corinthians. And yet he is too wise to indulge in mere rebuke.
Like Jesus, he penetrates to the spirit that is back of the
fault and then sets up the principle of the higher life. He
confronts the quarrelsome Philippians with his great appeal:
"Have this mind in you, which was also in Christ Jesus"
(Phil 2. 5-11). Before the immoral Corinthians he holds
up the great spiritual principle: "Your body is a temple of
the Holy Spirit which is in you, and ye are not your own"
(1 Cor 6. 19, 20).

There is one other great service which Paul rendered The church organizer
besides this personal oversight, and that was the organization of his churches. Christianity was more than a new
faith implanted in the hearts of so many men and women.
It was a new fellowship, a society which bound its members
together with the closest ties. And these people were joined
not simply locally in scattered communities; they were one
in a growing brotherhood that stretched throughout the
empire, a brotherhood of such strength that it stood firm
when the storms of later years swept the empire itself from
its foundations. There are three questions to be asked
concerning this work of Paul. How were the local Christian communities organized by him? How were these
scattered communities related to each other? And what
was the relation of the Pauline churches to the other Christian communities, especially the churches under the Jerusalem apostles?

What strikes us first in reading Paul's letters is that so Little about mere organization
little is said about organization or officers. No doubt this

is partly due to the fact that Paul felt that the present age was to last but a short time. The more important reason, however, lay in Paul's thought of the church. The church for him was not a matter of officials and organization; it was a fellowship in the Spirit. It was the Spirit that was the life of the church and that gave it guidance.

Many gifts, one Spirit

This Spirit belonged to all Christians as such. There was no higher or lower among them, for one Spirit filled them all. This same Spirit, however, showed itself in different manner with different people, fitting them for different forms of service. "Now there are diversities of gifts, but the same Spirit. And there are diversities of ministrations, and the same Lord. . . . To one is given through the Spirit the word of wisdom; and to another the word of knowledge, according to the same Spirit; to another faith, in the same Spirit; and to another gifts of healings, in the one Spirit; and to another workings of miracles; and to another prophecy; and to another discernings of spirits; to another divers kinds of tongues; and to another the interpretations of tongues. God hath set some in the church, first apostles, secondly prophets, thirdly teachers, then miracles, then gifts of healings, helps, governments, divers kinds of tongues" (1 Cor 12. 4-10, 28).

Overseers

In this long list we have the various kinds of activities represented in the Corinthian church. The apostles stand first, men specially commissioned to preach the gospel throughout the whole church. The prophets are the inspired preachers. The teachers are those who have the task of instruction, probably explaining the Old Testament in its Christian meaning and applying Christian truths to daily conduct. The speaking with tongues has already been considered. In the midst of this list occurs the word "governments" (1 Cor 12. 28). It probably refers to those who directed the temporal affairs of the little Christian community. Even in the simplest community, some one was needed to provide the place of meeting, to arrange for the care of visiting apostles or prophets or other brethren, to collect and distribute the money for the poor, and attend to similar duties. Stephanas was such a man, of whom Paul writes, "I beseech you, brethren (ye know the house of Stephanas, that it is the first fruits of Achaia, and that they have set themselves to minister unto the saints), that ye also be in subjection unto such, and to every one that helpeth in the work and laboreth" (1 Cor 16. 15, 16). In Cenchreæ it was a woman, Phœbe, who performed this service (Rom 16. 1, 2). In a larger community there would be several such. These are meant by the "overseers" mentioned in Phil 1. 1, translated "bishops" in our version. There is little doubt that in Paul's usage of the terms these are the same as the presbyters, or elders. This work would naturally fall to people of means and liberal spirit, such as those in whose houses the little groups of disciples gathered, or to the older disciples.

If we consider all these passages, certain interesting facts stand out. (1) These officers are for Paul not so much people of authority as people who serve. It is the service, not the authority, that Paul emphasizes with Stephanas. That is, Paul's test here as with every gift is, "To each one is given the manifestation of the Spirit to profit withal." It is the service of the church, and not authority over the church, that Paul is concerned with. He is expressing here simply the principle of Jesus: "If any man would be first, he shall be last of all, and servant of all" (Mark 9. 35). (2) These offices, like all others, are gifts of the Spirit. God helps one man to prophesy, he helps another to serve the church in these practical affairs. (3) These men are not placed above others in the church. In direct contrast with the later thought of the church, these overseers, or bishops, seem to have been placed pretty well down in the list. In Corinth, at least, the church seems to have thought more of the gifts of prophecy and of tongues. Paul finds it necessary here and elsewhere to exhort the church to appre-

Their place and meaning

ciation of the service of these men and to a proper respect for them. It was natural that the people should think more of the spiritual gifts than of these everyday affairs with which the overseers, or bishops, concerned themselves.

Increasing importance

As the church grew the work of these men increased in importance. The supervision of the poor funds, the provision for place of meeting, for the common meals, and other church matters added to their influence. The other gifts were matters of individual endowment and would change; these men formed a permanent body. Other duties would naturally be added, such as the supervision of the worship and matters of church discipline. Meanwhile, as the church at Corinth shows, the gifts of prophecy and of tongues might easily lead to excesses and even fraud. After Paul's day conflict arose between the men who appealed to their inspiration by the Spirit and the regular officials, and the church decided for the officials.

Early democracy

Paul's day was still one of freedom and spontaneity. The life of the local church was democratic. The picture of the worship in the Corinthian church shows that any one might take part as he felt moved by the Spirit. More significant is the fact that when matters are to be decided Paul calls upon the church as a whole. It is to the congregation as a whole that he addresses his letters and arguments and appeals. Nowhere does he ask any officer or body of officials to take any action or pass any decision. Furthermore, Paul himself does not decide for the church. It is true, he is an apostle and these are his churches, the children whom he has begotten in toil and pain. He argues and appeals, he praises and censures, he sometimes makes demands; but he never comes forward simply with command and the assertion of authority. They are a church of God and the Spirit of God is in them. When Paul has a word of Jesus to quote, then that is final (1 Cor 7. 10). He distinguishes carefully between this and his own authority (1 Cor 7. 12, 25, 40). As for the authority of any central church council or other body, that is nowhere so much as suggested. Neither the church at Jerusalem nor the twelve apostles have any right of rule in Paul's churches.

What, then, was the relation between the scattered com- The Spirit and church unity munities? Were they simply so many individual congrega- tions? On the contrary, no man of his generation seems to have had so clear an idea of the unity of the church or laid such stress upon it as Paul. It is the doctrine of the Spirit again which gives the answer. The churches are one in a real sense, not because of officers placed over them or a central authority which unites them, but because they have one spirit which is their life and which unites them in the one body of Christ.

This spirit of unity Paul seeks to further in every possible Paul's interest in unity manner. He knows no Christian life that is not a life in the Christian fellowship. He seeks to promote that fellow- ship in every possible way, and first of all within the single Christian community. His letters abound in exhortations to kindliness and patience and mutual helpfulness and serv- ice, and no man has ever so glorified the spirit of love and fraternal loyalty. He seeks to promote the same spirit among the churches, that they may all be united in one fellowship. His collection for the Jerusalem church is the great evidence of this desire. The space which this occupies in his letters shows how much pains he gave himself in this. And no opposition of the Judaizing brethren from Jerusalem ever made him swerve from this self-assumed task.

The constant travel of Christians was the most important Practical unity, how secured, its value practical means of securing this unity among the scattered brotherhoods. First among these were the twelve and the other apostles. Two of these he found in Ephesus (Rom 16. 7). We know little of the work of the twelve, but it seems that others besides Peter traveled about the church (1 Cor 9. 5). The prophets too went from church to church. But more important still were the travels of disciples of the rank and file. Such were Priscilla and Aquila, whose names we find connected in turn with Pontus, Rome, Corinth, and Ephesus. One of their moves was due to persecution suffered as Jews; the others were presumably for reasons of business. Such traveling and visiting kept alive the sense of brotherhood and of a vital unity. The Christians knew what was happening to their brethren all through the empire. Paul tells the Thessalonians that their faith is known not only in Macedonia and Achaia, but in every place. He informs the Corinthians that the Macedonians know of their first collections for Jerusalem. To the Romans he writes that their "faith is proclaimed throughout the whole world" (Rom 1. 8). By such mutual acquaintance and interest the bond of brotherhood became very definite and very strong. Nothing added more to the power and attractiveness of the new religion than this spirit of fraternity, both in the local church and throughout the empire. The new disciple found himself at once received into a community that was more of a family than a mere organization. On the first day of the week they met for worship in which each might have a part. During the week they sat down at common meals. When one disciple was in need, the love, the sympathy, and the material help of the whole brotherhood were behind him. And he soon realized that the little fellowship of his own city was part of a greater fellowship that embraced the Roman realm. Rome itself began at last to take notice, not so much of Christianity's creed, as of the power of this great fraternity.

DIRECTIONS FOR READING AND STUDY

Note Paul's qualities as a pastor as revealed in 1 Thess 2. 5-12.

Select two good illustrations of Paul's praise of his churches. In what letter does Paul omit this praise from the introduction?

Read 2 Cor 8 and 9 and make a list of the different motives to which Paul here appeals.

Read 1 Cor 12. 4-10, 28; Eph 4. 11, 12; Phil 1. 1; Acts 14. 23. Make a list of the gifts, or offices, mentioned in these passages.

Which of these are represented in the accounts of the Jerusalem church?

What significance, if any, is there in the fact that no two of these lists agree? Does it suggest the absence of fixed forms of church life and organization?

CHAPTER XXXVII

PAUL THE LETTER-WRITER

Importance of the letters   A STUDY of the New Testament shows that about one fourth of its contents are assigned to the apostle Paul. The influence of these writings has been in even greater proportion. The writings of no other Christian man can be set beside those of Paul in this regard. The great leaders of Christian thought, like Augustine and Calvin, have always looked to him. In the great religious movements within the church, like those led by Luther and Wesley, it is Paul's message that has been revived. There is not a city where Paul founded Christianity that could be called a great Christian center to-day; but these letters, directed to these churches, have been a ferment for Christian thought and a guide for Christian life through all these years; nor do they show signs of diminishing power to-day. If the test of inspiration be the power to inspire men, then these writings must be placed among the first of all writings wrought by the Spirit of God.

All due to special occasions   Probably no one dreamed less of such a future for these writings than Paul himself. A distant posterity was farthest from his mind when he wrote. Certainly he had no thought that his letters would ever be included in a new collection of sacred writings to be placed side by side with the Sacred Scriptures of his people. He never thought of his words as being on the same plane with the Old Testament or the words of Jesus. Neither did Paul ever think of his letters as words of literature or treatises on theology. Paul's writings all had a special occasion for their composition in some practical need. They were simply a part of his missionary work. Paul was not theologian and not author; he was

254

just apostle and missionary. These letters are all connected with a definite situation. Now he writes to thank the Philippians for their gifts, or to send his love to the Thessalonians and encourage them in their persecutions. Now it is to answer questions that the Corinthians have sent him, or to call the Galatians back from their errors. Usually, he has more than one purpose. But always there is a definite end, and the letters move on toward this and in earnest and practical fashion.

If we ask why these letters have lived, they themselves will give us the answer. It is not due to any claim that Paul made for them or any theory of inspiration that his churches held about them. It is due to what the letters are in themselves. They are the noblest expression of that Spirit of God which Paul and his disciples believed was working in their midst. It is true that Paul is treating matters that are local and questions that were often temporary. We are not troubled to-day about meats offered to idols, nor are we divided about the question of keeping the Jewish law. But these passing questions were all considered by Paul in the light of great Christian principles. We do not need Paul's discussion as to whether a Christian may eat such meats, but we need his great principle still: Knowledge puffeth up, but love buildeth up. The Jewish law is behind us, but we have not yet caught up with Paul's great truth, that life is a spirit lived out in freedom and not a matter of rule and routine. And as in matters of conduct, so in matters of faith: the varying needs of each one of these little brotherhoods is only another occasion for Paul to set forth in new form the eternal truths of his gospel. Paul himself was not unconscious of what he was offering. He sees the larger company behind those whom he is immediately addressing. He directs this letter not to one church, but to a whole province (2 Cor 1. 1). He arranges to have his letters passed on from church to church, or exchanged among them (Col 4. 16).

Why the letters lived

How
written

Paul's letters were dictated (Rom 16. 22; Gal 6. 11; 1 Cor 16. 21). This may have been due to trouble with his eyes, or to the fact that his hands roughened with work were not adapted to the pen, or simply that he let another write for him while he plied his tent-maker's needle. The habit, in any case, explains some qualities in Paul's style. They have a certain lack of literary finish, but there are a directness and vigor and vividness that more than compensate for this. We hear Paul speaking as we read. His arguments are often dramatic. He sets his opponents before him and questions them. He breaks out in impassioned utterance. Sometimes he begins sentences without completing them, as though he had been interrupted in his dictation. To be fully appreciated, these letters should be read aloud, or recited.

The usual
arrangement

While Paul follows no rule, most of his letters fall naturally into three parts, aside from the salutation. (1) The introductions are used by Paul to establish relations with his readers. They are models of Christian courtesy and tact and skill. Here is the letter to the Romans. Paul is paving the way for a later visit. He begins with an appreciation of their faith, which "is proclaimed throughout the whole world." He tells them how he has long since wished to see them, and has been prevented. He wants to preach his gospel to them also, to "impart some spiritual gift." And then, lest he might seem to assume too much, he hastens to make the service mutual: he is to comfort them and they are to comfort him (Rom 1. 8-15). In these modest, friendly, appreciative words Paul strikes just the right note for the letter to a church upon which he had no claim as founder. (2) The doctrinal part comes second. It is never abstract or general, but always a discussion of Christian truth in relation to the particular needs of a given church. (3) The practical exhortations come last. They form the finest body of ethical teachings and practical maxims to be found in Christian literature. They are Paul's answer to the important questions as to the meaning of the new faith for the relations of daily life.

Though the letters almost all have these three elements of the personal, the doctrinal, and the practical, yet Paul follows no fixed rule in writing. Each letter, indeed, stands by itself and reveals a new aspect of this great man. Some are written to churches which he does not personally know and so are less personal and more objective, as well as more doctrinal: such are Romans, Colossians, and Ephesians. Some are mainly practical and ethical, like First Corinthians. Two are letters of controversy and self-defense—Galatians and what we have called Third Corinthians, that is, 2 Cor 10 to 13. These are full of passionate appeal, of argument and denunciation. And, finally, there are the more intimate personal letters: First Thessalonians, written to the little company of Christians which he had been compelled to leave so suddenly but a few months before; Philippians, the letter of friendship to his most loyal church; and Philemon, the only letter preserved which Paul wrote to a private individual. The last two may be taken for closer study as examples of Paul's art as a letter-writer. *Differences in the letters*

Paul's letter to the Philippians is the great friendship letter of the New Testament. With no church did Paul have so close a relation. Here he had accepted private entertainment from Lydia contrary to his rule. And they formed an exception also in the gifts which they sent him again and again. He had revisited them twice and no doubt had written them as well, but these earlier letters are lost. At the time of this letter Paul had reached Rome as a prisoner. The Philippian friends had learned of his situation and had sent one of their number, Epaphroditus, to bring him money and to help care for him. Epaphroditus had fallen seriously ill at Rome. He was recovered now, but was homesick, and Paul prepares to send him back. He plans also to send Timothy to them a little later, as soon as he knows how his trial is coming out. Meanwhile he *The friendship letter* writes this letter, Paul's love letter some German scholars have called it. He tells them of his affection, of his need, of his appreciation. And yet he is still the faithful missionary and pastor, who tells them frankly of their needs at the same time. We may outline the epistle as follows:

Outline of
Philippians
Personal

1. Introduction and personal items: In my every prayer I thank God for you, remembering your help. May God make your love abound more and more and add to it wisdom. My imprisonment has been really an opportunity. It has given me the chance to preach to all the soldiers of the pretorian guard and it has encouraged others. I do not know what the end of my trial will be, whether life or death. I do not even know which I wish for myself. I should like to go and be with Christ, but I am ready to stay here and serve (1. 1-26).

Exhortation

2. An exhortation: Live worthily of the gospel of Christ, undisturbed by persecutions. And complete my joy by giving up all divisions and jealousies and pride. Instead of such selfish quarrelings, let each show in his life the spirit that Jesus showed. He left his high estate and became a servant of men, though that service led him even to death. That is why God has exalted him and why every knee is to bow before him. Work out your salvation with fear and trembling. Live the pure life despite the sin that is about you (1. 27 to 2. 18).

A message

3. A message: I expect to send Timothy to you in a little while. I am hoping to come to you myself before long. It seemed necessary to send back Epaphroditus now. Honor him for his work (2. 19-30).

Warnings

4. Some warnings: Beware of those Judaizers who teach that you must be circumcised and keep the law. If the law were worth anything, I should have been saved. No one can boast purer Hebrew blood or stricter obedience than I. But when I found Christ, these things were mere refuse to me. Now I have only one purpose—to gain the life that is in him. Like the runner I have only one goal; I press on

to lay hold of that for which Jesus once laid hold of me. Beware also of those who say we are delivered from all law, whose only law is self-indulgence. We are citizens of heaven; we must not follow things of earth (3. 1-21).

5. Further exhortations: Stand fast. Let Euodia and Syntyche agree. Live in joy and in trust, and God's peace shall keep you. Whatever is good, note and follow; and what I have stood for, that do (4. 1-9). **Final exhortations**

6. Thanksgiving: I rejoice in your gift to me; you have not had the chance for some time to send to me. For myself I do not complain; I can do all things in God's strength. You are the only church that has ever thus served me. And all your needs shall be supplied from God's riches as they are in Christ (4. 10-23). **A message of thanks**

The letter to Philemon stands alone in the New Testament. It shows the value placed upon Paul's words from the first that such a letter should have been preserved, for it is purely personal and has no discussion of doctrine or declarations as to moral principles. It is probably from the same period as Philippians. Paul is a prisoner at Rome. As that letter shows us, Paul was free to preach not only to the soldiers of his guard but to any who might visit his rooms. Men called the Rome of that day the sewer into which all the empire emptied its filth. Then, as now, the big city was a better hiding place for the runaway than was the desert. Among Paul's hearers one day was a runaway slave, such a man as might loiter idly on the edge of a Salvation Army street meeting in our time. Some word of Paul's gospel reached this man. He became a disciple. Very naturally, he told his story and confessed his fault. Then it appeared that this slave belonged to an old friend of Paul, one, indeed, who had been converted by the apostle, a certain Philemon who lived in Colossæ, and who was probably won by Paul while the latter was at Ephesus. Philemon was well to do. He not only had servants but was able to entertain. Paul writes asking him to have lodgings ready for him, for he **Letter to Philemon** **A runaway slave** was evidently expecting to be released and to travel to Macedonia and Asia. Philemon was not only a Christian but had been an active helper of Paul. Archippus, to whom Paul twice refers, may have been his son (Col 4. 17). Apphia was probably his wife. The letter suggests a Christian home of the best type.

A unique letter

Under the circumstances Paul writes this brief epistle. This charming letter, playful yet serious, appealing as a friend when he might have demanded as an apostle, honoring the friendship by his confident request, pathetically referring to himself as "being such a one as Paul the aged, and now a prisoner also of Christ Jesus," the next moment punning upon the name of the slave—this letter is not outranked by any letter of friendship in literature, and at the same time throws still further light upon this many-sided man.

The appeal for a slave

"I thank my God always for you," Paul writes, "remembering your faith and your service to the church. I might come with a command; instead I am bringing a request for friendship's sake on behalf of this convert of mine, your slave Useful (that is, Onesimus). So far, indeed, he has been Useless to you; now, however, he is useful to both you and me. I should have liked to keep him, but I wanted your goodness to be free and not of compulsion. And this may be why he left you as a slave—that he might return as a brother. If you count me a partner, receive him as you would myself. If you have lost anything by him, charge that to my account. I know you will do even more than I ask. Prepare a lodging for me, for I hope to come to you soon."

DIRECTIONS FOR READING AND STUDY

Read and compare the introductions to First Corinthians, Colossians, and First Thessalonians. What is common to them? Why should that of First Thessalonians be longer?

Read carefully Philippians and note its intimate and personal character. Make a list of the passages in which Paul sets forth his personal faith and purpose. Write an account of Paul's relations with the Philippians on the basis of Acts 16. 11-40; 2 Cor 11. 8, 9; and Philippians. Select eight or ten passages from Philippians which reveal his personal regard for this church.

Read Philemon. Does Paul expect Philemon to set Onesimus free? What bearing has the Christian religion had upon the problem of slavery?

CHAPTER XXXVIII

PAUL THE PRISONER

The close THE seven great years of Paul's work were drawing to a close. Long before this Paul had fixed his eye upon Rome and the West. It was about this time that he wrote to Rome and told them of his plans: He had fully preached the gospel from Jerusalem and round about even to Illyricum. Now he was planning for Rome and Spain. To Rome, indeed, Paul was to come, but only as a prisoner.

Last visit to Macedonia and Corinth Luke tells us that Paul left Ephesus after the tumult which Demetrius had stirred up. His missionary work in these regions was finished, but there were two reasons why he could not go at once to Rome. In the first place, he wished to revisit the churches in Macedonia and Greece. It was about this time that affairs at Corinth had reached a crisis. Timothy's visit had been followed by Paul's. Paul had written again (2 Cor 10 to 13). He had sent Titus and was anxiously awaiting word from him. Now he prepares to go to Corinth himself by way of Macedonia. Troas is his first stop, but he has not heard from Titus and so goes on to Macedonia to meet him. There he hears good news at last and writes his last letter to the Corinthians (2 Cor 1 to 9). The letter did not reach Corinth very much before Paul.

The collection Paul's second reason for delay was the collection that he was making for the Jerusalem church. This was one reason for his visit to the Macedonian churches. With all his insistence upon his independent authority as an apostle and the truth of his gospel, Paul never once surrendered his ideal of the church as one body of Christ and one fellowship. Under his direction the churches had been gathering these offerings for some time. Now the money was all to be brought together and taken to Jerusalem. The big offering was to be Paul's proof of loyalty, and Paul looked forward to it as the means that should cement the Gentile churches and the Jewish churches together. And yet Paul was not wholly sure of the issue. He knew the element in Judæa that had sought almost everywhere to block his work, that had attacked him by every possible means both in his gospel and in his person. These men would oppose him when he returned; how would the church as a whole stand? He knew too that he would be in danger from the Jews. How deeply concerned he was is seen from his letter to the Romans written at this time: "I beseech you, brethren, by our Lord Jesus Christ, and by the love of the Spirit, that ye strive together with me in your prayers to God for me; that I may be delivered from them that are disobedient in Judæa, and that my ministration which I have for Jerusalem may be acceptable to the saints" (Rom 15. 30, 31).

Paul had intended to sail directly from Corinth to Syria. The company A plot laid against him by the Jews compelled him to leave earlier than he intended. He had apparently fixed the date when he wished to arrive in Jerusalem, and now he uses the extra time at his disposal and returns through Macedonia. At Troas he is joined by those who are to accompany him to Jerusalem, and the group that starts for Jerusalem numbers at least nine. Luke was probably with Paul, and in addition there were seven representatives of the churches whose offerings were being taken. From Macedonia there came Sopater of the Berean church, and Aristarchus and Secundus of Thessalonica. Gaius of Derbe and Timothy of Lystra represented Galatia, while from Ephesus there came Tychicus and Trophimus (Acts 20. 4). These men were to be the living testimony to Paul's work which he could show to the Judæan Christians. But Paul's chief desire for their presence was that he might prevent all possible criticism as if he were profiting by these collections. These men were themselves to bear the funds. They were witnesses to Paul's disinterestedness.

Warnings of danger

As the journey to Jerusalem proceeded, Paul received repeated warnings of the danger to which he was exposing himself. Everywhere that Paul had labored his attitude against the law was known by the Jews. It was not a case of Judaizing Christians, but of the hostility of the Jews themselves. Paul had asserted that Jesus was the end of the law to those that believed. His mission had everywhere been in competition with the Jews. They had seen him lead away their best adherents and sympathizers among the Gentiles, the people who had given the synagogue standing and support. They were his bitter enemies. Restrained elsewhere by Roman authority, would they not here in Judæa wreak their vengeance upon him? Some of these men would be at Jerusalem, for the city always held large numbers of Jews of the dispersion returning for a longer or shorter stay. In any case, his work had long since been reported. Characteristic was the warning which Paul received when the party landed at Cæsarea. Here a Christian prophet from Judæa took Paul's girdle and bound the hands and feet of the apostle. It was his symbolic way of declaring the captivity that awaited Paul.

Meetings by the way

The story of this journey as given by Luke shows also that Paul's deep affection for his churches was returned by them. We read of the meeting at Troas, from which place the company started, and how Paul spoke till midnight and then till morning. It was their last time together and they found it hard to part. At Miletus he meets the Ephesian elders. "And they all wept sore, and fell on Paul's neck and kissed him." At Cæsarea they pleaded with Paul not to go on to Jerusalem. His answer shows the mutual affection: "What do ye, weeping and breaking my heart?" But all this could not move Paul from his purpose: "I am ready not to be bound only, but also to die at Jerusalem for the name of the Lord Jesus."

From Cæsarea Paul went up to Jerusalem, his little With the Jerusalem church company being increased by some members of the Cæsarean church and by one Mnason, a native of Cyprus and an early convert, who was to be Paul's host in the city. To the assembled church Paul reported his work. He had not seen them for three years. He told them of the establishment of the work in Ephesus, of its spread throughout Asia, and of its continued development in Macedonia and Achaia. Then his associates handed over their gifts. It must have been a large offering. It had been two years in the gathering. Much of it had come out of the poverty of its donors. The apostle, who would not take a penny for himself, had given constant care and effort to this. Would the Jerusalem church accept it in like spirit? Would the gift with his story of the work make them feel that his churches were really one with them? And would they overlook their scruples on the one hand and overrule the little group that had been making him so much trouble by their attack?

Paul was doomed to a measure of disappointment. They The request of the church received him kindly and they praised God for the progress of the gospel, but they could not forget their concern for the law. James, the brother of Jesus, seems now to have become the recognized head of the church. No one else is mentioned beside him. It is a striking fact that the two leaders who now faced each other, James and Paul, were neither of them of the twelve. James stood for reverence for the law. The church had become more conservative. The Jewish leaders now saw no cause for persecution. Many thousands of the Jews had joined the new faith, which did not mean to them any separation from the old. And so the leaders made a request of Paul. What troubled them was not the reception of the Gentiles, nor even that Paul had not required the law of these. "The report is around," they said, "that you tell the Jews that are converted that they do not need to keep the law. We have something to propose that will show that you keep the law as a faithful Jew. Here are four poor men who have just completed their term of the Nazirite vow. Do you now join them, shaving your head and paying for their offerings." Paul has been criticised for entering upon this plan. He had certainly not been walking "orderly, keeping the law." And yet this accommodation to the prejudices or weakness of others was in line with his practice all these years; he had been a Jew to the Jews, and to those without the law as without law.

The tumult in the temple It was this decision, however, that brought on the crisis. Following the old law in this case (Num 6. 13-20), Paul had gone into the temple. Certain Jews, who had known him in Ephesus, had seen him a few days before in company with Trophimus of Ephesus, a Gentile and one of those who had come with the offering. Evidently, they had recognized Trophimus also. Now, seeing Paul in the temple, they concluded at once that he had taken Trophimus also into the sacred place. It was an offense punishable by death, and they would have inflicted the penalty at the time had not the Roman guards rescued him. It was not simply hatred of Paul that was involved here. Most of the mob probably knew no more than that some one was charged with desecrating the holy place. But that was enough. The sanctity of the temple was more to them than life, and the experience of the last years with the Romans had kept their fear of desecration alive and their passions aflame. The captain himself could make nothing of the tumult. Only one man was cool; that was Paul. It was not the first time he had faced an angry mob, or even death. He was not thinking of safety now. He asked of the Roman captain permission to speak, and before the angry mob he undertook a defense of his life and his faith.

Addresses to people and Sanhedrin It speaks eloquently of the courage and commanding power of the man that he could win a hearing at such a

moment, but one need not wonder that his words did not
help his case with the excited crowd, or that they did not
listen long. They heard him while he told of his conversion. It was not the reference to Jesus as the Messiah that
brought the speech to an abrupt end, but the mention of
the Gentiles. At that all the excitement broke loose again.
The captain, seeing that no light was to be gotten here,
carried off his prisoner and prepared to scourge him. It
was the brutal method used in some cases to secure a confession. With a Roman citizen, however, it was never
permitted, and Paul's declaration of his citizenship stopped
the proceeding. The captain made a final attempt to get
light upon the matter the next day by calling a meeting
of the Sanhedrin and setting Paul before it. This too ended
in a tumult. They were in no mood to give such a man
a hearing, and Paul soon saw this. Luke reports that he
divided the enemy by his declaration that the trouble arose
because he believed in the resurrection, thus setting the
Pharisees of the council against the Sadducees; the ground
for such a declaration would be his preaching of the resurrection of Christ.

In this way Paul's imprisonment began. It was per- *In prison*
haps the most trying period of his life. Dangers Paul
did not fear, nor even the threat of death. He had long
since given himself up to his Master for life or death.
It was from prison that he wrote, "For me to live is
Christ, and to die is gain." But this was neither life nor
death. Beyond the sea were his churches still needing
his guidance. To the west were fields that he had planned
to reach. But he must remain for five years a prisoner,
held by the bitterness of his foes on the one hand, on the
other by the weakness, selfishness, or indifference of his
judges.

A plot against Paul's life, which his nephew brought to *Before Felix*
the captain, caused his immediate transference out of Jewish territory to the safer confines of Cæsarea, the official

residence of the procurator. Thus Paul retraced his journey of a few days before. The procurator at this time was Antonius Felix, a man who had once been a slave. Cruel and incompetent, the historian Tacitus declares that he kept the temper of a slave while wielding kingly power. Here Paul's enemies from Jerusalem, led by the high priest Ananias, brought their charges against him, having engaged as advocate one Tertullus, apparently a Roman. They charged him with stirring up insurrection, with profaning the temple, and with being a ringleader of the new sect of the Nazarenes. Paul admits the last, though denying any wrong in it. The two first he challenges them to prove. Felix simply postponed the case. He held Paul, however, as a prisoner with a double motive, Luke says—desiring to placate the Jews, with whom he had had trouble enough, and hoping for money from Paul. Apparently, he was not unkindly disposed toward Paul. The latter had considerable liberty, his friends were permitted access to him, and Felix himself called Paul to him more than once.

Before Festus After two years Felix was succeeded by Festus. The first visit which the latter made in his province was to Jerusalem. This was his chief city and the chief problem of his administration. To the demand of the Jews that Paul should be sent to Jerusalem for trial, Festus replied that he would try him in Cæsarea. So there was another trial at Cæsarea which established as little against Paul as the first. Instead, however, of setting Paul free, Festus now proposed to agree to the request of the Jews and take the case to Jerusalem. And so at length Paul made use of his privilege as a Roman citizen and demanded that he be tried at the imperial court at Rome.

Speeches before Felix and Agrippa Luke tells us of two other speeches that Paul made during this time. The first was before Felix and his wife Drusilla, the other was after the coming of Festus on the occasion of a visit from Agrippa and his sister Bernice. Drusilla, Agrippa, and Bernice were children of Agrippa I and great-grandchildren of Herod the Great, the last two especially of notorious immorality. It was significant of Paul that he should be willing to speak to them, that he should reason of "righteousness, and self-control, and judgment to come," and that his defense before Agrippa should become a sermon on repentance and faith in Christ. Paul could forget his own safety and everything else in the one passion of his life—the preaching of his gospel.

The journey to Rome was destined to prove a long one. We have a vivid and detailed account of it, which gives us a better picture of sea travel in that day than any other writing that has come down to us. We owe this to the fact that Luke was Paul's companion. Aristarchus of Thessalonica was also with him. There were a number of other prisoners, which presupposes a good company of soldiers by way of guard. The centurion in charge was named Julius. It was not possible to get a ship direct to Italy, and so a coasting vessel was taken which would take them to a port from which they could transship for the longer voyage. This latter was done at Myra, a port on the southern coast of Asia Minor, where they found one of the many vessels that plied between Alexandria and Italy and with the usual cargo of wheat. It must have been a large vessel for that day, as it had in addition to its cargo two hundred and seventy-six people on board. *The voyage to Rome*

From the first the voyagers suffered through untoward winds. They beat along the coast until they reached Cnidus, from which place they made for the island of Crete, reaching at last the harbor Fair Havens. The season was advanced and Paul urged that they winter here. But the harbor hardly deserved its good name, and it was decided to make for Phœnix, further along the coast. They had not gotten far from Fair Havens when a storm from the northeast swept down upon them. The task of the seaman, without compass or steam, was hard enough in that day in any case. Now they were swept on day after day with- *Storm and shipwreck* out sun or stars even to let them know their course. The ship's company seems to have reached a stage of despair where they would not even eat. In the night Paul had one of those visions which marked more than one turning point in his life. He told them of the vision the next day, how the angel of the God "whose I am, whom also I serve," had told him to be without fear, that he was to reach Rome and that the company should also be saved. The shipwreck itself is described with vivid detail by Luke. In these moments of peril the commanding figure was not captain of vessel or of soldiers, but the prisoner, Paul. He prevented the sailors from leaving the boat, and it was consideration for him that caused the centurion to check the plan of the soldiers, who wanted to kill the prisoners lest they escape.

Malta to Rome

It was the island of Malta, south of Sicily, where they landed. The winter season was spent here, three months in all, after which they shipped for Rome in another Alexandrian vessel which had wintered in the island. At the port of Puteoli they left the boat, the remaining journey of about one hundred and thirty miles being made on foot. They found disciples at Puteoli and the kindly centurion permitted a stay of a week. Meanwhile word was sent on to Rome. Some of the Roman brethren came out forty miles on the road, as far as the Market of Appius, to meet Paul, and still others were waiting him at The Three Taverns, a little farther on.

Prisoner at Rome

For two years Paul was kept a prisoner in Rome awaiting his trial. They were not idle years. We know of at least four letters dispatched during this time—those to the Philippians, the Colossians, the Ephesians, and Philemon. A large measure of freedom was allowed him. A soldier, a member of the pretorian guard, was with him constantly, but Paul lived in his own rented quarters and could receive visitors as he wished. Of these there must have been a great number. Luke tells of the conference that

Paul had with the leaders of the Roman Jews. The Christians would naturally come to him, and, in addition, Paul used his opportunity to preach the gospel to guard and visitor and whomever he might reach.

The church at Rome is one of the signs of the rapid spread of Christianity. We have no knowledge at all as to how it was founded. Its membership was largely Gentile. It was from this church that Priscilla and Aquila had come, and Paul had probably met other members before this. His letter to this church had been written from Corinth some three years before. There must have been a considerable Christian community even then. Paul's own labors added to that number. The constant change of his guard enabled him to give his message to the Pretorian troopers (Phil 1. 13). Onesimus must have been a type of others from the lower classes that he won. The message spread even to the servants of the imperial household (Phil 4. 22), and Paul's courage emboldened other disciples to a more active ministry (Phil 1. 14). Nero's persecution a little later shows that the church had become strong enough to attract public attention. *The church at Rome*

The close of Paul's life is hidden from us. Of one thing we are certain, though it is not told us in the New Testament itself: Paul suffered martyrdom at Rome. This we learn from the letter written by Clement of Rome, a message of the Roman church to that at Corinth dating from the last years of the first century. But what the events were connected with his death we do not know. There are two theories which scholars hold. Some consider that Paul was acquitted at his first trial, that he carried out his plan of a visit to Spain and to his old churches in the East, and suffered martyrdom at Rome after a second imprisonment and trial. Others hold that Paul was condemned and suffered death at the close of this first imprisonment. *The close*

Connected with this question is the problem of what

are called the pastoral epistles—First and Second Timothy and Titus. Many scholars hold that these letters do not come from Paul's hand in the form in which we now have them. Their argument is that the conditions reflected here indicate a later period in the life of the church, and that the language and the form of teaching do not correspond with Paul's other writings. Many of these scholars, however, hold that we have here portions of Pauline letters to which other matter was later added.

In any case, these letters do not describe for us the actual close of Paul's life or determine the time. That remains hidden from us. We do know, however, that which concerns us most. That is the character and life and achievement of this man. He has drawn for us his own picture in those letters in which he pours out his soul. Luke has portrayed him for us in such scenes as those of his voyage to Rome: the kindliness, the helpfulness, the faith, the courage, the mastery of himself and of others, the natural leadership that made him inevitably the first in any company whether of ship and soldiery or of his own disciples. And most eloquent of all, we have the witness of what he wrought, a Christianity made conscious of its independence and its power, of its world-saving message and its world-embracing fellowship, and established on firm foundations throughout the empire.

DIRECTIONS FOR READING AND STUDY

Read Acts 20 to 28.

Make a list of Paul's addresses as reported in these chapters, giving for each the place, the occasion, and the persons present.

Trace upon the map Paul's journey from Troas to Jerusalem and from Cæsarea to Rome. Make a list of the places stopped at upon each journey.

CHAPTER XXXIX

PAUL THE MAN

PAUL is the best-known man of his age and one of the The many, sided Paul most interesting men of all ages. He had the greatness of a man with a single purpose. His life was given to only one end—he was a missionary of the gospel of Christ. But to that one task he brought a marvelous diversity of gifts, and it is this many-sided character of the man that makes his personality so interesting. Preacher, teacher, theologian, missionary, church founder and organizer, poet, logician, mystic, moralist: he was all these and more.

I. We may study him first as man of mind, the great The man of mind thinker and teacher of Christianity. He had the keenness and mental alertness which belonged to the Greek, joined to the spiritual vision of a Hebrew prophet. His first great deed was to interpret Christianity. It is one of the The interpreter of Christianity strange facts of history, that this man who never knew Jesus personally saw the meaning of Christianity as none of the twelve did. He awoke Christianity to self-consciousness. He gave her a message and a voice. He interpreted Christianity to the mind of the Roman world. He showed them Jesus not simply as Jewish Messiah but as the Saviour of the world. Christianity was first of all a great experience to him, but he had also the power to interpret that experience.

But this man of mind was not a man of mere logic. Life, and not mere logic With all his keen intellect, he was not concerned with theory or speculation. His concern is with truth as it bears upon life. His great conceptions of religion all root in his own experience. And Paul was a psychologist; he knew how to read the meaning of what his own soul had

NEW TESTAMENT HISTORY

gone through and to draw its lesson for others. To this was joined his experience as missionary, preaching to others the truth that had made his own life. Sometimes, it is true, we hear the Jewish rabbi speaking in his arguments, but the great truths for which Paul stands had this vital source. It is this that has made Paul so great an influence in the Christian thinking of the centuries.

Will and character

II. We may consider Paul, in the second place, as a man of will. It is his strength of will that first of all impresses us. We feel that the personality of Paul is one of the great forces of history. This man had a clear purpose and an indomitable spirit back of it. The will of the man is seen in the greatness of that purpose. It is no less than the establishment of the new faith throughout the empire, and that by his own effort. No hardship, no toil, no danger holds him back. Beaten by Jews and by Romans, stoned, shipwrecked, imprisoned, fighting against illness, against the doubt of fellow Christians and the relentless hostility of the Jews, he moves on unswerving and with undaunted will. He had no organization back of him. To disarm criticism he supported himself by labor. And for this great work he had but a few years at command. Yet he carried out his plan in the main. His great campaign might well be placed beside that of Alexander or Napoleon, while in the permanency of his work he surpassed them both.

The leader

The study of Paul's life shows his strength as a leader at every stage. He is everywhere the master of men and of circumstances. In rude Galatia or cultured Athens, before the Philippian prætors or the angry mob of his countrymen, facing royal judges or in the presence of imminent death, he is always the same, unmoved by danger, unawed by authority. His independence is the more remarkable when we think of his position. His only credentials as he began his mission were his story of a vision. That was enough, however, for him. That vision and call lie back of his independence and his courage. He was an apostle "not from men, neither through man, but through Jesus Christ and God the Father." For that reason there was a deep humility joined to his independence. It is not his own strength but God's grace. "When I am weak, then am I strong," he said. "I can do all things in him that strengtheneth me." "We have this treasure in earthen vessels," he declares, "that the exceeding greatness of the power may be of God."

On its moral side, then, this strength of will is simply an absolute devotion to high purpose. His life has but one meaning—the preaching of the gospel. "One thing I do," he says. He has no other interest in life. We hear nothing of his family, except a casual reference to his nephew. He seems to have cut the ties of home as of nation. He has no friends except his fellow workers. "I count all things to be loss for the excellency of the knowledge of Christ Jesus my Lord. I press on, if so be that I may lay hold on that for which also I was laid hold on by Christ Jesus. For me to live is Christ." **Devotion**

III. And yet this man of keen intellect and inflexible will was also a man of heart. Indeed, it is here that we find the real Paul. In depth of feeling and range of religious experience and emotion it would be hard to find another to place beside him. Not that Paul is a flawless saint. His passionate feeling seems sometimes to have led him to a severity of judgment and a denunciation of his opponents which do not accord with his own teachings; and he may have erred on the other side in indulgence toward those he loved. If there be such defects, they are only incident to his strength. And in this emotional side of his nature Paul's strength largely lay. He was no man of cold calculation and shrewd prudence. He loved with the tenderness of a woman and the devotion of a mother, and he could fight with all the passion of his nature. It made him the most loved and the most hated of men. He **The man of heart** bound his friends to him for life, and he gained enemies who pursued him to his death.

Paul's religious experience is the first and deepest element in this side of his nature. Out of this experience came his message and his restless activity. Paul will never be understood so long as men think of him as primarily a great theologian or church organizer. He was first of all a Christian. Doctrine and institution are always simply forms in which life expresses itself. The life itself is greater than all its forms. Paul did an incalculable service to the church in expounding the meaning of the new faith, but we must always distinguish between these doctrines of Paul and the living faith which they seek to set forth. His letters show us again and again how all his thought and service flow out of this inner spring. "For the love of Christ constraineth us; because we thus judge, that one died for all, therefore all died; and he died for all, that they that live should no longer live unto themselves, but unto him who for their sakes died and rose again. Wherefore if any man is in Christ, he is a new creature: the old things are passed away; behold, they are become new. We are ambassadors therefore on behalf of Christ, as though God were entreating by us" (2 Cor 5. 14, 15, 17, 20).

With this depth of Paul's religious life there went an equally wonderful range. What he preached to men he himself had passed through. His speech may have lacked polish, but we do not wonder that it was with power. He himself was the sinner, like those to whom he spoke. Out of his own heart he spoke of the burden of guilt and the bondage of evil: "The good which I would I do not: but the evil which I would not, that I practice. Wretched man that I am! who shall deliver me out of the body of this death?" (Rom 7. 19, 24). The deliverance which he proclaimed he himself rejoiced in: "I thank God through Jesus Christ our Lord. There is therefore now no condemnation to them that are in Christ Jesus. For the law

of the Spirit of life in Christ Jesus made me free from the
law of sin and death" (Rom 7. 25; 8. 1, 2). When Paul
speaks of the new life that is given to the believer, of
the new spirit that lives in man's heart and makes a new
creature, this too is out of his own experience: "It is no
longer I that live, but Christ liveth in me: and that life
which I now live in the flesh I live in faith, the faith which
is in the Son of God, who loved me, and gave himself up
for me" (Gal 2. 20).

Besides the religious life, Paul's emotional nature may **Patriot**
be studied in his relations with men. Whichever way we
turn, we note his depth and power of feeling. He loved
his nation. This man who made Christianity universal,
who made it his life task to carry the gospel to the Gentiles, who was held as a traitor to his race for so doing,
was, in fact, the most ardent of patriots. He declares that
devotion in the most solemn words: "I say the truth in
Christ, I lie not, my conscience bearing witness with me
in the Holy Spirit, that I have great sorrow and unceas-
ing pain in my heart. For I could wish that I myself were
anathema from Christ for my brethren's sake, my kinsmen
according to the flesh." And with all his work for the
Gentiles, Israel yet remained for him a nation by herself: "Whose is the adoption, and the glory, and the cov-
enants, and the giving of the law, and the services of God,
and the promises, whose are the fathers, and of whom is
Christ as concerning the flesh" (Rom 9. 1-5).

Here, as elsewhere, Paul is a man of contrasts. His **Contrasts**
depth of feeling could show itself in fierce indignation and
bitter denunciation, overwhelming his antagonists. "Beware of the dogs, beware of the evil workers, beware of
the concision." "Such men are false apostles, deceitful
workers, fashioning themselves into apostles of Christ. And
no marvel; for even Satan fashioneth himself into an angel
of light." "If any man preacheth unto you any gospel other
than that which ye received, let him be anathema" (Phil

3. 2; 2 Cor 11. 13, 14; Gal 1. 9). Yet side by side with this he shows the greatest tenderness and patience and personal humility. In the very midst of the rebuke of his Galatians he calls out to them, "My little children, of whom I am again in travail until Christ be formed in you" (Gal 4. 19). In the same section in which he writes so sternly to the Corinthians, he declares: "I seek not yours, but you: for the children ought not to lay up for the parents, but the parents for the children. And I will most gladly spend and be spent for your souls" (2 Cor 12. 14, 15). Nor could anything suggest a more beautiful relation than the passage addressed to the Thessalonians where he speaks of his relation to them as being like that of a father with his sons, a nurse with her own children (1 Thess 2. 7-12). Equally attractive is the picture of his unselfish devotion, that weighs him down at the thought of their sorrow, and makes him forget his own troubles in the joy over their welfare: "Ye are our glory and our joy. Now we live, if ye stand fast in the Lord. For what thanksgiving can we render again unto God for you, for all the joy wherewith we joy for your sakes before our God?" (1 Thess 2. 20; 3. 8, 9).

The friend   Of Paul's tact and thoughtfulness and courtesy, mention has already been made. We have yet to speak of him as a friend. The traditional view pictures Paul as a stern and lonely man, pursuing his solitary task as he traverses land and sea. Nothing could be farther from the truth. He could stand alone when needed, but that was the measure of his courage and devotion, not the sign of his desire. One is surprised in counting up the names of his associates and friends that appear in his letters. They are here by the score. They appear first of all as the companions of his journeys and assistants in the supervision of his churches. Barnabas is the first of these whom we meet. Titus, Timothy, Silas, and Luke are others. Paul looked for young men especially to help him in this work.

They were not subordinate officials to the great apostle. They were his friends, his sons, and he pours the wealth of his affection upon them. How considerate he was of them is shown, for example, by his thoughtful treatment of Epaphroditus (Phil 2. 25-30), and by the letter with which he sent Onesimus back to Philemon. And the letters show how this strong man craved the sympathy and companionship of these coworkers. In addition to these were the associates whom Paul found in every place where he remained any length of time for work. Of these too there is a long list: Lydia of Philippi, whose guest Paul was; Priscilla and Aquila, of tried devotion; Stephanas, Paul's first convert in Corinth; Philemon, convert and friend and prospective host; Rufus of Ephesus, whose mother was a mother to Paul; and with them many others.

It is not hard to understand how Paul drew such people to himself. It was because the love which was central in his teaching was also central in his life. No one quality of the Christian life was so emphasized by Paul in his writings. For him it was the supreme element in the Christian character. At the same time it was the very life of the Christian fellowship. It was not organization and officers that made the church with Paul, but the indwelling spirit of Christ which was love. So love is "the bond of perfectness" for the individual as for the church. "Put on therefore, as God's elect, holy and beloved, a heart of compassion, kindness, lowliness, meekness, long-suffering; forbearing one other, and forgiving each other, if any have a complaint against any; even as the Lord forgave you, so also do ye; and above all these things put on love, which is the bond of perfectness" (Col 3. 12-14). Such fine exhortations come again and again, finding their fitting climax in the great chapter on love (1 Cor 13). And all this teaching is but the expression of the apostle's own spirit.

Love in life and teaching

Such was Paul the man, the most human figure, next to Jesus, that the New Testament or the whole Bible brings

A human saint

to us. It is this intensely human character that has made him so attractive to those who have really come to know him. In his words echo the deepest needs of the human heart, its cries and its despair. He shows us our aspirations too, man aiming at the highest. He makes us feel that we too may die to sin and live to God and so run as to attain. And yet there is no cold flawlessness about him. This man of deep passions and broad sympathies and human weakness and need lived upon our own earth. "Not that I have already attained, or am already made perfect: but I press on."

DIRECTIONS FOR READING AND STUDY

Find in Romans or Galatians a chapter which illustrates Paul's power of thought or argument.

Select three scenes from Acts which illustrate Paul's self-possession or strength of will.

Name two letters which show Paul as a friend, and mark several appropriate passages in each.

Make a list of friends and associates of Paul as given in Romans, First Corinthians, Philippians, and Colossians. Note that these names occur regularly in the closing chapter.

From the book of Acts find the names of one or more companions of Paul for each of his missionary journeys, his last trip to Jerusalem, and his voyage to Rome.

PART V
THE LATER CHURCH

CHAPTER XL

THE FAITH OF THE LATER CHURCH

THE years between 60 and 70 mark a turning point in the life of the first-century church. The three greatest leaders were taken away, Paul, Peter, and James. Paul suffered martyrdom in Rome between 64 and 68. Peter met the same fate, according to ancient tradition, at about the same time. James, the brother of Jesus, had been put to death by the Jews just before this, despite his faithful observance of the law. The Jewish war began in 66, and in 70 the city was taken and the temple destroyed; thus the link was broken which had joined the Gentile churches to the mother church at Jerusalem.

When we move past this year 70 into the second genera- tion of the Christian Church, we find no books to guide us like the Gospels and the Acts and the letters of Paul. We have a good many New Testament writings from this period, but they do not give us history. We do not know the leaders who took the place of Paul and Peter and James. The author of the letter to the Hebrews must have been a man of learning and ability, but not even his name is preserved. The many workers mentioned by Paul all pass from our sight. We hear no more of the gifted and eloquent Apollos. On this account the treatment of this period in a New Testament history may be brief. There is a second reason for brevity. Deeply interesting though the story would be if we could read it, it could not compare in importance with that already considered. The vital history of the beginnings of Christianity is forever linked to two names. The first is its Founder, whose message and spirit and life and death were the creative fact that brought forth all that followed. The second is the great apostle, who saw the meaning of that life, who proclaimed the good news throughout the world, who set forth for all time the great truths of the faith, and who established the fellowship which we call the church.

Three subjects

While we have little in the way of historical events, there are other matters of interest to consider in this closing period of New Testament history. These will be taken up under three heads: the faith of the later church, the life of the later church, and its writings.

Jewish Christianity

In taking up the faith of this second period, we turn first to Jewish Christianity. The great controversy within the church of the first generation was that concerning the law: Was the Christian bound to keep the Jewish law? In the second generation this question entirely disappears. One reason for this was the great and steady advance of Gentile Christianity. The other was the lessening importance of Jewish Christianity. The Jerusalem Christians left the city before its capture and so escaped destruction; by so doing they gained, however, the bitter enmity of their fellow Jews and had to suffer a great deal of persecution.

James: Christianity as a new law

The epistle of James gives us a good picture of the faith of these Jewish Christians. It was formerly held by many scholars that this letter was an attack upon Paul and his doctrine that man was saved by faith: "Ye see that by works a man is justified, and not only by faith" (James 2. 24). But there is no thought of opposition to Paul here. The writer has not really grasped Paul's great doctrine. To him religion is essentially a law according to which men are to live. True, it is a higher law; he calls it "the perfect law, the law of liberty." But Paul's great words of grace and the Spirit are wanting here. Religion is something to be done. Within these limits it is full of fine maxims and practical truth, with many echoes of the Sermon on the Mount and other gospel passages; but it is not the good news that conquered the world. In later years this idea

of Christianity as a new law gained an increasing place in the whole church. At this time it seems especially characteristic of Jewish Christianity.

Turning to the Gentile churches, the first question is, Did Paul's influence last? Did the great doctrines for which he stood remain as the church's conception of Christianity? In large measure, yes. (1) Christianity remained the universal religion for which Paul fought, not a mere variety of the Jewish faith. (2) Paul established once for all the conception of Christ as being on the one hand truly man, born of woman, and on the other the eternal Son of God and the Saviour of men. (3) Paul's doctrine of the Spirit as ethical remained. He saved Christianity from the danger of fanaticism by insisting that the Spirit was the Spirit of Christ, that it meant love and righteousness and not emotional ecstasy and physical excitement. (4) The Gentile church remained as Paul had founded it; Christianity stood, not simply for individual faith and experience, but for an ordered and organized fellowship, embracing all believers in its unity, and joined in a life of mutual love and service.

Gentile Christianity Paul's influence

And yet the church did not keep the level of Paul's highest thought. That was Paul's answer to the question, How shall a man be saved? Paul said: (1) A man is saved by God's grace. God is the Father. He is not a master whose help men must first earn. He is not an unwilling power, whom men must compel by sacrifice. He is the God of mercy, loving the world, giving his Son, forgiving the sins of men. "God was in Christ, reconciling the world unto himself." (2) A man is saved through faith; we might say trust instead. God's part is graciously to give; man's part is with love and trust to receive. Religion is not a proud and self-satisfied doing. It is a loving, self-surrendering trust of the soul. (3) All this means a new spirit in a man. It is the man made over, the "new creation," Paul says; but not made over from without by effort

Paul's central teaching

or knowledge. The new spirit which makes the man is God's Spirit in him. You may also call it the spirit of Christ. That is what it is: the love and purity and obedience and kindness which were the spirit of Jesus upon earth. (4) And this spirit which is God's gift, is our task at the same time. The Christian must live it out day by day: "If we live by the Spirit, by the Spirit let us also walk." It means obedience, but not to an outer rule. The law is within us, and the life is one of freedom.

The lower level In three respects the church moved down to a lower level: (1) Faith instead of being a personal trust came to be a belief in the doctrines of the church. Faith as a personal deed gives place to "the faith," which is a sum of doctrines. First Timothy shows the beginnings of this. (2) There appear, as has been noted in James, the beginners of a new legalism. It is not a falling back into the Jewish law, but it is an overemphasis upon Christianity as a new law, and a failure to see clearly that the right doing must spring from an inner spirit. (3) The freedom of the spirit gives place more and more to the authority of the church as an external and legal institution, whose officers are to rule and govern in all things. In the period which we are studying only the beginnings of this movement are apparent. In part it was inevitable. Indeed, Paul himself helped prepare the way. The church had to move forward on these three lines: to define its faith in creeds, to emphasize rules of conduct and require obedience, and to perfect and establish its organization. Paul himself, however, was not lost from the church. Though the church fell below his standards, yet he remained as a leaven within her life, even in the Roman Catholic Church. His religion of the spirit has always been a protest against the overemphasis of creed and rules and organization, and has broken forth successfully again and again in the great reformation movements.

Hebrews The New Testament contains two monuments which wit-

ness to the abiding influence of Paul in this period. The
first is the writing called "The Epistle to the Hebrews."
The title, which is not a part of the book itself, is hardly
correct. It is a treatise rather than an epistle, and it was
probably for Christians in general rather than for Jewish
Christians. It was not written by Paul, but it shows his
spirit and influence. Christianity is set forth as the world-
religion, existing from the beginning. Judaism was simply
its stage of preparation; after the prophets comes the Son.
And all the ceremony of Judaism is only the symbol of the
spiritual and eternal which is in the Son. Christianity is
the religion of redemption, and Christ is the final sacrifice
which puts an end to all others. Paul wrote merely letters;
this is a literary and theological product, but it has not the
freshness or life or power that Paul's letters possess.

Far greater than the letter to the Hebrews is the group of **Johannine writings**
writings which includes the Gospel and the three epistles
of John. These four writings belong together, and they too
bear eloquent witness to Paul's influence. Ancient tradition
ascribes them to the apostle John. Many scholars think
that while they represent the tradition of John's teaching,
the writings themselves were composed by one of his disciples, or by another John than the apostle. We know but
little of John's life. One tradition states that he suffered
early death as martyr like his brother James. The more
common tradition holds that he spent his last years in
Ephesus, beloved by all and of great influence; that he
wrote the Gospel and epistles at Ephesus and the Revelation
while in exile at Patmos; and that he died an aged man at
the close of the century.

Why was the Gospel of John written? For twenty or **The fourth Gospel: purpose and character**
thirty years the church had had three accounts of the words
and deeds of Jesus, our present synoptic Gospels. Though
the fourth Gospel gives us mainly incidents from Jerusalem,
instead of from Galilee, it does not add enough to the knowledge of Jesus' life to have been written simply as a supple-

ment to the other three. The author himself gives us his purpose. Out of the many wonders which Jesus wrought he has selected certain "signs"; and "these are written, that ye may believe that Jesus is the Christ, the Son of God; and that believing ye may have life in his name" (John 20. 30, 31). This is the double purpose—to set forth Christ and to show the life that men have through him. As we read this Gospel carefully we see that it is quite a different work from the synoptics. It is still in the form of a story of Jesus' words and deeds; but it is far more of a sermon than a biography. Each sign or saying of Jesus is like a text from which John preaches his sermon and proclaims his faith in Christ and his conception of Christ. For that reason he does not concern himself to distinguish sharply between his own words and those of Jesus. This can be seen, for example, in the third chapter, where one cannot separate definitely the words of Jesus, of John the Baptist, and of the evangelist. The Gospel is a great confession of faith, a great sermon like one of Paul's. The words and deeds of Jesus are like a window, through which the evangelist seeks to show us his vision of the eternal. He is neither biographer nor theologian; he is a preacher. Whatever he writes he sets forth that we "may believe," and that we "may have life in his name."

The occasion for the Gospel
The faith that is here set forth is nothing more than Paul's teaching concerning Christ, but there was special reason for its declaration at this time. Almost all the later writings of the New Testament show us that with the last years of the first century many different forms of doctrine arose which claimed to be Christian teaching, but which differed from the earlier faith of the church. There were teachers who declared that because Jesus was divine he could not have suffered and died. These men made his life a mere show, and so denied the actual humanity of our Lord. This was called docetism. There were others, on the contrary, especially among the Jewish Christians, who

denied his divinity. He was to them simply a great teacher, a prophet as others before him.

Over against these two, John sets forth his great message in his epistles and Gospel. Jesus is for him the eternal Son of God who was with the Father from the beginning, and who has come to be the life and light of men. This is the message of his prologue (1. 1-18). This is his theme, whether he reports the words of Jesus or tells of his deeds. Thus the deeds which he reports are "signs." They are not thought of primarily as deeds of mercy wrought to help men, but as signs of the divine power and majesty of Jesus. There are seven such deeds, finding their climax in the raising of Lazarus. Similarly, the words of Jesus which he reports do not concern themselves so much with the duties of men, as in the sermon on the mount, but are, rather, a setting forth of the same theme of Jesus' own person and its meaning. In lofty speech and beautiful figure this is proclaimed again and again: "I am the living bread"; "Whosoever drinketh of the water that I shall give him shall never thirst"; "I am the light of the world"; "I am the door of the sheep"; "I am the good shepherd"; "I am the resurrection, and the life"; "I am the way, the truth, and the life"; "I am the true vine"; "I have overcome the world." At the same time John sets forth just as clearly the real humanity of Jesus. He shows him to us hungry and weary as he rests by the well, weeping by the grave of his friend, struggling in the garden, suffering and dying upon the cross. All this is but Paul's great message of the Christ "who was born of the seed of David according to the flesh, who was declared to be the Son of God with power, according to the spirit of holiness, by the resurrection from the dead" (Rom 1. 3, 4). But while Paul finds his theme in the resurrection and the living Christ, John turns back to the Jesus who walked on earth, and shows us his glory in that earthly life. That was John's great service, to join together the Jesus of Nazareth whom the

Jesus as eternal Son of God and as true man

Gospels set forth with the divine Christ whom Paul proclaimed, and to declare that these two were one.

John's other purpose was, as he states it, to set forth Christ so that men believing might have life. As we read these pages, we feel the same spirit that speaks to us in Paul's letters: this man writes of that which is his own life, and which he wishes us to have. Chapters 14 to 17 set this truth forth especially. No passages in the New Testament have been more cherished by Christians or have had a deeper influence. That is why this Gospel has been called from early days "the spiritual Gospel." It has been the great book of personal devotion. One need only begin with the fourteenth chapter and mark the familiar passages to realize the place that this book has filled: "Let not your heart be troubled. In my Father's house are many mansions. I am the way, and the truth, and the life; no one cometh unto the Father, but by me. Whatsoever ye shall ask in my name, that will I do. I will pray the Father, and he will give you another Comforter, even the Spirit of truth. If a man love me, he will keep my word: and my Father will love him, and we will come unto him, and make our abode with him. Peace I leave with you; my peace I give unto you: not as the world giveth, give I unto you. I am the vine, ye are the branches: he that abideth in me, and I in him, the same beareth much fruit." And in all this, the question is not whether John is giving us the literal speech of Jesus, any more than Paul in his preaching. The message of John is essentially that of Paul, and the real question is whether they are setting forth the mind and spirit of Jesus. That such a book should come from the closing years of the first century is testimony, not only to the abiding influence of Paul's teaching, but even more to the abiding power of the spirit of Christ.

DIRECTIONS FOR READING AND STUDY

Mention six dangers or faults against which the readers are warned in James. Here as elsewhere cite chapter and verse.

Make a list of the passages in First Timothy which refer to doctrine or teaching or the faith.

Read the prologue of the fourth Gospel, John 1. 1-18, and make a list of John's various statements about Christ.

Make a list of the seven miracles, or "signs," recorded in John, beginning with the marriage feast at Cana and ending with the raising of Lazarus.

Make a list of at least eight of the sayings of Jesus concerning himself, such as "I am the living bread," as found in John.

From John 14 to 17 select ten or more individual verses or passages which set forth the ideal of the life of the disciple in relation to God or Christ.

CHAPTER XLI

THE LIFE OF THE LATER CHURCH

WE have no such writings as Paul's letters to the Corinthians to give us the picture of the life of the church in the last part of the century. Some facts we may gather from the late epistles and the book of Revelation. Aside from these we have only the writings outside the New Testament which come from the early part of the second century. Two questions call for answer: (1) What was the inner life of the church? (2) What was its place in the empire?

There are two words around which we may gather the story of these last years of the first century and opening decades of the second. They are bishops and martyrs. The first word suggests the change that took place in the inner life and organization of the church. The different steps of this change we cannot tell, but we do know the marked contrast between the church of 150 and the churches at the time of Paul's death. The churches of Paul had only the simplest organization, as we have seen. Men talked of service, not of authority. This service was of many kinds, but it was all the gift of one Spirit. The inspired prophets and teachers of the Word stood first. But the Spirit belonged to the whole church. A century later all this is changed. We find three offices in each church—bishop, elders, and deacons; but the authority is in the hands of the one man, the bishop. He is no longer the simple overseer. He has taken up within himself the various duties that at first belonged to different men or to the church as a whole. The practical affairs of the church are still in his hands, but these are of greatly increased importance. He has charge of the worship. Men are beginning to feel that the inspiration is no longer in the church as a whole, or in certain prophets and teachers, but in the bishop. The simple, unregulated worship is gone. There is no longer any chance for the irregularities that appeared at Corinth. The bishop presides at the service, which follows a regular order, and it is he that preaches. He has charge of the church discipline. The apostles and eyewitnesses are gone. He represents the tradition of what the true faith is. Instead of a group of overseers or elders, this bishop stands alone. Just what the position of the elders is we do not know. The deacons are simply the officers who carry out the bishop's directions. As yet, however, the bishop is not placed over any district or diocese; he simply directs the life of the one congregation.

All this took place very gradually. We do not know the steps, but we know some of the causes. (1) There was the decline of faith in immediate inspiration. The first outburst of enthusiasm gradually passed. There was a lessening number of prophets who felt themselves directly inspired. (2) There was found to be a need of regulating these inspired leaders. Paul had met this at Corinth. The inspiration did not always seem to be genuine or profitable to the church. All manner of things could be said and done and the claim made that they were inspired. Early writings show that some of these "prophets" made their inspiration a means of living off the church, and rules had to be adopted to guard against this. The conflict between the "officials" and the "inspired" leaders lasted through the second century, but long before the end the regularly chosen officials had taken the first place. (3) The same need of order appeared in other respects. As the church grew, its practical interests increased in importance and number. Matters of discipline, of the care of the poor, of protection in times of persecution, of representation of the local church so that it could act with other churches, and other like interests demanded responsible men in per-

Some causes

manent position. With the second century questions of doctrine became ever more important. Over against all manner of vagaries and strange teachings these officials stood as the custodians and guarantors of the faith handed down from the apostles.

The case of Diotrephes

It has been suggested by some that the third epistle of John is a witness of the early stage of the controversy between the regular official, or bishop, and the inspired prophets. Diotrephes seems to have been such an official who refused to welcome the traveling prophets when they came: "Neither doth he himself receive the brethren, and them that would he forbiddeth and casteth them out of the church" (3 John 10). He is censured as a church boss, "who loveth to have the preeminence." Gaius, to whom the letter is addressed, is bidden to receive the "brethren and strangers," and to set them forward on their journey. All these changes occurred gradually, and they were in process during the last years of the first century.

Moral life; charity

In its moral life the church seems to have made steady advance. Roman critics of Christianity like Pliny admit the moral excellence of the life of its followers. The writings of this time all show the constant emphasis upon the pure and true life. The charity of the church was especially rich and beautiful. And yet there was wisdom in its exercise. The traveling brother was cared for two or three days. If he did not pass on then, he was to work; but the church was to help him find employment. The church had followed in the line of Paul's teaching: "If any will not work, neither let him eat" (2 Thess 3. 10). No doubt the industry and sobriety which the church inculcated helped to make it an economic force in the empire.

Public worship

The regular worship of the church was on the first day of the week. Though more and more under the direct leadership of one official, it was still a very simple service. Lessons were read from the prophets of the Old Testament. New Testament writings were not yet placed by the side of this as Sacred Scripture, but there is little doubt that in different parts of the church letters of Paul or portions of gospel story were read, the latter being called the "memoirs of the apostles." In earlier days the prophets and other inspired leaders would speak; later this fell to the officials. The church had inherited the psalms from the synagogue and used these in her service. To these she added Christian hymns. It is perhaps a portion of one of these that we have in 1 Tim 3. 16:

> He who was manifested in the flesh,
>   Justified in the spirit,
>   Seen of angels,
> Preached among the nations,
>   Believed on in the world,
>   Received up in glory.

The Lord's Supper was celebrated in the morning. The regular church supper, known as the love feast, or *agape,* had been separated from the former and was held in the evening.

From the close of this period, that is, about the middle of the second century, dates the first formal creed of the church so far as known, probably originating in Rome. It was used by the candidate for baptism. The earliest baptism was with the simple words, "in the name of Jesus." Later the baptism was "in the name of the Father and of the Son and of the Holy Spirit." This trinitarian formula was now expanded into a creed which still moved about the three persons of the Trinity. "I believe in God the Father almighty; and in Christ Jesus his only begotten Son, our Lord; born of the Holy Spirit and the Virgin Mary, crucified under Pontius Pilate and buried, arising on the third day from the dead, seated on the right hand of God, whence he cometh to judge the living and the dead. And I believe in the Holy Spirit, the holy church, the forgiveness of sins, the resurrection of the flesh." Like everything else at this

The "Apostles' Creed"

time, this creed was referred back to the apostles and so was called the Apostles' Creed.

Lord's Day and Sabbath

The first day of the week was regularly used for worship, and this may have been the case from the first. Its Christian name was Lord's Day (Rev 1. 10). It was never called the Sabbath day, and was never by the early Christians identified with the latter. Paul had classed the Sabbath days with other Jewish customs made obsolete by the gospel (Col 2. 16, 17; Gal 4. 9, 10). As Sunday was not the Sabbath day, the Christians did not refrain from labor upon it. It was first of all a day of worship and gladness. Gradually it came to be a day of rest. But it was centuries before any one thought of confounding the Christian Lord's Day with the Jewish Sabbath, or of applying the fourth commandment to the former.

Martyr beginnings under Nero

The other word about which the history of this period may be centered is that of martyr. It is the time of beginning persecutions on the part of the state. The word "martyr" means simply "witness," and the martyr was one who gave witness to his faith at peril or at cost of his life. It was Nero that began this persecution. The great conflagration at Rome occurred in the year 64. Rightly or wrongly, the popular mind charged Nero with the deed. Nor were the people satisfied even when he began to reimburse those that had suffered loss and to rebuild the city in splendid manner. They wanted some one to suffer for the crime. Nero picked upon the Christians for this purpose. They were poor, they were disliked. The people were ready to see them suffer, especially as their death was made a public sport; and Nero diverted attention from himself.

Continued hostility

This of itself was simply an episode, but it seems that what Nero began in this special manner became a more or less settled attitude of hostility to the Christians on the part of the state. We are not sure of the date of the later writings of the New Testament, but Peter, large portions of

First Timothy, James, and Revelation all come within this time, and all of these refer to persecutions.

Almost exactly a century after the burning of Rome, Pliny was sent by the emperor Trajan to be governor of Bithynia and Pontus in Asia Minor. There he found that the Christian religion had spread very widely, not simply in the cities where it was always strongest, but in villages and country also. The temples were being deserted, and trades that depended upon the temple patronage were being interfered with, such as the sale of fodder for animals kept for sacrifice. Pliny writes to inquire just how he is to proceed against the Christians, and whether he has been taking the right course. He does not ask whether he should proceed against them, but simply how; and the whole correspondence, which has been preserved for us, suggests that the hostile attitude of the state toward the Christians was a recognized policy. Evidence from Pliny

Why should the empire have persecuted the Christians? It was not religious intolerance, for the empire welcomed and adopted all manner of faiths from all lands. It was not the crimes of the Christians. Whenever serious investigation was made, as by Pliny, the popular charges were seen to be unfounded. The real reason was political, with popular hatred pushing on the officers of the state. The one thing upon which Rome insisted was the unity of the empire and absolute reverence for her laws and order. With these interests Christianity seemed to interfere. Reasons for Roman hostility

And first with the principle of unity. The first fault of the Christians was that they stood for a unity which was not that of the empire. It was the unity of their faith, their brotherhood, of the kingdom of God. The Romans wanted no other bond of unity than that of the empire. With religious societies and religious meetings there was no interference. But other associations were most carefully watched. Benefit clubs among the poor, such as those with burial funds, were about the only associations tolerated, and Opposition to Christian fellowship and organization these were strictly controlled. It was the fear of anything like a common political association among the people which countries like Russia and Turkey show in our own day. The Christians kept the laws of the empire. They planned no insurrection. The church was no political organization. And yet the government discerned rightly that here was a force that in its final spirit was opposed to the spirit of autocracy that belonged to Rome. Nevertheless the church in the end might have saved the empire, if her help had been called upon soon enough. Rome relied upon an external and autocratic power to hold the empire. That was not enough. It was the decay of the people that caused her doom, and the church might have changed that decay into life.

The emperor cult

Later on the refusal of the Christians to worship the emperor was a charge brought against them. But this too was looked upon as political and not religious. The worship of the emperor was simply one part of the plan to assert and secure the political unity of the empire. This emperor cult is referred to in Rev 13 as the worship of the beast.

Opposition and prejudices

Back of this principle of the state there lay the strong prejudice of the people which was shared by officers and emperors as well. The prejudice took many forms. (1) There was the opposition, such as Paul met at Ephesus, of tradesmen whose business suffered by the spread of Christianity with its hostility to pagan worship and to the practice of vice. Then, as now, there were large profits joined to such practices, and we need only think of the hostility shown to-day by those who make profit from commercialized vice in saloon and gambling den and brothel. (2) There was no doubt personal opposition from those whose families had been divided, who saw believers separating from fathers and mothers and brothers and sisters because of the new faith. Enemies could only explain this strange power over converts by charging sorcery and magic. (3) There were unfounded charges that were raised against

the Christians for centuries. The Lord's Supper, with its
wine used as symbol of blood, was made the occasion for
the story that Christians killed little children and drank
their blood, just as the charge of ritual murder against the
Jews still persists in Russia to-day. Profligacy was charged
because of the secret meetings at which both sexes were
present. (4) More than anything else, it was the inflexible
attitude of the Christians about certain matters that angered
the people and brought the severe condemnation of even
men like Pliny and later on the emperor Marcus Aurelius.
Aside from Judaism, Christianity represented here something wholly new in religion, for which even Marcus
Aurelius had no comprehension. For the Romans religion
was a matter of social custom and convention. Its forms
could be changed or added to at will. To add a new form
or a new god might be very wise and safe. It might even
be well to erect an altar to an "unknown god," lest one
should have been overlooked. In any case, there was no
possible harm in such conformity. For the Christians religion was a principle of conscience and a supreme loyalty
to one God: "We must obey God rather than men." To
others the attitude of the Christians seemed nothing short
of willful perversity and wicked obstinacy. Especially did
this appear when they were brought up for trial. Often all
that was asked was to pour out a little wine before a shrine
of the emperor, or to deny the Name with which they were
called, the name of Christ. Such refusal angered officials
as well as people. To the former it seemed highly
dangerous: it was the spirit of insubordination which in an
individual might not be serious, but in a great and growing
fellowship meant danger to the empire.

For this reason, as we learn from Pliny's letters, it was
thought enough to convict a man of being a Christian, even
though no special crimes were charged against him. Over
against this, the Christian leaders of the second century
pleaded that they might be convicted upon the proof of

The crime
of being a
Christian

crime, not by the charges of prejudice. Their position is nobly voiced by a word of Justin Martyr that has come down from the middle of this century: "It is our maxim that we can suffer harm from none, unless we be convicted as doers of evil, or proved to be wicked. You may slay us, indeed, but you cannot hurt us. But, lest any should say that this is a senseless and rash assertion, I entreat that the charges against us may be examined; and if they be substantiated, let us be punished as is right." He pleads that "neither by prejudice nor desire of popularity from the superstitious, nor by any unthinking impulse of zeal, nor by that evil report which has so long kept possession of your minds, you may be urged to give a decision against yourselves."

Apocalypses and their character

The book of Revelation is a writing born out of this situation of persecution and danger. It may be studied either as an apocalypse of the future, giving us prediction of what is to be, or as a book of religion written to strengthen faith and give comfort. All apocalypses have this double character. They come out of times of great persecution and danger. Their purpose is to encourage the faithful lest they fall away. The method of these books is that of visions. The writers are prophets who see. They use pictures and symbols constantly. These pictures are not original with the individual writer. They are more or less the common language of such productions.

The meaning of Revelation

While we cannot interpret with certainty all the symbols of the book, its general meaning on the apocalyptic side is clear. It sets forth the story of the future in pictures. Rome has been persecuting the Christians. Her time is now fulfilled. She is the Babylon that is to be destroyed. The world is hopelessly evil. Salvation is to come not by the growth and spread of the Christian faith, but by a great catastrophe which is to destroy the present world. Then the New Jerusalem is to be let down out of heaven. In it the saints are to be gathered together and God is to dwell with them in the city of light.

All this apocalypticism represents something taken over from the Jewish church of which Christianity was gradually ridding itself. More and more the church saw that the world was to be changed and the kingdom was to come by gradual moral and spiritual conquest, and for this reason many opposed the reception of this book into the New Testament.

But all this must not hide from us the real message of the work. That lies in its practical purpose which is apparent all the way through. The book was probably written about 95, in the reign of Domitian, but it reflects the conditions of Nero's persecution as well. The disciples are in danger. They are facing the demand that they should worship the beast, that is, the image of the emperor, or else be put to death (Rev 13. 15). The writer sets before them the end that is near at hand. He brings a message of warning: the Lord is coming as a thief in the night; let his followers cleanse themselves from all evil, for he will give to each one according to his works. But above all he writes for encouragement, that he may help believers to remain faithful.

The words of warning are found especially in the messages to the seven churches of Asia Minor to which the writing is addressed. These opening chapters give us a picture of the church life of the time. On the whole, the picture is encouraging. Three dangers are in these warnings. There was the danger of simple indifference, the loss of spiritual life: "Thou hast a name that thou livest, and art dead" (3. 1). "I know thy works, that thou art neither cold nor hot" (3. 15). There was the danger of sinful laxness, such as appeared at Corinth, joining in the old idol feasts and pagan practices. This is probably what is meant by the reference to the Nicolaitans (2. 6), to Balaam (2. 14, 15), and to "the woman Jezebel" (2. 20). Such faithlessness is called fornication, after the manner of the Old Testament prophets. The third danger was that of apostasy. It is significant of the higher moral life of the churches that the references are not to common immoralities.

Three causes of encouragement

The dominant note, however, is that of encouragement. Let the disciples be faithful, first of all, because of the sure reward. "To him that overcometh, to him will I give to eat of the tree of life, which is in the paradise of God." "Be thou faithful unto death, and I will give thee the crown of life" (2. 7, 10). In varied phrase there is set forth again and again the reward for "him that overcometh." The second cause for encouragement for the persecuted Christians is the coming overthrow of Rome and the powers of evil. Rome is "Babylon the Great," "the woman drunken with the blood of the saints," "the great city, which reigneth over the kings of the earth" (17. 5, 6, 18). But her hour is come. The kings of the earth and the merchants who shared in her wealth shall look on and mourn her destruction and her torment. Not so the saints: "Rejoice over her, thou heaven and ye saints, and ye apostles, and ye prophets; for God hath judged your judgment upon her" (18. 9-20). The final cause for encouragement is the vision of the glory that awaits the saints, the new heaven and new earth that are to come when the old is destroyed. "And I saw the holy city, new Jerusalem, coming down out of heaven from God, made ready as a bride adorned for her husband. And I heard a great voice out of the throne saying, Behold, the tabernacle of God is with men, and he shall dwell with them, and they shall be his peoples, and God himself shall be with them, and be their God" (21. 1-4).

The faith of the book

The real message of the book lies not in the visions of destruction nor in other prophecies of things to come. Neither do we find it in the elaborate pictures of the new Jerusalem, with its equal length and breadth and height. Rather it is in that great faith which breathes through all Messianic and apocalyptic hope from the Old Testament prophets on: No forces of evil can stand out against the power of God. Whatever the oppression and the burden now, God and good and righteousness shall rule in the earth.

The persecution of the Christians continued intermittently long after this period. The actual number of the martyred was not so large. There were probably fewer Christians that lost their lives in any one persecution than there were Chinese Christians who suffered at the hands of the Boxers or Armenian believers at the hands of the Turks in these last years. But the danger was an always present one, though active persecution came and went; and it was held over the Christians by the all-embracing power of the great empire. *Extent of persecution*

More important than the actual number slain was the effect upon the life of the church. In times of active persecution not a few fell away. The church as a whole proved steadfast, and the noble example of loyal martyrs was of the deepest influence. Men remembered such words as those of Polycarp, who suffered in 166: "Fourscore and six years have I served him, and he has done me no wrong. How, then, can I speak evil of my King, who saved me?" Through all these years Christianity spread steadily. It entered the army. From the cities it spread to village and country. It began with the lowest ranks, but it reached some of wealth and high station. There is good reason to hold that Flavius Clemens, consul and cousin of the emperor, who was executed by Domitian, suffered that fate for being a Christian, as was also his wife Flavia Domitilla. "We are but of yesterday," writes Tertullian proudly a century or so later, "and yet we already fill your cities, islands, camps, your palace, senate, and forum. We have left you only your temples." *Effects*   *Spread of Christianity*

DIRECTIONS FOR READING AND STUDY

Look carefully through James, First Peter, and Heb 10 to 12, finding in each of these one or more references to persecution of the Christians. Note especially Heb 11. It is not a theological study of faith, but has a practical purpose. What is this?

Read Rev 1 to 3. Make a list of some things commended and some criticized in these churches, giving references. Make a list of the passages containing the word "overcometh," and note the different rewards promised.

Read Rev 7. 9-17 and 14. 1-5. Note that these passages reflect the impression made upon the church by the death of the martyrs, and offer encouragement by the picture of their reward.

Read Rev 18 as to the fall of Rome. Compare Isa 14. 3-20 and the lament over the fall of Babylon.

Read Rev 21. 1 to 22. 5 for the description of the New Jerusalem. Note the effort that is made to picture this to the eye.

CHAPTER XLII

THE MAKING OF THE NEW TESTAMENT

I<small>F</small> the church at the time of Paul's death be compared Two great changes with the church of the year 200, two great changes will be noted. The first of these has just been discussed. It is the change from the simple brotherhood to the ecclesiastical institution, from the free guidance of the Spirit and its democracy to the single bishop in each church with his supreme authority. The second change came with the making of a Christian Scripture, our own New Testament. The church of the year 50 had its gospel, but it was not a writing or a book. The church of the year 200 had its collection of sacred writings which it placed by the side of the Old Testament.

No other deed of the early church was so important as The New Testament as the great gift from the early church this. We cannot conceive the history of Christianity without these Christian writings. Nor can we overestimate what the treasure is that has been thus bequeathed to us. We need only think of two of its parts—the Gospels and Paul. The great fact of Christianity is Christ. It is not some doctrine about him, nor some institution developed by his followers. The great creative fact from which all else sprang is the life and spirit and teaching of Jesus. That is what the Gospels bring us. They simply set Jesus before us, and let him walk and speak and work his great deeds. Next to him stands Paul, not the creator but the matchless interpreter. No one experienced the meaning of the new faith in such fullness and depth as he; no one set it forth with such clearness and power. Every religious movement undergoes change. It develops creeds and ceremonies and institutions, and it has need of these. But often the life itself dies beneath the weight of all this, or else its spirit is radically changed. Christianity has not escaped this danger, but it has always had its New Testament, the writings that set forth the great creative source in Jesus and the first and greatest interpretation in Paul. And so it has always kept the means for its own reformation.

Dangers

The gaining of the New Testament as a fixed collection of sacred writings was not without its danger as well, as history has shown. There was the danger that men should worship the letter of these writings and lose the spirit which they were meant to preserve. There was the danger of the idea of the sacredness of the letter, a theory that was taken from Judaism. There was the possibility that the book and its words might take the place of the Christ and his gospel as Paul stood for them. But the making of the New Testament, in any case, was inevitable, and we have simply to ask how it came about. Here, again, we must go beyond the apostolic age into the second century in order to understand what the first century had begun.

Two questions

There are two distinct questions to be considered: First, How did these writings come to be composed? Second, How did the church come to regard these writings as sacred, to form them into a collection, and to set them by the side of the Old Testament?

The gospel at first not written

It was the living word that counted in the early church and not the writing. Jesus himself neither wrote nor ordered the writing of his sayings. When he sent his disciples forth it was to preach. They were to win men by the living word. They needed no authority of book. They had simply to bear the good news to men. It was the same with Paul as with the first disciples, and it remained the same for the first century and longer. It was a practical necessity that caused men to take the pen, and the writing was distinctly secondary to the spoken word. How this came about with Paul has already been seen. The apostle could not always be present with the various churches. Sometimes he sent special messengers. Often he wrote to them to say what he would otherwise have spoken face to face.

The story of the writing of the Gospels is largely hidden from us. What Luke tells us in his opening verses is very interesting. He says that many had undertaken to write the gospel story before him. He indicates that these, like himself, were not eyewitnesses, but had to depend upon what had been handed down by those who were, and he seems to imply that he had used all these accounts as well as other material to make a complete and ordered story. What these earliest accounts were we do not know. They probably precede all of our Gospels except, possibly, Mark. We have one ancient tradition coming indirectly from a church father named Papias, and dating about a century after Jesus' death. Papias says: "Matthew composed the oracles [or sayings] in the Hebrew language, and each one interpreted them as he could." He also tells us that Mark wrote down accurately, though not in order, everything that Peter related of the things said or done by Christ. In addition to this, scholars have carefully compared the Gospels themselves to gain what light they could. They have found evidence that at least two of these Gospels, Matthew and Luke, have used earlier writings, and not simply as sources, but by incorporating their materials with very little change. One of these sources was Mark's Gospel itself. Another seems to have been a collection of the sayings of Jesus.

With these suggestions we can outline the probable story of the forming of our present gospel accounts, dividing this into three stages:

1. The oral period came first. The disciples who had known Jesus told the story of his life and death in preaching to others, and repeated his teachings for the instruction and guidance of believers. Repeated over and over again, the parables of Jesus, his pointed sayings, and stories like those of his healings, would come to have fixed forms. There was no thought of writing and for two reasons: first,

The beginnings

The oral period

because the church would naturally prefer the living voice of one who had seen and heard Jesus; and, second, because all were expecting the speedy return of Christ and so had no thought of writings to preserve his words for the future. This may have lasted for years, but the need of writings soon appeared. The church was spreading rapidly. There were not enough of these eyewitnesses to go around. As the years passed too they began to diminish by death. What was more natural than to secure in writing brief collections of the sayings of Jesus, or stories of his deeds and particularly of his death? Before this individual believers had probably written down for their own use sayings or stories heard from a Peter, a John, or another first disciple.

The first writings

2. Thus we have the period of the first writings. One of these was the collection of sayings of which Papias speaks, made by Matthew or by some disciple upon the basis of Matthew's teaching. Another was the simple story of Jesus' deeds as we have it in the Gospel of Mark, written probably by John Mark, with Peter as his sponsor. Other and briefer collections of sayings and accounts of incidents were made, but we have no individual knowledge of them.

Completed Gospels

3. As a third stage we have our present completed Gospels. It should be remembered that none of these gives in itself the name of the author. The names at the head of these writings in our English Bibles are simply the tradition of the church. Here, again, we can only speak of probabilities. Mark is probably the oldest Gospel and substantially the same as the story just referred to. Matthew comes next, bearing this name because it contains the collection of sayings which came from the apostle. The compiler, however, used not only this collection, but large portions of Mark, and other materials as well. Luke also used these two sources, the sayings and Mark. He had other sources, however, in addition, as he indicates, and from these he gets such stories as those of Dives and Lazarus, the good Samaritan, and the prodigal son, which

he alone gives. These three Gospels, in the order named, were probably written in the years between 50 and 90, such a source as Matthew's collection of sayings being still earlier.

It is quite probable that the other New Testament writings all had some special occasion for their composition, just as the letters of Paul. Revelation was written to strengthen the Christians against persecutions. First John was directed against particular heresies which it attacks specifically. The fourth Gospel had a similar practical and immediate purpose.

But the story of how these writings were composed does not answer our second and main question: How did the church come to make a special collection of them, to include these and no others, and to set them on a level with the Old Testament as sacred writings? Nothing was farther than this from the minds of the writers. The early church had two authorities. The first was the Old Testament, especially the prophets, which it interpreted from the Christian point of view. The Old Testament was the Bible of the early church, and for over a hundred years it was its only Bible. This alone was read in its worship as Sacred Scripture. To it the appeal was made in argument as we see from Paul. The second authority was the words of Jesus. This too was final, and stood even above the Old Testament. Nothing shows more the complete mastery that Jesus had over his disciples than this fact. These Jews, brought up from childhood to reverence the law and the prophets as the absolute and final word of God, yet retained and accepted the word of Jesus when he set himself above this and declared, "But I say unto you." Neither Paul nor any of the evangelists thought of putting their words as final authority for the church by the side of the Old Testament or the words of Jesus. *What was final authority in the early church: Old Testament and Jesus?*

In a sense too the word about Jesus, the gospel, or good news, was authority. This was what they believed, the faith that made the Christians one. But this authority belongs to the gospel as a living word, not to any writing as *The gospel message as authority*

such that brings it, whether the story according to Mark or
the sermon according to Paul as given in his letters. For
a century and more this remains true. The early writers are
very careful to quote the exact words of the Old Testament.
Not so with the writings of the New Testament. Here it
is the thought that counts, not the words. It is not these
writings that they hold sacred, but the gospel in these
writings. "I delivered unto you first of all," Paul says, "that
which I received" (1 Cor 15. 3). These men were anxious
to hand down the message that they had received, the pure
gospel, and the writings were a help to this, but they had
not made a Bible of the writings.

Authority and inspiration   All this does not mean that the writers did not feel that
they were inspired, that they were moved by the Spirit of
God. They felt this just as truly as did the teachers and
prophets at Corinth of whom we have studied. That faith
was universal in the early church. Nor did it cease with
our writings. Clement, who writes about 95 for the Roman
church to the church at Corinth, makes the same kind of
claim that the writer of Revelation makes (22. 18, 19).
But neither of these men would have put their writings on
a level with the Old Testament. Such a declaration as
that of 1 Tim 3. 15-17 refers plainly to the Old Testament,
the sacred writings which Timothy had studied from his
youth. We see the same distinction in First Corinthians.
Paul feels that he has the Spirit of God, but he distinguishes
carefully between the Old Testament to which he appeals,
the words of Jesus, and his own judgment (1 Cor 7. 10, 12,
25, 40; 9. 9). Aside from the sense of inspiration, there was
a special respect given to the authority of the apostles
from the beginning, and this grew with the passing years.
Clement of Rome feels that he is speaking by the Spirit of
God, but he does not think of placing himself beside an
apostle like Paul.

Letters and Gospels used in worship   The use of these writings in the worship of the church
was the first step that prepared the way for their valuation

as Scripture. Such a use must have been very early, and came about very naturally. When one of Paul's churches received a letter from him, they were certainly not contented with reading it once. It would be read again and again as they met for worship, till it was fixed in their minds. It would be referred to later to help settle questions that arose. Thus Clement in his letter from Rome advises the Corinthians to take up again Paul's letter to them. What Paul suggests to the Colossians (4. 16), that they exchange letters with the Laodiceans, must have taken place between other churches. Small collections of Paul's letters would thus be made. In the absence of Paul these would be read to the congregation. In the same manner any church might count itself fortunate to possess one of the Gospels, so that they might hear the words of Jesus or stories of his deeds.

Such use does not imply that these writings were as yet regarded as "Bible." The Old Testament was the Bible and was read as such in the service. The epistles and Gospels came in the place of the sermon. They were not the sacred text from which men preached; they were rather the message itself, the gospel which was read when no one was present to give it with living voice. It was in the second century that the change took place. It was a gradual and natural change. Read so long by the side of the Old Testament, the writings began to share the position of the former. The church, moreover, began to see that her real message, the truth which justified her, lay in these Christian books; and more and more reverence was being attached to the men of the first age who wrote them. *They come to be regarded as Scripture*

It was another cause that hastened this process and compelled the church to take definite action. We have noted the rise of heresies in connection with the writings of John by which they were opposed. About the middle of the second century these began to seriously threaten the church. The most notable leader was Marcion. He joined an appreciation of Paul with a strange mixture of wild specula- *Marcion and his New Testament* tion. He claimed, of course, to represent the true Christian tradition. The Old Testament he threw out altogether. Then he set up a Christian collection, or canon, in its stead. This included the Gospel of Luke with ten epistles of Paul, omitting the pastoral letters. Even from these he cut out the passages that did not agree with his position.

He compels the church to act

The first Christian canon was thus made by a heretic. The word "canon" originally meant a rule for measuring. As applied to the Scriptures it means the collection made according to a given rule and including the writings that are held as sacred and authoritative. The church was thus compelled to face the question which for years had really been present: What are the writings that really represent the Christian tradition and authority? It needed a definite body of Scriptures to oppose to Marcion and others like him.

The task of the church

The first task of the church here was not to make a collection. That was already made, for the church possessed all these writings. The real problem was that of exclusion. There were many other writings current among the churches besides those of our present New Testament. Some of these had only local currency. Others were quite widely used. The epistle of Hermas and the Gospel of the Hebrews were among the latter. On the other hand, some of the books of our New Testament were not generally accepted. Such were Revelation, Hebrews, Jude, Second Peter, and Second and Third John. Two influences seem to have shaped the decision of the church in its selections. One was the extent to which these writings had been used in the worship of the church. The other was the apostolic character of the writings. What the church wanted was to state and to guard the true tradition. Marcion had appealed to one apostle. They wished to bring forward the authority of them all. The book of Acts aided in this, as it was held to set forth the acts of all the apostles. There were, of course, writings long held in high esteem and used in the worship of the church that did not come or claim

The two standards

to come from the apostles. In case of Mark the authority
of Peter was called upon; in case of Luke and Acts the
author was vouched for by his association with Paul.

We must not picture this work as being done at one time When and how done
or by unanimous consent. It was not decided by some
universal church council. The discussion and differences as
to the books mentioned above continued for a matter of two
centuries. The main work, however, was done within a
period of fifty years. By the year 200 the large part of the
church accepted the canon substantially as we have it now.
Two great divisions were taken in without question: the
four Gospels with Acts, and the thirteen letters of Paul.
Of the other writings First John and First Peter were
generally received. Revelation was opposed in some quarters because of its views on the second coming. Hebrews
was not generally received until it was attributed to Paul.
There was thus practically no question about the great and
essential parts of our New Testament.

Looking back, one cannot but say that the church was
guided in this work by the same Spirit by which the early
church had felt itself controlled. It is our duty, it is true,
to distinguish between the various writings in the New
Testament. Some of these works, like James and Revelation, were criticized by the great reformers, especially
Luther. But this was because they tried to apply one fixed
standard to them all. The relative value of these books is
suggested by the attitude of the early church. We place
first, as they did, the Gospels and Paul, and in this order.
Roughly speaking, the books about whose acceptance there
was some question are those which are of lesser value to-
day. An equally important question is often asked: Were
not valuable writings omitted, writings that might have
equal claim to be inspired? There were other Christian
writings of value, some of them preserved for us, but there
is not one of these which could command the support of
scholars if the canon were being formed anew to-day.

A BRIEF BIBLIOGRAPHY

Introductory and General

Huck: Synopsis of the First Three Gospels.
Hastings or Standard: Dictionary of the Bible, one volume.
Angus: Environment of the Early Church.
Fairweather: The Background of the Gospels.
Wade: New Testament History.
Mathews: History of New Testament Times.
Wood and Grant: The Bible as Literature: An Introduction.
Introduction to the New Testament; briefer, by Peake, Bacon, McClymont; larger, by Moffatt or Jülicher.

Jesus

Life of Jesus, Rhees, Gilbert, Holtzmann.
Kent: Life and Teaching of Jesus.
Stevens: Teaching of Jesus.
Headlam: Life and Teachings of Jesus.
Smith: The Days of His Flesh.

Paul and the Apostolic Age

Histories of the Apostolic Age; briefer, by Ropes and Purves; larger, by McGiffert and Weizsäcker.
Dobschütz: Christian Life in the Primitive Church.
Smith: The Life and Letters of St. Paul.
Rhees: Life of Paul.
Weinel: Saint Paul, the Man and His Work.
Ramsay: The Church in the Roman Empire, and Saint Paul the Traveler and Roman Citizen.
Deissmann: Saint Paul.

Huck's Synopsis is of special value in the study of the Gospels. The student who can buy but one book should have the Dictionary of the Bible.